Teaching Students Thinking Skills and Strategies

of related interest

Count Me In!
Ideas for Actively Engaging Students in Inclusive Classrooms
Richard Rose and Michael Shevlin
Foreword by Paul Cooper
ISBN 978 1 84310 955 6
Innovative Learning for All series

Language Function
An Introduction to Pragmatic Assessment and Intervention for Higher Order Thinking and Better Literacy
Ellyn Lucas Arwood
ISBN 978 1 84905 800 1

Educational Psychology Casework
A Practice Guide
2nd edition
Rick Beaver
ISBN 978 1 84905 173 6

Frameworks for Practice in Educational Psychology
A Textbook for Trainees and Practitioners
Edited by Barbara Kelly, Lisa Woolfson and James Boyle
Foreword by Sue Morris
ISBN 978 1 84310 600 5

How to Help Children and Young People with Complex Behavioural Difficulties
A Guide for Practitioners Working in Educational Settings
Ted Cole and Barbara Knowles
Foreword by Joan Pritchard
ISBN 978 1 84905 049 4

Common SENse for the Inclusive Classroom
How Teachers Can Maximise Existing Skills to Support Special Educational Needs
Richard Hanks
ISBN 978 1 84905 057 9

Promoting Emotional Education
Engaging Children and Young People with Social, Emotional and Behavioural Difficulties
Edited by Carmel Cefai and Paul Cooper
ISBN 978 1 84310 996 9
Innovative Learning for All series

Teaching Students Thinking Skills and Strategies

A Framework for Cognitive Education in Inclusive Settings

Dorothy Howie

Jessica Kingsley *Publishers*
London and Philadelphia

Figure 4.2 from Sternberg 1995 on p.73 is reproduced by permission of Professor Robert Sternberg.

First published in 2011
by Jessica Kingsley Publishers
116 Pentonville Road
London N1 9JB, UK
and
400 Market Street, Suite 400
Philadelphia, PA 19106, USA

www.jkp.com

Library of Congress Cataloging in Publication Data
Howie, Dorothy R. (Dorothy Ruth), 1945-
  Teaching students thinking skills and strategies : a framework for cognitive education in inclusive settings / Dorothy Howie.
    p. cm.
  Includes bibliographical references and index.
  ISBN 978-1-84310-950-1 (alk. paper)
  1. Teaching. 2. Education--Experimental methods. 3. Thought and thinking--Study and teaching. 4. Learning, Psychology of. 5. Critical thinking--Study and teaching. 6. Cognition in children. I. Title.
  LB1590.3.H68 2011
  371.102--dc22
                               2011007095

British Library Cataloguing in Publication Data
A CIP catalogue record for this book is available from the British Library

ISBN 978 1 84310 950 1

Printed and bound in Great Britain

Dedicated to my three grandsons, Thomas, Reuben,
and Theo, each a unique thinker.

Contents

Acknowledgements

Thanking people who have contributed to my writing of this book, and whose ideas are central to this book, takes me through my own learning in my long academic life. There are those leading researchers in learning and thinking who have taught me, starting with Dame Marie Clay, who supervised my PhD on imitative learning, and whose own internationally used Reading Recovery programme is firmly based on Vygotskian theory. Professor Michael Corballis taught me in his Master's paper on cognitive psychology, made sure that I was well acquainted with Professor Robert Sternberg's theory of the Nature of Mental Abilities, and has always been supportive of my writing. Professor Robert Sternberg agreed to my use of his figure on the problem-solving cycle, and his creative model making and keynote addresses have personally inspired me.

An introduction to the work of Professor Reuven Feuerstein began my long learning and apprenticeship in his Theory of Mediated Learning Experience, with his guidance and support, and that of his research colleague, Professor Alex Kozulin, who is also a Vygotskian expert, and more recently, his son Rabbi Raphael (Rafi) Feuerstein.

I have been privileged to have learnt much from Professor Carol McGuinness and Professor David Perkins, particularly while attending a British Council workshop in Belfast, where they took leadership roles. They have both consented to use of their materials.

I have also learnt much from my colleagues who have supported me in research on the teaching of thinking, including in particular John Thickpenny, Joint-Director with me of the Australasian Institute for Learning Enhancement, who joined with me in our early research in New Zealand with Feuerstein's Instrumental Enrichment programme. Other research colleagues with whom I have worked on New Zealand projects and whom I particularly wish to thank are Ruhi Richards for her partnership with me, and Philip Coombe for agreeing to use of research materials. Professor Robert Burden, a colleague who is at Exeter University, continues to guide me in the use of his SPARE wheel model for evaluating cognitive implementations. Sue Robson and Professor Vivienne Baumfield have been other valued UK colleagues in the teaching of thinking. Professor Jo Lebeer has supported me in the publication of this book and contributed the endorsement on the back cover. Dr Mogens Jensen has been a supportive colleague and agreed to the coverage of his Mindladder model for the teaching of thinking. I make particular mention of Professor Peter Mittler, who has encouraged me in my research on inclusion throughout my academic life.

I have learnt much from my PhD and Master's students while teaching postgraduate papers in learning and inclusion at the University of Hull. Special thanks are due to those whose research I have drawn on in this book as fine examples of thinking and of the teaching of thinking: Dr Mary Barry-Joyce, Robert Bolton, Julie Cattle, Rhys Davies, Associate-Professor Kenneth Fong, Nicola O'Riordan, Cheri Pattison, Dr Tony Tam, and Joy Thompson. Mere Vadei, a Master's student when I taught at the University of the South Pacific, agreed to the use of material from a seminar she presented as part of that Master's programme.

Finally, I would like to thank those who have supported me through the writing and publication process itself. Professor Paul Cooper encouraged my initial involvement in the book. Stephen Jones, Caroline Walton, and Alexandra Higson, of Jessica Kingsley Publishers, gave consistent patience and care throughout the publication process. My family and close friends gave love and support throughout this journey.

Dr Dorothy Howie
E-mail: D.R.Howie@hull.ac.uk

CHAPTER 1

Rationale for the Teaching of Thinking

Introduction

This book is about the teaching of thinking for all learners in the classroom. It brings together the teaching of thinking, a key need for every learner, with the concept of inclusion.

We need to define what we mean by the teaching of thinking. It involves teaching learners about their mental processes and how these can be used for problem solving. It requires us as teachers to 'intervene at the level of the mental process and teach individuals what processes to use when, how to use them, and how to combine them into workable strategies for task solution' according to Professor Robert Sternberg, an international leader in the field of cognitive enhancement, or the teaching of thinking (Sternberg 1984, p.39).

A broader approach to the teaching of thinking is taken by Harpaz (2007) in his interesting conceptual mapping of the field of teaching of thinking. He sees it as made up of three main types of approaches to the teaching of thinking: the *skills* type of approach (teaching various thinking means, such as strategies, that render thinking process more effective, fast and precise); the *dispositions* type of approach (a thinking disposition being, in his terms, a reasoned motivation for a certain thinking pattern, a thinking quality such as open-mindedness, depth, systematic thinking); and the *understanding* type of approach (he considers that knowledge and thinking are interconnected, and this type of approach makes clear the conditions under which knowledge becomes understanding). Sternberg's definition above fits into the first approach to the teaching of thinking proposed by Harpaz. Metacognition, or 'thinking about thinking', is one of the key ideas in the literature on the teaching of thinking. It is of interest to us that the mapping of the teaching of thinking by Harpaz lines up somewhat with the three main aspects of metacognitive knowledge: knowledge of strategy, knowledge of the self as learner, and knowledge of the task (Meichenbaum *et al.* 1985).

We also need to define what we mean by inclusion. It is defined by Frederickson and Cline (2002) as a radical set of changes whereby schools restructure themselves so as to be able to embrace the needs of all children. The *Index for Inclusion*, now used widely internationally to explore the progress of a school towards inclusion, and which will be drawn on in this book to help us to think about inclusion, was jointly authored by Booth and Ainscow (2002). Ainscow gives us a similar definition of inclusion, where he compares *integration*, which is giving support to children with special educational needs to enable them to fit into an ordinary school, and *inclusion*, where the school is restructured to meet the needs of all learners, including those with special educational needs (Ainscow 1995).

The teaching of thinking and inclusion

This chapter presents fourteen key reasons as rationale for our teaching of thinking to all learners in the classroom. Each rationale is treated as a dimension or aspect, and for each dimension, first, a rationale for the teaching of thinking will be given, followed by a rationale for inclusion (for all learners in the classroom), and then a drawing of the relationship between the two.

Rationale 1: The right to the teaching of thinking and inclusion

The United Nations has given us relevant rights in what can be called 'supreme law' which cuts across cultures and countries. In the *Convention on the Rights of the Child* (United Nations 1989), Article 29, the child is stated to have the right to develop his/her abilities to their potential, as follows: the right to 'the development of the child's personality, talents, and mental and physical abilities to their fullest potential'.

In terms of inclusion, a new *United Nations Convention on the Protection and Promotion of the Rights and Dignity of Persons with Disabilities* (United Nations 2006), Article 24 on education, states that signatory countries shall 'ensure an inclusive education system at all levels, and lifelong learning, directed to: The full development of the human potential and sense of dignity and self worth and the strengthening of respect for human rights, fundamental freedoms and human diversity.' The same article goes on to reiterate the clause from the 1989 *Convention on the Rights of the Child*, with even stronger emphasis which relates to the teaching of thinking as follows: 'the development of persons with disabilities of their personality, talents, and creativity, as well as their mental and physical abilities to their fullest potential'. This clause then states a strong concept with an inclusive goal and a goal for lifetime participation, 'enabling persons with disabilities to participate effectively in a free society'.

We can therefore see in this recent 2006 Convention that the United Nations itself is drawing the link between a right to realising one's potential, including in 'mental abilities', and a right to inclusion, not only in all levels of schooling, but in fullest participation in society, which is a key goal of inclusion.

Rationale 2: The requirements by governments for the teaching of thinking and inclusion

There is a move internationally for countries to establish within their national school curriculum statements the teaching of thinking as a key requirement. For example, the United Kingdom's new *National Curriculum Primary Handbook* (Department for Children, Schools and Families 2010), which was proposed by the then Labour Government but has not become policy under the new Government, is progressive in its approach towards the teaching of thinking. It outlines its aims as being to enable young people to be successful learners, confident individuals, and responsible citizens. It wants to 'instil in children a positive disposition to learning and a commitment to learning' (p.5). It includes in the first main section, 'Essentials for Learning and Life', the 'skills, attitudes and dispositions that children need to become well-rounded individuals and lifelong learners' (p.13). These include literacy, numeracy, ICT capacity, learning and thinking skills, and personal, social and emotional skills, which are prioritised in this new curriculum. The focus of the 'learning and thinking' skills is that 'children have the skills to learn effectively. They can plan, research and critically evaluate, using reasoned arguments to support conclusions. They think creatively, making original connections and generating ideas. They consider alternative solutions to problems' (p.15). In the following areas for learning, specific thinking skills are further mentioned – for example, under the heading of 'Understanding physical development, health and wellbeing', key skills include 'reflect on and evaluate evidence when making personal choices or bringing about improvements in performance and behaviour' and 'generate and implement ideas, plans and strategies, exploring alternatives' (p.53).

In the UK National Curriculum (DfES 2002) a list of thinking skills is given consisting of information processing, reasoning, inquiry, creativity and evaluation. A number of approaches covered in this book address these skills, but it is not an exhaustive list, and in the writer's view should not limit the range of choice of methods for the teaching of thinking that can be considered appropriate for the meeting of identified learner needs.

Another recent example is that of New Zealand, where the teaching of thinking is required in the new National Curriculum (New Zealand Ministry of Education 2007) as a first key competency aspect.

Similarly, there is a move internationally for countries to progress towards inclusion in their provision of education, through legislation. In the United Kingdom, the 2001 *Special Educational Needs and Disability Act* (DfEE 2001) sets out 'a duty to educate children with special educational needs in mainstream school including a child with a statement', with only two caveats: the wishes of the parents, and the provision of efficient education for other children (rigorously interpreted).

Although these two areas of the teaching of thinking and inclusion remain separate in the relevant policy documents, they both appear to be driven by the aim of the fullest possible participation in society for every learner.

Rationale 3: The importance of shaping the learning environment for the learning and thinking of all children

Some approaches to the teaching of thinking consider the importance of the wider learning environment of the community and the school in the teaching of thinking. For example, an important paper, 'Transforming schools into communities of thinking and learning about serious matters' was written by the late Professor Ann Brown (1997), an expert on metacognition. Similarly, in an important book, *Smart Schools: From Training Memories to Educating Minds*, Professor David Perkins (1992) looks at the ways in which we in schools can put thinking at the centre of all that happens.

One approach to the teaching of thinking which has 'shaping modifying/changing environments' as an important aspect, is that of Professor Reuven Feuerstein. He sees this aspect as ensuring an environment which has a great heterogeneity of people, with a variety of levels of functioning, thinking, emotions and interests. This exposes the learner to a need to change themselves, to go beyond what they are (Feuerstein 2008). Such a modifying (or changing) environment is seen as having a high degree of openness; conditions of positive stress to which the learner needs to adapt; planned and controlled encounters with new tasks; and individualised and specialised/customised instruction and mediation (Feuerstein, Rand and Rynders 1988; Feuerstein, Rand and Feuerstein 2006).

The *Index for Inclusion* (Booth and Ainscow 2002) also recognises the importance of the wider cultural and contextual aspects for inclusion. It has three main dimensions, with the cultural dimension informing the other two dimensions of inclusive policies and inclusive practices.

As early as 1989, in a groundbreaking paper within the *Oxford Review of Education*, Kaniel and Feuerstein stated: 'the prevalent perception is that the student must adjust to the teachers and the school, while the latter remain fixed and unchanging. It is important to develop the reverse and opposite approach which focuses on the need of the system for structural modifiability and maximum flexibility' (Kaniel and Feuerstein 1989, p.177).

That recognition of the importance of the wider community and school environment (especially in working towards it being an inclusive environment) will be required in the teaching of thinking, is clear from the comments of Professor Reuven Feuerstein, quoted above and also from a chapter written by his son, Raphael Feuerstein, 'Mainstreaming Special Needs Children According to the Criteria of Mediated Learning Experience and Shaping Modifying Environments', in Feuerstein, Rand and Feuerstein (2006).

There is also some evidence that if the teaching of thinking is not supported by such an environment, with its openness, then learners undergoing change in their thinking may encounter difficulties – as suggested by the research findings of Blagg in the UK in an early, Oxfordshire-wide project with Feuerstein's 'Instrumental Enrichment' approach (Blagg 1991), and in New Zealand by evaluation of the use of de Bono's Cognitive Research Trust (CoRT) approach (Howie, Coombe and Lonergan 1998). We need research which demonstrates how a systematic, whole-school/community approach to the teaching of thinking supports the teaching of thinking at both teacher and learner level.

Rationale 4: The importance of learning how to learn, in preparation for lifelong learning

The teaching of thinking enables individuals to develop their own self-monitoring and self-regulation of learning, and to manage their own thinking (metacognition). The development of self-regulation is a cornerstone of learner autonomy and lifelong learning, which involves the learner in being active and responsible, rather than passive (Presseisen, Smey-Richman and Beyer 1994).

In relation to inclusion, pupil partnership – a central tenet in the recent 'personalisation' policy in the UK – relates to the agency of learners in their own learning and development. 'Greater personalisation and choice', with 'the wishes and needs of children, parents and learners centre stage' is a key principle for reform of schools, especially in relation to the individual needs of learners (i.e. for inclusion) in the *Five-Year Strategy for Children and Learners* (DfES 2004, Foreword).

We need to recognise the partnership of learners in their learning, and the development of their self-agency, in the legislation which underpins our education (Howie 2010). We need to address the self-management of learning and thinking, as it is a key rationale both for the teaching of thinking, and for addressing the learning needs of all learners.

Rationale 5: The importance of developing thinking in order to cope with change positively, in lifelong learning

This rationale point links to the previous one. The importance of reflective, flexible and creative thinking in order not only to adapt to change, but to be involved in creating positive change, is presented to us by Sternberg, in discussing his triarchic theory of intelligence (Sternberg and Lubart 1995).

In terms of inclusion, we need to prepare all learners not only for the challenges, both academic and social, of an inclusive classroom and school, but for their fullest participation in their future in wider society (Feuerstein, Rand and Feuerstein 2006). We all experience the challenges presented by, and the transitions needed for, our swiftly changing society, as noted by Feuerstein (2008). These include cultural and moral challenges.

In bringing together developing thinking for change, and inclusion, Lebeer states, 'In an ever-changing world, all children need to develop cognitive competencies which enable them to adapt to a variety of technical, social and cultural changes' (Lebeer 2006, p.13).

Rationale 6: The importance of developing general problem-solving skills which can be applied to both academic and real-life problem solving

A useful model of the problem-solving process is presented to us by Sternberg, arising from his model of mental abilities, and he reminds us of the importance of three aspects of intelligence – analytical, practical and creative – in real-life problem solving (Sternberg 1997).

It is of interest that in our traditional assessment of the need of children for special educational services, assessment of adaptation to real life was a requirement. Under that system, the evidence of well-developed, real-life problem-solving skills would mean the child could not be labelled as having a learning disability or placed within special (non-inclusive) services. In writing about intelligence assessment needs for this new millennium, we were reminded of the need to analyse real-life problem-solving needs, and to develop the tools to assess them, by Brown and French (1979).

The UK Green Paper *Every Child Matters* (House of Commons 2004) sets out five outcomes which services for children should work towards, and which have particular implications for both the teaching of thinking and for inclusion of all children in such teaching: being healthy, staying safe, enjoying and achieving, making a positive contribution, and economic well-being. This is a key UK policy paper with long-term import.

It is clear that the learning of problem-solving skills is central to achieving all of these goals, and that there is a strong emphasis on equipping *every* child with these goals, implicit in the title of the policy document *Every Child Matters*.

Rationale 7: The importance of acquiring the underpinning cognitive skills needed for academic learning

In our present climate of school accountability for standards of academic achievement, the role of the teaching of thinking in relation to acquiring academic skills has assumed considerable importance. We need to realise that the learning of academic skills can be enhanced by acquisition of the underpinning cognitive skills that are prerequisites for that academic learning. A compelling argument for the importance of enhancing these underpinning cognitive skills (especially as learners enter the more abstract levels of learning required at the secondary school level) is made by Adey and Shayer (1994) in their book *Really Raising Standards: Cognitive Intervention and Academic Achievement*. They see it as important to challenge learners to transcend their present levels of thinking in order to bring about higher achievement. The development of the thinking skill programmes *Cognitive Acceleration in Maths (CAME)* and *Cognitive Acceleration in Science (CASE)* by Adey and Shayer aimed to enhance the underpinning cognitive skills in these two subject areas.

In terms of the academic achievement of *all* children (i.e. inclusion), we recognise the importance of the Vygotskian (1978) concept of working with mediation and support within each child's 'zone of proximal development', to ensure that all children develop their cognitive potential with the aim of academic achievement to their fullest ability.

Also, it is important to ensure that in using approaches such as Gardner's Multiple Intelligences (Gardner 2006) and learning style theories, we are careful not to label children as particular types of learner, such as a 'kinaesthetic learner', possibly limiting the input made available to them just at the very time when they need to be developing more abstract, verbal, conceptual skills in order to master the demands of academic learning.

In terms of inclusion, Lebeer (2006), in his book about inclusion and cognitive education, notes that the 'the focus is on cognitive education because it helps to develop the mind of the child in acquiring basic pre-requisites of thinking' (p.24). Particular attention is drawn in that publication to the learning of mathematics as a problematic area for all children within the inclusive classroom, and work on the teaching of thinking specifically in relation to mathematics, by Kinard and Kozulin (2008) and Ben-Hur (2005), is noted.

Rationale 8: The importance of thinking analytically and critically in order to evaluate, including evaluation of best courses of action

As part of the agency of the learner, the learner in this increasingly complex academic and social world needs to be able to engage in analysis and criticism. These are skills which are clearly required in higher levels of academic learning, but are also required to achieve the positive participation outcomes in real life, as aimed for in the *Every Child Matters* policy document. An increasing number of approaches to the teaching of thinking consider the importance of thinking critically for the development of a more moral society. This has always been the aim of the 'Philosophy for Children' approach, which has development of ethical understandings as a key aim (Lipman, Sharp and Oscanyon 1980).

In Sternberg's triarchic theory of intelligence, which is made up of analytic, practical and creative intelligence, we might consider that a systematic analysis of different courses of action in solving a problem, along key dimensions (e.g. cost, feasibility, probable reactions from key persons involved, and personal preference) may lead to an effective practical solution. Similarly, developing an idea creatively could involve not only the lateral thinking suggested by de Bono, but its enhancement by developing ideas and concepts systematically along key dimensions.

The link to inclusion is suggested in the reference to the positive participation in the *Every Child Matters* outcomes above. It is also of interest to us that the *Index for Inclusion* (Booth and Ainscow 2002) has as key aspects of an inclusive school culture 'overcoming barriers to discrimination', and the 'valuing of all children'. Such an inclusive culture requires us to understand the positive meanings of difference, and to be able not only to evaluate where barriers to learning and inclusion are occurring, but also to develop effective ways of overcoming them. This requires our own ability to think analytically and critically, including self-evaluation and self-criticism. In relation to this, Lebeer (2006) notes that the teaching of thinking helps in both valuing of, and valuing by, learners (p.52).

Rationale 9: The importance of focus on the learning process, not only on the learning outcome

This focus begins with Vygotsky (1978), who taught us much about the importance of the process of learning. Further, an information-processing approach underpins most current approaches to the teaching of thinking. Such a focus on the 'how' of thinking is clearly important for all learners, not only in terms of the strategies engaged in a learning task, but in the views of self while learning (both key metacognitive aspects).

The importance of this process approach is emphasised in relation to the learner dealing with frustration in an inclusive setting, by Feuerstein, Rand and Feuerstein (2006). They state: 'Change the attitude which caused these feelings from the beginning, i.e. change from a product-oriented approach to a process-oriented approach.' This includes comparing the learner's learning progress to his/her own previous progress, rather than to that of others (p.388). There is actually research evidence that teachers who use a teaching thinking approach such as Feuerstein's Instrumental Enrichment programme, which looks at the learning process, make a general shift in attitude towards a more process-oriented education (Tebar Belmonte 2003, cited in Lebeer 2006, p.21).

Rationale 10: The teaching of thinking is supported by our knowledge that thinking can be enhanced, and we should have an optimistic view of this for all learners

Again, Vygotsky's (1978) theory is key to this understanding – for example, with its idea of the zone of proximal development, where support and mediation is aimed at achieving the level of next, or proximal, development. This focus on the modifiability of the individual, with an optimistic view of the learning possibilities of each learner, is central to some approaches to the teaching of thinking, such as Feuerstein's. Not only should such an optimistic view underpin our use of a teaching of thinking approach, but, conversely, we can expect that the use of such an approach will confirm our optimistic attitude.

Within the *Index for Inclusion*, a key aspect of the inclusive culture is having high expectations for all learners (Booth and Ainscow 2002). This high expectation is also a tenant of the UK 'personalised learning' policy, and mirrors the political view of the government responsible for the policy that each child should fulfil their potential.

The linking of the two areas, teaching of thinking and inclusion, comes with the consideration of the aim of inclusion as the fulfilment of every child's potential, as stated in the supreme law. The teaching of thinking is how to achieve this goal. We all, as key players – school staff, parents and learners – need an optimistic view to achieve this, in order to act as important mediators not only of this attitude, but of the thinking itself.

Rationale 11: There should be an interest in the unique potential of every individual, and individual differences in learning and thinking

Vygotsky (1978) recognised the importance of unique individual differences in thinking, including the unique thinking of learners from minority cultures in Russia. We have a number of approaches to the teaching of thinking which have taught us the importance of each person's unique profile of cognitive abilities, such as Gardner's theory of Multiple Intelligences (2006), and Sternberg's theory of the triarchic intelligence (2000). Theories of learning styles have further drawn our attention to individual differences in learning preferences.

Within the *Index for Inclusion* (Booth and Ainscow 2002) there is an indicator concerning the role of recognition and value of individual difference in enhancing learning. It states 'pupils' diversities are accepted and used as a resource in learning activities for all'. This encourages us to take a positive approach to individual differences in learning and thinking, rather than a limiting, labelling one. Difference is to be celebrated, and provides a rich learning context in which the diversity of learning strengths, strategies and styles is used for the benefit of all.

Rationale 12: There should be a shared construction of meanings, and empathy for a shared contribution to the social world

Vygotsky (1978) has taught us that the learning and thinking of each individual is embedded in their social and historical context, through the internalisation of shared meanings gained through social interaction. More recent thinking about 'emotional intelligence' reminds us of the importance of understanding and managing our own emotions, along with understanding and empathy in relation to others (Goleman 1998).

In thinking about the inclusion of all learners, a vital role is played by collaborative activities, including at the level of an inclusive culture, a philosophy of inclusion shared by all of the key players (school staff, parents and learners). This is a key requirement in the *Index for Inclusion* (Booth and Ainscow 2002). When it comes down to teaching and learning practices, not only do we need to provide appropriate and sensitive mediation by staff, through social interaction, but opportunities for the fullest possible participation in classroom peer activities, so that the learner is exposed to strong models of thinking and learning. The *Every Child Matters* (House of Commons 2004) UK policy document requires us to think about how every child is making a positive contribution within the inclusive school and classroom context, and this means in both academic and social activities. It is important that we do not underestimate the value of each child as a mediator, and an interesting study by Kaufman (2001) has demonstrated how, with adult support, young people with Down's syndrome have been able to deliver a peer-mediated thinking programme.

Rationale 13: The role of teaching thinking in raising learners' self-esteem and positive sense of identity

This rationale is proposed by a number of approaches for the teaching of thinking. For example, it is claimed that the Philosophy for Children approach raises self-esteem (Fisher 1998). However, it is notoriously difficult to provide evidence of this, to some extent because the types of global measures of self-esteem often used to evaluate shifts are not finely enough tuned to measure changes brought about by a particular approach to the teaching of thinking.

A good example of using an approach to the teaching of thinking in relation to developing a positive sense of identity is provided by a South African study by Skuy, Goldstein, Mentis and Fridjhon (1997) which used selected instruments from Feuerstein's thinking programme to help to develop the four stages of multicultural awareness outlined in Hoopes' (1979) four stage model of multicultural development. The first 'isolate' stage is 'knowing me', the second 'inquire' stage is 'knowing others', the third 'contact' stage is 'me and others' and the fourth 'integration' stage is 'this is us'.

The United Nations (2006) *Convention on the Protection and Promotion of the Rights and Dignity of Persons with Disabilities* links inclusion to the full development of the person, including a sense of dignity and self-worth. It would seem that the aims of inclusion in such a statement match well with this rationale for the teaching of thinking, including a respecting of difference, both in oneself and others. Lebeer (2006) includes the following aspects of inclusive education as they connect to the teaching of thinking: the starting point is the learner's own competencies and experiences; there is relevance to the learner's life at present and in the future; and there is valuing of and by the learner.

Rationale 14: The value of the teaching of thinking in teachers' professional development

Where teacher attitudes have been explored in association with the use of an approach to the teaching of thinking, the value of this for their professional development is usually affirmed. For example, in the present author's own work with Maori teachers in the use of Feuerstein's Instrumental Enrichment programme, teacher statements while using the programme included a considerable number relating to professional and personal gains from their involvement with the programme (Howie

2003, p.57). Of these, the highest proportion involved help in 'tackling and exposing problems in teaching method', followed by 'development of confidence in skills'.

Similarly, international studies on progress towards inclusion generally identify teachers' professional development as a key related issue. The *Index for Inclusion* stresses the importance of collaborative professional development activities for support to teachers in meeting the needs of all learners (Booth and Ainscow 2002). In fact, when we have the responsibility of meeting a great variety of learner needs in an inclusive classroom, we ourselves experience professional and personal challenges and needs, which should be addressed by professional development and support.

According to Lebeer (2006), 'one has to change teachers' minds alongside changing children's minds' (p.35). Inclusion is seen as 'improving schools for staff as well as for students' (p.12). The preparation for, and experience of, the teaching of thinking, should be professionally and personally enriching for all of us, and encourage the fullest development of our own unique teaching and research strengths.

In their chapter on restructuring classroom environments for students at risk, Presseisen, Smey-Richman and Beyer (1994) state 'Restructured schools...are places in which teachers strive to be cognitively creative in their instruction, where, as life-long learners themselves, they seek to refine their professional ability to enhance every student's autonomy and ability to think, and where they constantly seek to create conditions for optimal student achievement' (p.198).

Self-reflective questions

- [ ] In your school context, which rationales for the teaching of thinking need to be given greater attention?

- [ ] Are there any further reasons for the teaching of thinking in your school context?

References

Adey, P. and Shayer, M. (1994) *Really Raising Standards: Cognitive Intervention and Academic Achievement.* London: Routledge.

Ainscow, M. (1995) 'Education for all: Making it happen.' *Support for Learning 10,* 147–153.

Ben-Hur, M. (2005) *Concept-rich Mathematics Instruction: Building a Strong Foundation for Reasoning and Problem Solving.* Alexandria, VA: Association for Supervision and Curriculum Development.

Blagg, N. (1991) *Can We Teach Intelligence?: A Comprehensive Evaluation of Feuerstein's Instrumental Enrichment.* Hillsdale, NJ: Erlbaum.

Booth, T. and Ainscow, M. (2002) *Index for Inclusion: Developing Learning and Participation in Schools.* London: CSIE.

Brown, A.L. (1997) 'Transforming schools into communities of thinking and learning about serious matters.' *American Psychologist 52,* 4, 399–413.

Brown, A.L. and French, L.A. (1979) 'The zone of potential development: Implications for intelligence testing in the year 2000.' *Intelligence 3,* 255–273.

Department for Children, Schools and Families (2010) *National Curriculum Primary Handbook.* Coventry: Qualifications and Curriculum Development Agency.

Department for Education and Employment (2001) *Special Educational Needs and Disability Act 2001.* London: HMSO.

Department for Education and Skills (DfES) (2002) *National Curriculum.* London: HMSO.

Department for Education and Skills (2004) *Five-Year Strategy for Children and Learners.* London: HMSO.

Feuerstein, R. (2008) Presentation to a seminar, Venice International Workshops, author's notes.

Feuerstein, R., Rand, Y. and Rynders, J.E. (1988) *Don't Accept Me as I Am: Helping 'Retarded' People to Excel.* New York: Plenum Press.

Feuerstein, R., Rand, Y. and Feuerstein, Ra.S. (2006) *You Love Me! Don't Accept Me as I Am: Helping the Low Functioning Person Excel.* Jerusalem: International Centre for the Enhancement of Learning Potential.

Fisher, R. (1998) *Teaching Thinking: Philosophical Enquiry in the Classroom.* London: Cassell.

Frederickson, N. and Cline, T. (2002) *Special Educational Needs, Inclusion and Diversity: A Textbook.* Oxford: Oxford University Press/Open University Press.

Gardner, H. (2006) *Multiple Intelligences: New Horizons.* New York: Basic Books.

Goleman, D. (1998) *Working with Emotional Intelligence.* New York: Bantam Books.

Harpaz, Y. (2007) 'Approaches to teaching thinking: Toward a conceptual mapping of the field.' *Teachers College Record 109,* 1845–1874.

Hoopes, D. (1979) 'Intercultural Communication Concepts and Psychology of Intercultural Experiences.' In M.D. Pusch (ed.) *Multicultural Education: A Cross Cultural Training Approach.* Yarmouth, ME: Intercultural Press.

House of Commons (2004) *Every Child Matters: Next Steps.* London: HMSO.

Howie, D.R. (2003) *Thinking about the Teaching of Thinking.* Wellington: New Zealand Council for Educational Research.

Howie, D.R. (2010) 'A comparative study of the positioning of children with special educational needs in the legislation of Britain, New Zealand and the Republic of Ireland.' *International Journal of Inclusive Education 14,* 8, 755–776.

Howie, D.R., Coombe, P. and Lonergan, J. (1998) 'Using single subject design in an Auckland study of the CoRT thinking skill programme.' Paper presented to the Conference on Teaching for Successful Intelligence, Auckland.

Kaniel, S. and Feuerstein, R. (1989) 'Special needs of children with learning difficulties.' *Oxford Review of Education 15*, 165–179.

Kaufman, R. (2001) 'The process of experiencing mediated learning as a result of peer collaboration between young adults with severe learning difficulties.' Unpublished doctoral dissertation, Exeter University.

Kinard, J.T. and Kozulin, A. (2008) *Rigorous Mathematical Thinking: Conceptual Formation.* Cambridge: Cambridge University Press.

Lebeer, J. (ed.) (2006) *In-clues: Clues to Inclusive and Cognitive Education.* Antwerpen-Apeldoorn: Garant.

Lipman, M., Sharp, A.M. and Oscanyon, F.S. (1980) *Philosophy in the Classroom.* Philadelphia, PA: Temple University Press.

Meichenbaum, D., Burland, S., Gruson, L. and Cameron, R. (1985) 'Metacognitive Assessment.' In S.R.Yussen (ed.) *The Growth of Reflection in Children.* London: Academic Press.

New Zealand Ministry of Education (2007) *National Curriculum.* Wellington: New Zealand Government.

Perkins, D. (1992) *Smart Schools: From Training Memories to Educating Minds.* New York: The Free Press.

Presseisen, B.Z., Smey-Richman, B. and Beyer, F.S. (1994) 'Cognitive Development Through Radical Change: Restructuring Classroom Environments for Students at Risk.' In M. Ben-Hur (ed.) *On Feuerstein's Instrumental Enrichment: A Collection.* Palatine, IL: IRI Skylight.

Skuy, M., Goldstein, I., Mentis, M. and Fridjhon, P. (1997) 'A cognitive approach to promoting multicultural awareness and co-existence in the classroom.' *Journal of Cognitive Education 6*, 47–56.

Sternberg, R.J. (1984) 'How can we teach intelligence?' *Educational Leadership 42*, 1, 38–48.

Sternberg, R.J. (1997) 'The concept of intelligence and its role in lifelong learning and success.' *American Psychologist 52*, 10, 1030–1037.

Sternberg, R.J. (2000) 'Group and Individual Differences in Intelligence: What Can and Should We Do about Them?' In A. Kozulin and Y. Rand (eds) *Experience of Mediated Learning.* Oxford: Pergamon.

Sternberg, R.J. and Lubart, T.I. (1995) 'An Investment Perspective on Creative Insight.' In R.J. Sternberg and J.E. Davison (eds) *The Nature of Insight.* Cambridge, MA: MIT Press.

Tebar Belmonte, L. (2003) *El Perfil del Profesor Mediator.* Madrid: Santillana.

United Nations (1989) *United Nations Convention on the Rights of the Child.* Geneva: United Nations.

United Nations (2006) *United Nations Convention on the Protection and Promotion of the Rights and Dignity of Persons with Disabilities.* Geneva: United Nations.

Vygotsky, L.S. (1978) *Mind in Society: The Development of Higher Psychological Processes.* Cambridge, MA: MIT Press.

CHAPTER 2

General Principles in Teaching Thinking for All Learners

Introduction

This chapter identifies some key principles which are helpful to us in guiding decision making in terms of teaching thinking for all learners. It draws on two particular approaches which are internationally recognised, theory-based, and informed by research. The first identifies for us the key dimensions in the teaching of thinking, illustrated in Figure 2.1 as a diagram with the central focus on a belief in the modifiability of intelligence (i.e. an optimistic view); the embracing learning environment; and the three triangle points of the mediator, the task, and the learner. They are drawn from one of the approaches to the teaching of thinking covered in the following chapters, that of Feuerstein *et al.* (2006).

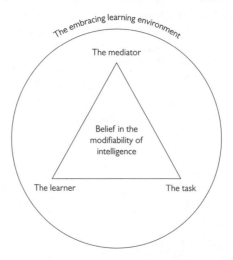

Figure 2.1 The key dimensions in the teaching of thinking

The second is the *Index for Inclusion*, which is increasingly used internationally to guide schools in self-evaluation of their progress towards inclusion for all learners. It was developed in the UK by Booth and Ainscow (2002).

The principles below follow the order of the key dimensions of thinking in Figure 2.1, and for each dimension, links will be made to appropriate indicators of the *Index for Inclusion*.

1. The belief system

Principle 1: A belief that all children can learn and change in their cognitive functioning

Central to the teaching of thinking for all learners is a belief that all children can learn and change in their cognitive functioning. There will be individual differences in the extent to which a child can change, but the full potential for change is usually unknown, and certainly not discernible through traditional approaches to cognitive assessment. Even with a more dynamic approach to the assessment of cognitive functioning, what is identified is the learner's response to skilled mediation and guidance, at a particular point in time, and what kinds of mediation and guidance most effectively facilitate that response. It will not be possible to predict future cognitive performance, because that is dependent on a wide and complex range of learning opportunities and learner motivations, which can change over time.

As pointed out in Chapter 1, it is the right of every child to develop to his or her fullest potential, and the belief and views of every key player in the child's learning, including each child, is critical to achieving that potential. It is important that we have high expectations concerning the future potential for the cognitive development of all learners, and need this to inform current assessment practices. For example, some UK schools use the Cognitive Abilities Test (CAT) (Mercer 2008) for predicting future achievement performance, individual target setting, and ability grouping of whole classrooms of learners. Prediction of learning for any one individual from such a standardised test result may fail to take into account possibilities of change for that individual, in both new learning opportunities and positive motivational factors. There is also a strong literature to support the understanding that such prediction acts as a 'self-fulfilling prophecy'.

The *Index for Inclusion* has, under the aspect of 'Equal valuing of all students', which is a key inclusive aspect, an indicator, 'There are high expectations for all students' (Booth and Ainscow 2002). This indicator clearly links to an optimistic view for every learner.

Principle 2: The use of any teaching of thinking approach should aim to improve thinking for all of the learners involved

A related principle is that the use of any teaching of thinking approach should aim for improved thinking for all of the learners involved, not just a selected few. In her chapter 'Thinking Skills: Identifying Generic Principles and Supporting Effective Implementation', Baumfield (1997), a leader in the teaching of thinking in the UK, states, 'In the classroom, thinking skills programmes require shared inquiry through group work, promote distributed thinking rather than private reflection, and expect improvement of all, not success for a few' (p.136).

There are also whole-school issues relating to this principle. If we expect improvement for all, and not just for a few, this leads us to think very carefully about the needs of all in terms of thinking enhancement, and what approaches are required to maximise the possibility of meeting these needs. The next four chapters of this book seek to help the reader in making such decisions.

Further, this principle has implications for the way we evaluate the outcomes of thinking enhancement approaches. A useful question we could ask is, 'To what extent did the approach meet the needs of all learners?' If there is evidence that those with higher levels of initial cognitive ability benefited from the approach, but that there was little benefit for those with barriers to learning, then we would need to ask serious questions about equity and inclusion in the use of this approach.

The importance of looking at individual differences in response to a thinking intervention, in order to identify to what extent each individual involved has benefited or not from each component of the programme, has been identified by Sternberg (2000). There are some examples of research carried out using both group control design and single subject research design, to facilitate such individual evaluation, including the systematic set of studies reported by the present writer (Howie 2003). The aim of tracking the learning of each individual during the intervention was to inform future work with the thinking approach used, so as to ensure more adequate meeting of each learner's needs.

In terms of inclusion, the principle of improving the thinking of all learners, and not just a selected few, relates to the *Index of Inclusion* aspect of 'removal of barriers to learning and participation' (Booth and Ainscow 2002). We need to ensure that the choice of a particular approach for the teaching of thinking does not unduly advantage an already advantaged group of learners, to the disadvantage of those experiencing barriers to learning. Particular choices may well need to be made to use approaches which help to overcome barriers to learning for particular groups of learners and individual learners who experience difficulties with traditional approaches used in the ordinary classroom setting. The following chapters identify a three-tier framework which aims to help us to think about needs and approaches for groups of learners experiencing shared difficulties, and for individuals with considerable unique learning needs.

Principle 3: Teachers need to believe in the positive possibilities for, and contributions from, all learners

All teachers and educators involved in the teaching of thinking need to have a belief system which affirms the positive possibilities for, and contributions from, all learners, including those from a wide range of cultural and socio-economic backgrounds. Leading international writers on the teaching of thinking, Presseisen, Smey-Richman and Beyer (1994), state that:

> teachers need a new belief system based on the current research. (p.231) ... Considering the cultural diversity evident in America's changing demographics, the demand for effective teachers who can relate to students of many backgrounds and varying personal histories will only increase in the coming decade…these are the instructors with the positive belief systems called for in restructured classrooms. (p.239)

This move towards greater cultural diversity in classrooms is worldwide, meaning that all of us as teachers must learn to value and utilise the unique thinking strengths of learners from varying cultural backgrounds.

The *Index for Inclusion* has a key inclusive value in the *culture* dimension of inclusion, concerning the equal valuing of all students; and it has a specific indicator in the *practice* dimension relating to this principle: 'Student difference is used as a resource for teaching and learning' (Booth and Ainscow 2002).

2. The learning environment

Principle 4: The learning environment needs to provide adequate learning challenges for all learners

We have already considered in Chapter 1 the importance of shaping a modifying environment, ensuring that it caters for the requirement of challenges to change (Feuerstein 2008; Feuerstein, Rand and Feuerstein 2006). Further, we are reminded in a key early paper in the *Oxford Review of Education* (Kaniel and Feuerstein1989) concerning the wider school environment, that in order to 'bring about cognitive modifiability the school must be changed so that the processes in it are dynamic and changing in accordance with the needs of those that attend it'(p.177).

We are living in a rapidly changing world, as already noted. In focusing on the inclusion of children in an ordinary classroom in relation to the teaching of thinking, according to the concept of shaping modifying environments, Raphael Feuerstein points out that the main goal of inclusion is to prepare learners for real inclusion in ordinary life. What is required in an ordinary classroom, in his view, is a 'normative' environment which will be geared 'to shaping a significant change in the child's developmental path in the realms of thinking, learning, emotions and behaviour' (2006, p.345). The broad goals of such an environment he sees as:

1.   providing exposure to normative stimulation

2.   increasing the ability to imitate

3.   creating positive environmental pressure

4.   mustering adaptation skills

5.   precipitating the process of change by internalising environmental pressures and identifying them, and

6.   changing the status [of the learners]…from a perpetual protected entity to a bearer of responsibility.

(Feuerstein 2006, p.346)

The *Index for Inclusion* aims to help schools identify how their school can be restructured to meet the needs of all students (Booth and Ainscow 2002), following Ainscow's (2005) definition of inclusion, which includes such restructuring. The first dimension of the *Index* focuses upon a culture of inclusion, where 'staff seek to remove barriers to learning and participation in all aspects of the school'. This then suggests the importance of a learning environment which presents all learners with both a wide range of challenges for learning, and support for meeting these challenges, in their school and local community.

In writing about inclusive education and the teaching of thinking, Lebeer notes that inclusive education involves 'restructuring the cultures, policies and practices in schools so that they respond to the diversity of students in their area' and 'increasing the participation of students in, and reducing their exclusion from, the cultures, curricula and communities of local schools' (Lebeer 2006, p.12).

Principle 5: The learning environment needs to be open to change

The learning environment needs to be open to change, new ideas and new directions, and to affirm the partnership of all key players, including parents and students, in the process of change.

One of the key characteristics of a modifying environment is that it has a high degree of openness (Feuerstein, Rand and Feuerstein 2006).

We need to move away from viewing schools as places where students, and especially learners who are vulnerable and disadvantaged, are regarded as recipients of provision, and towards viewing them as active partners in planning and producing changes in the learning environment. The education legislation of some developed countries, such as Britain and New Zealand, needs to affirm such partnership with the learner, as does recent education legislation in Scotland and the Republic of Ireland which provides the learner with a more active decision-making role (Howie 2010).

As pointed out in Chapter 1, it is important that we match the teaching of thinking, and particularly decision-making skills, with a wider learning environment, which includes teachers who are open to, and encourage, the active use of such skills in many facets of school life.

The *Index for Inclusion* acknowledges the importance of students' partnership in their own learning. There is an indicator in the practices dimension, that 'students are actively involved in their own learning' (Booth and Ainscow 2002). Of particular interest to teachers will be *The Manchester Inclusion Standard: School Improvement*, in which ideas for, and tools for assessment of, such partnership are presented by Ainscow, Fox and Moore (2007).

Principle 6: The learning environment includes the wider community

The learning environment includes the learning community in which the school is placed. Not only should we see the school as a whole 'community of thinking and learning' (Brown 1997), we should also involve the wider school community (i.e. including parents and the local community served by the school). In the present writer's work with Feuerstein's approach to the teaching of thinking in a large South Auckland school with a high percentage of Maori students, the programme was delivered by a team that included the students' key Maori teachers. Agreement for the thinking approach was obtained from the parents of all of the students involved. However, at the end of four years of research with the programme, the writer regretted not having involved the wider community as real partners in the programme – for example, in identifying the aims of the project; actively participating in teaching and learning processes, in order to generalise (or, as Feuerstein puts it, to 'bridge') learning to real life; and jointly evaluating the outcomes of the programme. (See Howie, Richards and Pirihi 1993, and Howie 2003).

The importance of attending to such wider learning links is affirmed by Presseisen and her colleagues. They state: 'the classroom is linked to life beyond its boundaries, i.e. to the school as a whole, to other educators and staff, and to the entire community, including parents and other agents' (Presseisen, Smey-Richman and Beyer 1994, p.205).

UK government policy strongly endorses a community-linked approach to learning in order to meet the holistic needs of all children. This is clearly signalled in the *Every Child Matters* policy (House of Commons 2003) which spells out the five outcomes which services for children, including schools, should work towards: being healthy, staying safe, enjoying and achieving, making a positive contribution, and economic well-being. It acknowledges the importance, for vulnerable children, of positive links between the school and the community, and this importance is endorsed by leading writers on inclusion, such as Dyson (1997), Mittler (2000) and Todd (2007).

In the *Index for Inclusion* the culture dimension includes several indicators relevant to this community-linked approach, such as 'staff, governors, students and parents/carers share a philosophy of inclusion' and 'all local communities are involved in the school' (Booth and Ainscow 2002).

3. The mediator and the mediation

Principle 7: The mediation of thinking involves the mediator in a shared, reciprocal learning relationship with the learner

That we share the intention of the learning focus in a reciprocal way is a central criterion of mediation in Feuerstein's theory of mediated learning experience (Feuerstein and Feuerstein 1991), which is important in Feuerstein's approach to the teaching of thinking. In reviewing the Instrumental Enrichment programme for the teaching of thinking, which arises from this theory of mediation, Sternberg and Ben-Zeev note that

> the main goal is for students to develop a sense that they are active and responsible for their own learning experiences, not passive recipients of knowledge. Feuerstein and his colleagues believe that it is this latter goal that is most strongly associated with desired changes in the attitudinal, emotional and motivational components of learning. (Sternberg and Ben-Zeev 2001, p.336)

(See Chapter 4, Section 2 for fuller discussion of Feuerstein's theory and programme.)

This reciprocal sharing of learning should have an important 'affective' value (Greenberg 1990, p.36) whereby the mediator, who in our case is the teacher, expresses an emotional attachment and involvement with the learner and the lesson activities. Six important parameters for the mediator's demeanour which relate to this attachment are humour, sensitivity, belief, energy, creativity, and love (Silver and Burden 2006.)

This sharing of intention links to a key indicator in the *Index for Inclusion* for the culture dimension: 'staff, governors, students and parents/carers share a philosophy of inclusion', and to more specific indicators, such as 'staff and students treat each other with respect', 'lessons encourage the participation of all students', and 'students learn collaboratively' (Booth and Ainscow 2002).

An example of how the mediator may ensure that a vulnerable child is engaged in the learning process and sharing the learning intention, is given to us by Raphael Feuerstein. He explains how the mediator would engage in dialogue with the learner to help him/her to be aware of the learning process being engaged in, the steps being taken, and the motives for taking them. He sees this as creating metacognitive thinking structures which help the learner to develop these structures independently for other learning occasions (Feuerstein 2006, p.409).

Principle 8: The mediation of thinking involves the mediator in making the learning meaningful to the learner

In mediating a programme for the teaching of thinking, we need to make clear to the learners the meaningfulness of the programme as a whole, and its value to the learners' real lives. When evaluating the programme we should explore its meaning for the learners. For example, a SPARE wheel model is used by Burden and Nichols (1997) to evaluate an intervention using the Somerset Thinking Skill Course (Blagg, Ballinger and Gardner 1988), a direct descendent of the Feuerstein Instrumental Enrichment programme. The authors asked Year Seven students to respond to the questionnaire in terms of their enjoyment of, and the perceived usefulness of, the programme. A further 20 students were interviewed in depth about their feelings about the programme. The students ranked the potential value of the programme higher than their enjoyment or interest in it. Students' responses included the extent to which they found the work helpful in other classes, and students valued their increased ability 'to break down and solve problems, to make hypotheses, and to think before rushing in' as well as recognising their 'improved vocabulary, and their ability to work together in pairs and groups' (Burden and Nichols 1997, p.40).

In his list of inclusive approaches in classrooms and school for the teaching of thinking, Lebeer (2006) notes that an important criterion is the relevance of the thinking approach for the learner's life at present and in the future, with a specific aspect that 'pupils experience the learning tasks meaningfully' (p.52).

The *Index for Inclusion* indicator 'student difference is used as a resource for teaching and learning' suggests a link to those meanings that are unique for each diverse learner, and a sharing of those meanings (Booth and Ainscow 2002).

The particular importance of emotional and social meaning of the learning for the inclusion of all children is stressed by Raphael Feuerstein (2006). The *emotional* meaning is seen as important for the motivation involved in the transmission of the learning content to the learner's own learning repertoire. The *social* meaning of the learning is seen as mediated by both teachers and peers, within the learning context. He gives an example of how teachers can emphasise the importance of the learners' imitation of new social skills, both in terms of the imitation itself, and its significance in the learners' lives (p.350).

Principle 9: The mediation of thinking involves the mediator in the transferring and generalising of new learning

Feuerstein and Feuerstein (1991) use the unique term 'transcendence' in the sense of going beyond the immediate learning situation, in teaching for transfer or generalisation. It involves a wider idea, in that it also involves the transcending of immediate learning needs to embrace wider goals, including more long-term goals for change of self and change in society.

No matter what approach we use for the teaching of thinking, our teaching for the transfer or generalisation of the thinking skills and strategies being taught will be key to their effective use. In her chapter on identifying generic principles for effective implementation of programmes for the teaching of thinking, Baumfield (1997) identifies transfer of these skills to other aspects of the curriculum as an aspect of key concern. We need to mediate for transfer to real-life problem solving as well. Excellent examples of transfer (or bridging) to current problems that young people face in their lives, including such issues as safe use of the internet, and protection of the environment, are given in *Bridging Learning-Thinking Skills to Unlock Cognitive Potential* by Mentis, Dunn-Bernstein, Mentis and Skuy (2009).

Another example of the importance of teaching for transfer or generalisation is given in relation to another widely used approach to the teaching of thinking. In the present author's evaluation of the transfer or bridging of de Bono's CoRT approach in one whole-school intervention with it (Howie, Coombe and Lonergan 1998), interviews with the learners involved suggested that, even though a number of them did report transfer of strategies learnt on the programme to their real-life problem solving, more use could have been made in actual teaching sessions of the learners' own ideas and examples of how such strategies could be applied in their real lives.

As one of his criteria for an inclusive approach to the teaching of thinking in the classroom, Lebeer (2006) includes 'cohesion between different parts of learning' (p.53). By this he means that the learning in a lesson on the thinking strategy is linked to other learning activities, including those at home in leisure time.

The *Index for Inclusion* has within its practices dimension several indicators which suggest the importance of this linking between classroom learning and real life, such as 'community resources are known and drawn upon' and 'lessons develop an understanding of difference'

(Booth and Ainscow 2002). If we, as mediators, invite learners to contribute examples of the ways in which thinking skills and strategies can be applied in their own wider life experiences, we not only foster a wider perception of how these skills and strategies can be applied, but also encourage the possibilities for new learning and change in terms of empathy, self-change, and change in society – all part of transcendence.

We are reminded that for vulnerable learners and learners with special educational needs, the ultimate goal of inclusion in an ordinary school and classroom is preparation for inclusion in ordinary real life (Feuerstein 2006). We need to give careful thought to the challenges which full participation in the community brings for vulnerable learners, with particular attention to practised transfer of the thinking skills and strategies needed to deal effectively with such challenges.

4. The Task

Principle 10: The tasks used in the teaching of thinking should foster challenging, high-level thinking and real-life problem solving

The tasks used in any approach to the teaching of thinking should foster challenging, high-level thinking about curriculum subjects and real-life problem solving, including the emotional and social aspects involved in the problem solving.

In a British Council seminar on thinking skills in the curriculum, called 'The Tame and the Wild', Perkins, an international expert on the teaching of thinking, discussed the importance of choice of topics and tasks for teaching which 'wild the tame' – which teach for understanding rather than only for knowledge, and which develop thinking dispositions such as curiosity, appropriate scepticism and open-mindedness. Such tasks and topics involve the teacher and learner in conceptual exploration – for example, by talking about the topic, and by application both in subject areas and in meaningful occasions in real life identified by the learners. The learners can move in their understanding from what they know, extending their knowledge through thinking. Powerful questions which we can use in doing this thinking encourage the learner in exploration, connection and conclusion. In development of such understanding 'high road' transfer is involved, which is 'dependent on reflective abstract and mindful connection making' (Perkins 2002, p.13).

In terms of including all learners, this principle links to an *Index for Inclusion* indicator already mentioned: 'there are high expectations for all learners' (Booth and Ainscow 2002). In using concepts like that of individual difference in learning profiles, drawn from theoretical approaches such as Gardner's Multiple Intelligences (see Chapter 4, Section 6) and some learning style approaches, it is important that we give all learners, no matter what their profile (e.g. those strong in 'kinaesthetic learning'), opportunities and tasks for challenging, high-level, abstract verbal and conceptual thinking.

Another indicator within the *culture* dimension of the *Index for Inclusion* is: 'staff seek to remove barriers to learning and participation in all aspects of the school'. This includes the task or curriculum aspect, including the 'hidden curriculum', meaning all activities in the school which involve learning including those with considerable emotional and social content.

Further, in notes relating to the *policy* dimension of the *Index for Inclusion*, Booth and Ainscow include as sample questions: '(i) Do all curriculum development activities address the participation of students differing in background experience, attainment or impairment?' and '(ii) Do all curriculum development activities address the reduction of barriers to learning and participation?'

A number of the indicators in the *practice* dimension of the *Index for Inclusion* relate to task challenge – for example, 'teaching is planned with the learning of all students in mind' and 'teachers are concerned to support the learning and participation of all students'.

Principle 11: The task needs to be fully understood in terms of its task dimensions and demands

This includes understanding in particular the processes involved in the task, so that the mediator can facilitate the most flexible and appropriate decision making in tailoring aspects of the task to individuals' learning needs.

The present writer has presented a rationale for using Feuerstein's cognitive map to help carry out a task analysis and adapt the task to meet the learners' needs, particularly when addressing real-life problem-solving tasks (Howie 2008). Key dimensions or parameters of the cognitive map are:

- the content around which the task is centred (its content focus should be fitting to the learning enhancement aimed at)
- the modality in which the content is presented (e.g. as concrete objects, pictures, figures, graphs, words or symbols etc.)
- the phases of the mental act involved (input, elaboration and output).

This processing approach is linked to another key parameter, the cognitive operations involved in the task, meaning the central mental operations which are required to carry out the task, such as comparison and categorisation. Finally, the remaining parameters (which we can readily change to fit the learners' needs) are the level of complexity of the task (in terms of both number of units of information involved and novelty of the task to the learner) and the level of abstraction of the task (ranging from more concrete to more abstract). (See Howie (2008) for examples of research-informed, real-life problem-solving tasks of varying degrees of complexity which are first analysed and then addressed with appropriate cognitive intervention.)

Principle 11 is not specifically addressed in the *Index for Inclusion* in terms of task analysis and understanding of the learning processes involved. However, one practice dimension indicator, 'assessment contributes to the achievement of all students', could include teacher assessment of task demands, and adequate differentiation of task demands to meet the needs of all learners (Booth and Ainscow 2002).

Lebeer states in writing on the teaching of thinking and inclusion: 'What is good inclusive practice? Differentiation of learning materials… according to [the] concept of [the] cognitive map: content, modality, complexity, phases [and] abstraction' (2006, p.33).

In relation to inclusion and the teaching of thinking, Raphael Feuerstein draws our attention to the ways in which task analysis is important for differentiation of the task to meet the unique learning needs of each learner (Feuerstein 2006). He states: 'Together with the children the teacher must analyse the meaning of the assignment [i.e. the task], its requirements, its level of difficulty (objectively and relative to the children's current level)' (p.389). He also stresses that it is important to change from a product-oriented approach (focusing on the learning outcome only) to a process-oriented approach, and sees this as important for overcoming feelings of frustration in inclusion.

Principle 12: The links between the teaching of thinking and curriculum tasks need to be as strong as possible

This point is made directly by Presseisen, Smey-Richman and Beyer (1994), and they also state that 'task-related knowledge (of skills and strategies) should be applied to other task content, contexts and setting. So cross-curricular links are very important in the teaching of thinking, in order to enhance the transfer of learning' (p.199).

The building of an integrated curriculum for the teaching of insight for transfer is important, according to Perkins (1991). Some key characteristics of mediation which will foster transfer from one task to another are outlined by Ben-Hur (2000). We need to include sufficient practice, we should use a variety of contents and contexts as a vehicle for learning skills or concepts, and we should facilitate development of the learners' deeper understanding (meaning) through teacher-led reflective discussions following the learners' experience. We need to encourage learners to connect new skills to their past experiences, to recognise where their newly acquired skills will be useful, and to apply them.

This principle links to the debate concerning whether the teaching of thinking should be by means of approaches such as de Bono's CoRT programme and Feuerstein's 'Instrumental Enrichment' programme which use task tools or instruments with content which is novel and non-curricular, and which also require maximum 'bridging' to curriculum tasks and real-life problem-solving tasks; or by means of approaches that 'infuse' the teaching of thinking through curriculum content (such as the approach developed by Swartz (Swartz and Parks 1994)).

Perkins (1995) states 'both are better'. A careful analysis of the advantages and disadvantages of both approaches was carried out by Sternberg as early as 1987. He argued for a 'mixed model in which thinking skills are taught as a separate course at the same time that they are infused and reinforced throughout the entire curriculum' (p.255).

In the present writer's view, the more independent approaches can be particularly useful in highlighting the thinking operations in novel and non-failed-at tasks, which then can be strongly bridged to ordinary curriculum subject tasks, and the same teacher can remind learners of these thinking operations when teaching the ordinary curriculum subjects.

The *Index for Inclusion* makes particular mention of the importance of the link to community learning for inclusion, with indicators such as 'all students take part in activities outside the classroom' and 'community resources are known and drawn upon' (Booth and Ainscow 2002).

Lebeer (2006) amplifies this in discussing the teaching of thinking and inclusion by stating: 'what pupils do in one sector of the learning activities is given place in other learning activities' (p.53).

Raphael Feuerstein (2006) is particularly keen to see an abundance of varied stimuli and intensity of stimulation in the tasks within an ordinary classroom, so that all children will be challenged to transfer and apply new thinking skills and strategies.

5. The learner

Principle 13: The mediator of thinking for all must address the unique learning needs of every individual learner

Presseisen, Smey-Richman and Beyer (1994) note that the approach to the teaching of thinking needs to 'meet the individual's unique learning needs while encouraging development of potential' (p.199).

This principle is in line with current educational policy in the UK and other countries (like New Zealand) for 'personalised learning'. A *Five-Year Strategy for Children and Learners* with a key principle, stated as 'greater personalisation and choice', was presented by the UK Secretary for Education and Skills (DfES 2004). This policy includes the 'personalisation of teaching and learning to the needs of the individual child' (Section 12). Within such an approach, we need to consider the learner's learning needs and rate of progress in relation to that child's previous progress, rather than in comparison with other learners. Individual choice is also an important component of 'personalised learning'.

Sensitivity to unique individual needs will involve us in programmes for the teaching of thinking in a flexible rather than a lock-step approach, and in evaluation in terms of individual response to that approach. We will need to pay particular attention to unique individual needs in terms of:

- cultural needs
- needs relating to socio-economic factors, such as disadvantage
- emotional and social needs.

This book presents a three-tiered approach to the teaching of thinking, which takes into account Norwich's (1996) conception of learning needs in terms of inclusive education. Chapter 3 outlines this three-tier approach and the common needs, exceptional needs, and individual needs, as conceptualised by Norwich, to which the approaches can be addressed.

The *Index for Inclusion* affirms the recognition of such individual needs in terms of the *culture* indicator 'staff and students treat one another as human beings as well as occupants of a role' (Booth and Ainscow 2002), involving a holistic and unique valuing of each individual. In the *policy* dimension, the indicator 'the school arranges teaching groups so that all students are valued' raises the complex issue of how support is offered through the grouping of students, to maximise the learning of all, as inclusively as possible. Within any grouping we need to ensure proper valuing of all students, as well as valuing of what each student can offer the others. Within the *practice* dimension of the *Index for Inclusion*, indicators such as 'teaching is planned with the learning of all students in mind' and 'lessons encourage the participation of all students' relate to this principle of addressing the unique learning needs of each learner.

In recognising unique learning strengths and needs, Gardner's (1983) theory of Multiple Intelligences has much to offer. It is an inclusive, rather than elitist, notion of intelligence, in which each learner has a unique profile of intelligence, or learning abilities, with learning strengths which can be capitalised on for enhancing learning, and abilities which are less strong and need to be strengthened. Further, there are a number of theories of learning style which suggest that we should capitalise on an individual's unique learning preferences. Some of these approaches are addressed in later chapters of this book.

Principle 14: The mediator of thinking needs to address the learning needs which the learner is experiencing in the learning process involved with the thinking interaction

As mediators we need not only to understand the processes involved in each thinking task, as covered in the previous section; we also need to observe the learner carefully to identify at what phase in those processes the learner is experiencing difficulty and needs guidance and support.

Feuerstein has given us a unique tool to help identify learners' needs in relation to functions and dysfunctions in the thinking process, which he sees as having *input, elaboration* and *output* phases. (Chapter 4, Section 2 discusses this 'Checklist for Cognitive Functions and Dysfunctions', as does Howie (2003, p.36)). In the input phase, for example, learners can experience difficulties in systematically exploring the learning situation, in the precise and accurate understanding of words and meanings, and in using information from more than one source. In the elaboration phase, learners can experience difficulties in defining the problem being addressed, in thinking about information relating to it already stored in the brain, in selecting relevant cues, in making comparisons, in summarising the information, and in using all of this elaboration to plan a solution. In the output phase there can be difficulties in controlled and planned expression of thoughts and actions to produce the thinking outcome (the solution to the problem), as well as in precise and accurate use of words and concepts to communicate that solution.

Complex factors may act as barriers to successful thinking in each of these phase aspects, including within-learner factors such as, for example, cognitive difficulties relating to a disability, or emotional and motivational difficulties; and more context-related factors such as disadvantage and inadequate previous mediation of the process skills.

The *Index for Inclusion* has an important indicator in its *culture* dimension: 'staff seek to remove barriers to learning and participation in all aspects of the school'. This includes barriers experienced by the learner in carrying out the thinking process. Further, a *practice* indicator states: 'assessment contributes to the achievements of all students' (Booth and Ainscow 2002). Learning process assessment, on which there is now a huge literature, is an essential tool for each of us as mediators. The present writer presents in her book *Thinking about the Teaching of Thinking* (Howie 2003) a chapter called 'Assessing and Meeting Learning Needs', in which a rationale is given for assessing the learner's learning process, with some examples from the author's own research studies. For example, using a 'think aloud' technique for observing a young person's learning process showed where there was metacognitive awareness of the difficulty of the task ('Oh my God, this one's hard'); where the young person perceived her own difficulties, that is, metacognition of the self ('I'm getting a wee bit tired' on her third mistake); where she was reflecting on a strategy ('I thought out loud before I could actually say this is my answer'); and self-evaluation ('Well, that one's kaput!') (p.32).

Principle 15: The mediator needs to work in partnership with the learner for the fullest self-regulation of their thinking and learning approaches

The importance of learner choice and self-building of their own learning techniques is emphasised by Sternberg, Okagaki and Jackson (1990). That the learner needs to consciously improve his/her learning techniques is stated by Presseisen *et al.* (1994), who see it as important to

> help students to trust their own minds, to build connections to what they know and do beyond the classroom, and to consider their own and their classmates' ways of thinking. Through such elaborative experience, the learner-as-self becomes defined, cognitive competence becomes owned, and commitment to learning is enjoined. (p.213–214)

The *Index for Inclusion* states as a *practice* indicator: 'students are actively involved in their own learning' (Booth and Ainscow 2002). This applies, of course, to all learners, but is particularly important for some more vulnerable learners who are disengaged from learning. Such disengagement can be affected by the apparent meaninglessness of the learning task, inadequate mediation of the task to meet the cognitive, emotional and social needs of the learner, and the experience of failure in learning tasks.

Some of the important factors in mediation of thinking in relation to motivational and emotional needs of learners have been identified by Tzuriel, Samuels and Feuerstein (1988). These link not only to needs related to within-learner characteristics, such as accessibility to mediation, need for mastery, tolerance of frustration, locus of control, overcoming fear of failure and defensiveness – but also to needs which relate to appropriate mediation of the task, so that aspects of the tasks are modified by us to meet the learners' needs, learners are prepared for difficulty, feedback is given on reasons for success (such as use of a strategy), and past failure is compared to present success.

Conclusion

This brings us back full circle to the original conceptualisation of the key dimensions in the teaching of thinking, illustrated at the beginning of this chapter. The principles covered address important challenges and opportunities for changes in the mediation itself, changes to the task, and changes aimed at for the learner, to maximise the effectiveness of a cognitive enhancement approach.

All these aspects are all underpinned by positive changes in our belief systems concerning the possibilities for cognitive change. These positive beliefs should be shared by all of the key players involved, including the mediator and the learner; and supported by positive restructuring of the learning environment in order to include all learners in enhancement of thinking and learning.

Self-reflective questions

☐ In your school context, which of these principles require greater attention?

☐ How adequately is each principle being expressed in your school's planning for the teaching of thinking?

References

Ainscow, M. (2005) 'Education for all: Making it happen.' *Support for Learning 10*, 147–153.

Ainscow, M., Fox, S. and Moore, M. (2007) *The Manchester Inclusion Standard: School Improvement.* Manchester: Manchester University.

Baumfield, V. (1997) 'Thinking Skills: Identifying Generic Principles and Supporting Effective Implementation.' In Q.M. Ling and H.W. Kam (eds) *7th International Conference on Thinking. Thinking Processes: Going Beyond the Surface Curriculum.* Singapore: Prentice Hall.

Ben-Hur, M. (2000) 'Learning and Transfer: A Tautology.' In B. Lighter (ed.) *Teaching for Intelligence II: A Collection of Articles.* Palatine, IL: Skylight Professional Development.

Blagg, N., Ballinger, M. and Gardner, R. (1988) *Somerset Thinking Skills Course.* Oxford: Basil Blackwell/Somerset County Council.

Booth, T. and Ainscow, M. (2002) *The Index for Inclusion: Developing Learning and Participation in Schools.* Bristol: CSIE.

Brown, A.L. (1997) 'Transforming schools into communities of thinking and learning about serious matters.' *American Psychologist 52*, 4, 399–413.

Burden, R.L. and Nichols, S.L. (1997) 'Evaluating the effects of introducing a thinking skills program into the secondary school curriculum.' *Journal of Cognitive Education 6*, 33–45.

Department for Education and Skills (2004) *Five-Year Strategy for Children and Learners.* London: HMSO.

Dyson, A. (1997) 'Social and educational disadvantage: Reconnecting special needs education.' *British Journal of Special Education 24*, 152–156.

Feuerstein, R. (2008) Presentation to a seminar, Venice International Workshops, author's notes.

Feuerstein, R. and Feuerstein, S. (1991) 'Mediated Learning Experience: A Theoretical Review.' In R. Feuerstein, P.S. Klein and A.J. Tannenbaum (eds) *Mediated Learning Experience (MLE): Theoretical, Psychological and Learning Implications.* London: Freund.

Feuerstein, R., Feuerstein, S., Falik, L.H. and Rand, Y. (eds) (2006) *Creating and Enhancing Cognitive Modifiability: The Feuerstein Instrumental Enrichment Program.* Jerusalem: International Centre for the Enhancement of Learning Potential.

Feuerstein, R., Rand, Y. and Feuerstein, Ra.S. (2006) *You Love Me! Don't Accept Me as I Am: Helping the Low Functioning Person Excel.* Jerusalem: International Centre for the Enhancement of Learning Potential.

Feuerstein, Ra.S. (2006) 'Mainstreaming Special Needs Children According to the Criteria of Mediating Learning Experience and Shaping Modifying Environments.' In R. Feuerstein, Y. Rand and Ra.S. Feuerstein (eds) *You Love me! Don't Accept Me as I Am: Helping the Low Functioning Person Excel.* Jerusalem: International Centre for the Enhancement of Learning Potential.

Gardner, H. (1983) *Frames of Mind: The Theory of Multiple Intelligences.* New York: Basic Books.

Greenberg, K.H. (1990) 'Mediated learning in the classroom.' *International Journal of Cognitive Education and Mediated Learning 1*, 33–44.

House of Commons (2003) *Every Child Matters.* London: House of Commons.

Howie, D.R. (2003) *Thinking about the Teaching of Thinking.* Wellington: New Zealand Council for Educational Research.

Howie, D.R. (2008) 'The Cognitive Map and Real-Life Problem Solving.' In O. Tan and A. Seng (eds) *Cognitive Modifiability in Learning and Assessment: International Perspectives.* Singapore: Cengage Learning.

Howie, D.R. (2010) 'A comparative study of the positioning of children with special educational needs in the legislation of Britain, New Zealand and the Republic of Ireland.' *International Journal of Inclusive Education 14*, 8, 755–776.

Howie, D.R., Coombe, P. and Lonergan, J. (1998) 'Using single subject design in an Auckland study of the CoRT thinking skill programme.' Paper presented to the Conference on Teaching for Successful Intelligence, Auckland.

Howie, D.R., Richards, R. and Pirihi, H. (1993) 'Teaching thinking skills to Maori adolescents.' *International Journal of Cognitive Education and Mediated Learning 3*, 70–91.

Kaniel, S. and Feuerstein, R. (1989) 'Special needs of children with learning difficulties.' *Oxford Review of Education 15*, 165–179.

Lebeer, J. (ed.) (2006) *In-clues: Clues to Inclusive and Cognitive Education.* Antwerpen-Apeldoorn: Garant.

Mentis, M., Dunn-Bernstein, M., Mentis, M. and Skuy, M. (2009) *Bridging Learning–Thinking Skills to Unlock Cognitive Potential.* London: Corwin Press (Sage).

Mercer (2008) *The Cognitive Abilities Test (CAT).* Mercer: Mercer Publishing.

Mittler, P. (2000) *Working Towards Inclusive Education: Social Contexts.* London: David Fulton.

Norwich, B. (1996) 'Special needs education or education for all: Connective specialism and ideological impurity.' *British Journal of Special Education 23*, 100–103.

Perkins, D.N. (1991) 'Educating for insight.' *Educational Leadership 49*, 2, 4–8.

Perkins, D.N. (1995) *Outsmarting IQ: The Emerging Science of Learnable Intelligence.* New York: The Free Press.

Perkins, D.N. (2002) 'The tame and the wild.' Presentation to a British Council seminar, Belfast.

Presseisen, B.Z., Smey-Richman, B. and Beyer, F.S. (1994) 'Cognitive Development Through Radical Change: Restructuring Classroom Environments for Students at Risk.' In M. Ben-Hur (ed.) *On Feuerstein's Instrumental Enrichment: A Collection.* Palatine, IL: IRI Skylight.

Silver, J. and Burden, R.L. (2006) 'Building Blocks of Learning: Dynamic Assessment and Cognitive Mediation with Children.' In O. Tan and A. Seng (eds) *Enhancing Cognitive Functions: Applications Across Contexts.* Singapore: McGraw-Hill Education.

Sternberg, R.J. (1987) 'Questions and Answers about the Nature and Teaching of Thinking Skills.' In J.B. Baron and R.J. Sternberg (eds) *Teaching Thinking Skills: Theory and Practice.* New York: Freeman and Company.

Sternberg, R.J. (2000) 'Group and Individual Differences in Intelligences: What Can and Should We Do about Them?' In A. Kozulin and Y. Rand (eds) *Experience of Mediated Learning: An Impact of Feuerstein's Theory in Education and Psychology.* Oxford: Pergamon.

Sternberg, R.J. and Ben-Zeev, T. (2001) 'Teaching Thinking.' In R.J. Sternberg and T. Ben-Zeev (eds) *Complex Cognition: The Psychology of Human Thought.* New York: Oxford University Press.

Sternberg, R.J., Okagaki, L. and Jackson, A.S. (1990) 'Practical intelligence for success in school.' *Educational Leadership 43*, 2, 69–74.

Swartz, R.J. and Parks, S. (1994) *Infusing the Teaching of Critical and Creative Thinking into Content Instruction.* Pacific Grove, CA: Critical Thinking Books and Software.

Todd, E. (2007) *Partnerships for Inclusive Education: A Critical Approach to Collaborative Working.* London: Routledge.

Tzuriel, D., Samuels, M.T. and Feuerstein, R. (1988) 'Non-intellectual Factors in Dynamic Assessment.' In R.M. Gupta and P. Coxhead (eds) *Cultural Diversity and Learning Efficiency.* London: Macmillan Press.

CHAPTER 3

The Three-tier Model for the Teaching of Thinking

Introduction

This chapter introduces the three-tier model for the teaching of thinking for all classroom learners. It first outlines what the three tiers are, then gives reasons for using a three-tier model. Within this rationale, the increasing use of a three-tier model internationally, to address the needs of all classroom learners in a variety of curriculum areas, is discussed, with examples from various countries.

The three-tier model

This model is depicted in Figure 3.1.

The three tiers are:

- Tier 1 – teaching thinking for all, with approaches which are integral to all classroom teaching and learning
- Tier 2 – working with small groups for those needing further particular attention to the teaching of thinking
- Tier 3 – working with individuals who need further individual attention, beyond Tier 2.

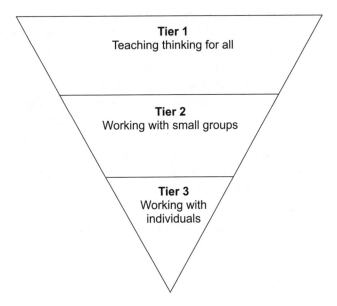

Figure 3.1 The three-tier model for the teaching of thinking

Why the three-tier model?

This book is about the teaching of thinking in an inclusive way, meaning a way that meets the needs of all classroom learners. In the field of inclusive education, three kinds of educational need have been identified by a leading UK writer (Norwich 1996) and endorsed by Mittler (2000), a key writer in inclusive education and international leader in the field of special education. (While based at the University of Manchester, Mittler visited and influenced many countries, including New Zealand.)

The three kinds of needs, as outlined by Norwich, are:

- common needs – arising from the characteristics shared by all (e.g. need for esteem)

- exceptional needs – arising from characteristics shared by some (e.g. visual impairment, high musical abilities)

- individual needs – arising from characteristics unique to the individual.

These three kinds of needs map well onto the 'three wave' model first proposed by the UK Department for Education and Skills (DfES 2003) when it suggested, in the policy document *Excellence and Enjoyment: A Strategy for Primary Schools*, that we should have an inclusive focus on learning for individual children, including those with special educational needs, using a 'three wave' model which addressed both literacy and mathematics. In *wave 1*, there was to be 'effective inclusion of all pupils in a high quality, daily literacy hour and mathematics lesson (Quality First Teaching)'. *Wave 2* would consist of small group, low-cost intervention. *Wave 3* would involve specific, targeted intervention for pupils requiring special educational needs (SEN) support (DfES 2003, Section 4.6).

This is similar to the model for literacy instruction presented in the final independent report into literacy by Rose (DfES 2006), where the provision is seen as:

- Wave 1, the effective inclusion of all children in daily 'quality first' teaching

- Wave 2, additional interventions to enable children to work at age-related expectations or above

- Wave 3, additional, highly personalised intervention – for example, specifically targeted approaches for children identified as requiring SEN support.

Rose is careful to state: 'It is important to recognise that these "waves" signify types of provision and not categories of children' (DfES 2006, para. 133).

The three kinds of needs are also in line with the UK three-tier model for the teaching material addressing social and emotional needs (SEAL) (DfES 2005). In this approach, presented diagrammatically as an inverted triangle, the first and largest tier is for 'quality first teaching of social, emotional and behavioural skills to all children', involving 'effective whole-school or setting policies and frameworks for promoting health and wellbeing'. The second tier involves 'small-group intervention for children who need additional help in developing skills, and for their families'. The third and smallest tier involves 'individual intervention' (DfES 2005, p.13, Figure 2).

The purpose of using a three-tier framework for the teaching of thinking is to ensure that we have first, an approach by a school which addresses the whole-school and school community needs, but one which also includes small group approaches and individualised interventions which address the exceptional and unique needs of learners, over and above the needs shared by all. It is expected that the three tiers will run concurrently in any school situation.

For example, the teaching of thinking in an inclusive way in a primary school in the Netherlands is described for us by Lebeer (2006). First, there is teaching of metacognitive skills (learning to learn) for all learners in the school. As part of this work, all children are encouraged to work in small groups and to reflect on their thinking work. A subgroup of these children also spends two extra hours per week on Feuerstein's Instrumental Enrichment programme for the teaching of thinking. A learner with severe language needs obtains further individual support through the 'Thinking Bears' approach developed by Camp and Bash (1985). (This is a metacognitive approach which provides self-regulation through private speech, based on cards depicting a bear using a series of problem-solving self-instructions.) As part of the more intensive levels of support, dynamic assessment with Feuerstein's Learning Potential Assessment Device is used, rather than traditional intelligence assessment (Lebeer 2006, p.32 and p.34).

The three-tier model in practice

An example of the teaching of thinking in what could be considered a three-tiered approach is seen in the teaching of thinking adopted as policy by the Scottish Borders, which makes systematic use of the Feuerstein approach. Community-wide Tier 1 coverage is provided by giving opportunities for training in the tools of the approach to all key community members, including parents, as well as involved professionals in partner agencies such as social work and health visitors, members of school management teams and teachers. This is seen by O'Neill, a leader in the development, as creating a 'modifying environment' with a common language and a common approach (O'Neill 2009).

In the initial pilot programme (O'Neill 2007) there was a particular focus on addressing underachievement by pupils as a result of social, emotional or behavioural problems. All newly qualified teachers (NQTs) are trained in the use of Feuerstein's mediated learning experience (MLE) criteria, and given support in teaching with the criteria, so that these can be used in an infused way in all classroom teaching. Each teacher is given a copy of the updated book by Mentis *et al.* (2009) on mediated learning, and especially bridging, using the MLE criteria, and develops lesson plans for incorporating the criteria into their teaching processes. Anne-Theresa Lawrie, Scottish Borders Learning and Teaching Development Officer, notes: 'what began as a pilot looking at underachievers is now involving mainstream subjects and whole-school teaching as practitioners began to see the benefit for everyone. This is for all children and it should be taught throughout the curriculum' (Lawrie, cited in Ross 2007).

At the Tier 2 and Tier 3 levels, support professionals and teachers can obtain training in a wide range of Feuerstein's tools, including Feuerstein's original Instrumental Enrichment (FIE) programme for the teaching of thinking, and the newer FIE-Basic programme for younger learners and learners with more severe learning difficulties, so that work that caters for groups of children with exceptional needs, and more intensive individual work, can be carried out. Again, in the initial pilot project, one of the aims was to equip teachers to deliver the FIE programme to the most vulnerable learners.

After only six months of the pilot project, evaluation was carried out independently by a local university to judge the impact of the programme on both teachers and pupils (O'Neill 2007). The teachers who were interviewed showed a significant shift in their attitudes towards both learning and learners, reporting that they were using mediated learning throughout the schools, and engaging in a more 'open and powerful type of dialogue that is likely to develop young people's ability to learn for themselves' (p.2).

They also saw the programme as likely to enhance other policy initiatives such as a 'curriculum for excellence'. When using the Feuerstein cognitive enhancement instruments, ratings made by the teachers indicated that 98 per cent of learners had improved their 'correction of deficient cognitive functions'. O'Neill's report notes: 'It appears that the FIE pupils, with a history of social, emotional and behavioural needs, not only retained what they had learned, but also generalised their learning to a new task' (O'Neill 2007, p.3).

We find further examples of the increasing use of a three-tier model in the USA, where states are developing models to address the 'Response to Intervention' (RtI)[1] policy requirement introduced in 2008, with an aim of avoiding assessment that leads mainly to special class placement (Ballanca 2009). It is seen as a multi-tiered, problem-solving approach that addresses the learning needs of all students; a school improvement approach which is to be used at all school levels. In one state, Colorado, the state Department of Education (undated) describes

---

1   Response to Intervention (RTI or RtI) is a method of intervention used in the United States to provide early and effective assistance to children having difficulty with learning. It seeks to prevent academic failure through early intervention, frequent progress measurement, and increasingly intensive research-based instructional intervention for children who continue to have difficulty.

the basic underpinning of the RtI approach as relying on the premise that all learners receive research-based instruction in general education, that learning is assessed early and often, with progress monitoring, and that if there are concerns about learner progress, a three-tier model is used to address the learning needs. These three tiers are as follows:

- Tier I instruction includes high-quality, research-based curricula and instruction strategies to meet the needs of all students. Within this tier flexible grouping that targets specific skills is included, so that the instructional goals of all students can be met.

- Tier II provides supplemental instruction in addition to that provided in Tier I, designed to meet the learning needs of students not progressing as expected at Tier I.

- Tier III provides more explicit instruction that is focused on a specific skill need, which could be either an acceleration need or a remedial need.

Shapiro, who is assisting the state of Pennsylvania in developing their response to the RtI policy, has presented a paper on the RtI Action website entitled 'Tiered instruction and intervention in a Response-to-Intervention model'. In this paper he notes that tiered instruction represents a model in which the instruction delivered to students varies on several dimensions that relate to the nature and severity of the student's difficulties. He raises some important issues which are of interest to us in decision making for each tier level:

- At Tier I, he notes the importance both of good choice of programme out of those available from commercial publishers, and of sufficient and ongoing professional development for staff developing the chosen programme/s.

- Tier II work is for children who do not reach minimal levels of expected competency ('benchmarks'), identified through an assessment, and instruction is focused on their identified needs in small groups of about five to eight children.

- Children who are identified to be at high risk of failure are provided with Tier III instruction, both in small groups of three to five children, and in one-to-one instruction.

- The differences in instruction in the three tiers can be in both intensity and frequency of the instruction. Progress monitoring also becomes more intensive at each tier level, with learners in Tier III provision monitored twice a week, in some examples.

Shapiro presents a very interesting account of how schools can be restructured in order to provide a flexible approach to RtI, with maximisation of school personnel resources across the tiers, and collaboration of teaching staff.

While the RtI policy in the USA relates to the general school curriculum, it is also providing an appropriate opportunity to incorporate the teaching of thinking into the school curriculum within a flexible restructuring of the interventions. For example, as reported by James Ballanca (2009), in the state of Michigan, Ben-Hur, as district consultant and an expert on Feuerstein's Instrumental Enrichment programme, is involved in the use of Feuerstein's programme for the teaching of thinking for all children. The programme is taught for a three-year intervention. All teachers are trained in the approach, and supported by consultants, both to initiate the intervention and to carry on with it. Ballanca reports that teachers are already noticing changes in learning, which probably relate to their own new teaching approaches. In this example, the usual standardised testing is being used, but Ballanca comments that the RtI policy allows for use of a more dynamic approach as well, such as Feuerstein's Learning Potential Assessment Device, intervention with Instrumental Enrichment, and reassessment with the Learning Potential Assessment Device.

Professor Elena Grigorenko (2005), in her keynote address to the 10th International Conference of the International Association for Cognitive Education and Psychology in Durham, commented that the new RtI approach, which involves collecting multiple measures over time, has the potential for identifying change, and considering learning more directly. It could look at learning in relation to other variables, such as type of instruction. She saw it as dynamic assessment reincarnated and restructured, and hoped that such dynamic assessment will make its way into the literature on RtI.

Another emerging example of a three-tier approach can be found in Hong Kong. The Education Bureau (2007), part of the Government of Hong Kong, has a policy on 'gifted education', which advocates a three-tier mode of operation for this area of education (which is often associated with the use of cognitive enhancement programmes).

- Tier 1 is whole-school based, aimed at the delivery of higher order thinking skills, creativity and personal–social competence within the curriculum for all learners. This level also aims at differentiation of teaching through appropriate grouping of learners, to meet their needs with enrichment and extension of curriculum areas in regular classrooms.

- Tier 2 involves pulling out from the regular classrooms homogeneous groups of learners, to allow for enhancement in specific areas, such as creativity training and leadership training, and in specific curriculum areas where there is outstanding performance, such as maths and arts.

- Tier 3 is for external support from bodies such as tertiary institutes, to provide expert resources for the exceptionally gifted, such as counselling, mentorship, early entry into advanced classes, etc.

Although this policy is aimed specifically at learners who are gifted, it also has a more inclusive Tier 1 approach.

Chapters 4, 5 and 6 cover each of the three tiers separately, identifying key issues for us to address in each tier, and possible approaches to the teaching of thinking which could be used for that tier. Each approach is supported with an extended practical example.

Self-reflective questions

☐ How well does the three-tier model for the teaching of thinking outlined above fit with the educational policies and practices of your country, in general?

☐ How well does the three-tier model fit with the philosophy, policies and practices on inclusion (i.e. meeting the needs of all learners), in your country?

References

Ballanca, J. (2009) Personal communication.

Camp, B. and Bash, M. (1985) *Think Aloud: Increasing Social and Cognitive Skills–Applying a Self-regulating Private Model to Classroom Settings.* Ardmore, PA: Workbook Publishing.

Colorado Department of Education (undated) *6 components of RtI–Curriculum and Instruction.* Available at www.cde.state.co.us/RtI/curriculum.htm, accessed on 8 June 2009.

Department for Education and Skills (DfES) (2003) *Excellence and Enjoyment: A Strategy for Primary Schools.* Norwich: DfES.

Department for Education and Skills (DfES) (2005) *Excellence and Enjoyment: Social and Emotional Aspects of Learning (SEAL)* Norwich: DfES.

Department for Education and Skills (DfES) (Rose, J.) (2006) *Independent Review of the Teaching of Early Reading: Final Report.* Norwich: DfES.

Education Bureau (2007) *Gifted Education.* Hong Kong: Education Bureau.

Grigorenko, E. (2005) 'Dynamic assessment: When assessment and instruction are two sides of the same coin.' Keynote address to the 10th International Association for Cognitive Education and Psychology, Durham, July 2005.

Lebeer, J. (ed.) (2006) *In-clues: Clues to Inclusive and Cognitive Education.* Antwerpen-Apeldoorn: Garant.

Mentis, M., Dunn-Bernstein, M.J., Mentis, M. and Skuy, M. (2009) *Bridging Learning: Unlocking Cognitive Potential In and Out of the Classroom.* London: Corwin Press.

Mittler, P. (2000) *Working Towards Inclusive Education: Social Contexts.* London: David Fulton.

Norwich, B. (1996) 'Special needs education or education for all: Connective specialism and ideological impurity.' *British Journal of Special Education 23,* 100–103.

O'Neill, B. (2007) *Feuerstein Partnership Evaluation Report.* Available at www.feuersteintraining.co.uk/article2.htm, accessed on 27 November 2009.

O'Neill, B. (2009) Personal communication.

Ross, R. (2007) 'Tools of the Learning Trade.' *Times Educational Supplement,* 16 February 2007.

Shapiro, E.S. (undated) *Tiered Instruction and Intervention in a Response to Intervention Model.* RTI Action Network. Available at www.rtinetwork.org/essential/tieredinstruction/tiered-instruction-and-intervention-rti-model, accessed on 25 March 2011.

CHAPTER 4

Tier 1 – Teaching Thinking for All

Approaches which are Integral to All Classroom Teaching and Learning

Introduction

This chapter addresses the first and most comprehensive tier as outlined in the three-tier model; see Figure 4.1 below.

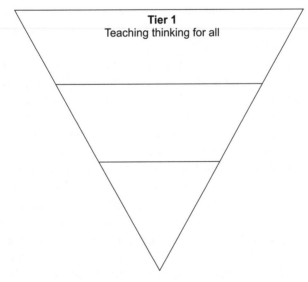

Figure 4.1 Tier 1 – Teaching thinking for all

It addresses the common needs of all classroom learners for high-quality teaching of thinking, and introduces, first, some important issues which we need to address in considering what approaches are best used for the teaching of thinking at Tier 1 level. It then presents a variety of approaches for the teaching of thinking which can be considered as appropriate at this level. The list is not exhaustive, but includes widely recognised approaches, and approaches with which the present writer is familiar and in many cases has engaged, in some capacity. For each approach the following is covered: the value that it has as an approach; an example of it in practical use in the classroom (generally drawn from the work of the writer and her colleagues); and references for the approach (at the end of the chapter).

Important issues in Tier 1 teaching of thinking

As a first step for our consideration, every school and its school community need to collaboratively develop a systematic approach to the teaching of thinking which will make it available to the whole-school community, as part of the ordinary classroom learning environment. Some of the principles that such a systematic, school-wide teaching of thinking would involve were developed by the present writer at the 'Breakthroughs' International Conference on Thinking in Auckland (Howie 2001), in partnership with the participants in the conference session. These included making available a thinking programme which teaches metacognitive knowledge, strategies and attitudes to all learners in the school, with formal training in the approach for all key staff and subject teachers in a school. They also included the principle that the teaching of thinking should begin at the earliest possible age, in order to maximise opportunities for learning, and involve parents, caregivers and members of the wider community in the mediation of that approach. Another principle is to consider the relationship between the teaching of thinking within a school, and the school-wide assessment approaches. This would include not only summative assessment, looking at both the processes and the outcomes of effective learning, thinking and problem solving; but also formative assessment, particularly in terms of identifying thinking processes which need to be addressed. Finally, the unique contributions which both the latest technology and the wider school community can make towards this systematic approach to the teaching of thinking were also acknowledged.

Next we need to ensure that all schools and their school communities develop an approach to the teaching of thinking for all children which reflects the values and cultural uniqueness of the school population. All of the key players in the school, including the learners, staff, parents, and wider community members, need to be able to identify the common need, or needs, for the teaching of thinking, and the ways these can be addressed, so that there is full ownership of them, in a partnership process. A detailed rationale for the importance of considering cultural issues when using a programme for the teaching of thinking was presented by the present writer in a paper to the International Conference on Thinking in Washington, Seattle (Howie 2003b). The rationale is as follows:

1. Thinking is culturally embedded, so any programme for the teaching of thinking needs to reflect the thinking embodied in the culture of the learners using the programme.

2. Thinking is carried out through the processes and tools of each person's culture, so the unique thinking processes and cultural tools involved in the learners' culture should be reflected in the key processes, content and tools of the programme used for those learners.

3. Cultural features unique to the interpersonal approaches in the community of learning and thinking should be reflected in the programme used.

4. The specific characteristics not only of the learners and the mediators or teachers, but also of the learning environment, should be explored in choosing a programme for the teaching of thinking.

5. In developing the teaching of thinking we are collaboratively constructing thinking, so the active role of all of the key players in this construction should be enhanced.

6. The learners should play a strong role as true partners in the learning and evaluation processes.

This all means that when we are deciding on a programme for the teaching of thinking for all learners, it should be one with a theoretical underpinning that suits the unique cultural group involved; the aims of the programme and the ways in which the programme is delivered should be collaboratively decided on, and culturally appropriate; and measures of the effectiveness of the programme should also be collaboratively decided on and culturally appropriate.

It is important to understand that different approaches to the teaching of thinking have different aims. For example, the Feuerstein

Instrumental Enrichment (FIE) programme for the teaching of thinking has as its aim cognitive restructuring, which requires intensive and long-term intervention. In contrast, de Bono's CoRT thinking programme aims at the development of creative thinking, and can be carried out within a much shorter time-frame. It is important that schools ensure that the programme chosen has aims which match the needs of the individual school. Evaluation of the effectiveness of the programme intervention also needs to be appropriate to the aim of the programme.

It would be helpful to use a systematic set of criteria to evaluate both the needs of the school community and its learners, and approaches which might address those needs. The criteria for evaluating approaches for the teaching of thinking offered by Professor Robert Sternberg (1983), an international leader in the field of thinking enhancement, may be particularly useful. Sternberg includes the following key criteria:

- the importance of socio-economic and cultural needs, and relevance of an approach to meeting those needs

- the basing of any approach in sound theory, and with research evidence of its value for the needs identified

- the need to provide for teaching not only of basic cognitive or thinking processes (such as comparison), but also of higher-level metacognitive or executive thinking, which addresses the learning of strategies, knowledge of task demands, and knowledge of the learner's unique learning needs

- the meeting of holistic needs relating to the fullest development of the individual learner, including motivational and emotional needs

- an analysis of needs, and approaches which may meet them, which takes fully into account needs not only for school achievement, but also for real-life learning.

Howie (2003a) has a chapter on evaluating programmes for the teaching of thinking, based on Sternberg's criteria.

In thinking through ways of approaching the teaching of thinking for the whole-school, it is important that we also consider ways of evaluating the approach that we have chosen. Of some help may be a section on 'Assessing Growth in Thinking Abilities' in Costa's edited book (2001, 2003) on the teaching of thinking.

One of the often cited questions of choice is whether to use a programme which is separate from the curriculum, or one which is infused in the curriculum. As early as 1987 this was discussed in depth, along with the advantages of each of the various types of programme (Sternberg 1987). Sternberg states:

> So long as the issue of infusion versus separation is presented as a contest, the debate is likely to continue. I doubt, however, that the model of the contest is ideal in this case. The points raised by both sides are persuasive enough to argue for a mixed model in which thinking skills are taught as a separate course at the same time as they are infused and reinforced throughout the entire curriculum. (p.255)

He concludes his section on choosing which approach to use by stating 'no matter what program is used, careful selection should be made, taking into consideration the needs of the school district and the children' (p.256).

Another important consideration is that the thinking strategies which are being taught need to be 'generalised', tested, and endorsed in a variety of school and community settings so as to become part of the everyday life of the learner. In Chapter 1 one rationale offered for the teaching of thinking was that it was important as preparation for lifelong learning. In Chapter 2 the need for learning environments which adequately challenge all learners, and which are open to change, new ideas and new directions, was addressed. There is a move in the UK to teach skills and competencies in a generic way – for example, with discussion about and identification of 'skills for learning and life' (Rose 2009), and in the QCA's 'big picture for the curriculum' which includes literacy, numeracy, ICT, personal, and learning and thinking skills (QCA 2007, p.31) that cut across the whole of the school curriculum. Mike Waters outlines his 'big picture' of the curriculum as having aims which enable all young people to become successful learners, with the curriculum organised as an entire planned learning experience underpinned by a broad set of values and purposes, and providing support for exploring diverse disciplines. Similarly, the new National Curriculum in New Zealand (Ministry of Education 2007) has the teaching of thinking as a key competency area taught across the curriculum.

In teaching thinking for Tier I work, in-class grouping may facilitate learning, through differentiation of the approach being used. However, it is very important that we do this without labelling and categorisation, and in a way that allows every learner to observe peer models working at a higher level of abstraction, and demonstrating thinking related to that higher level. We need to take care to personalise the approach to meet the needs of each individual learner and not to 'depersonalise' it – for example, by using terms like 'kinaesthetics' for learners with this ability strength (Gardner's Multiple Intelligences approach); or 'visualisers' for learners with this learning style preference (Riding's cognitive style approach). In inclusion the learner comes first, with a particular, personal profile of learning needs, strengths and styles.

Approaches which have a strong theoretical base

1. Lev Vygotsky's socio-cultural approach

Lev Vygotsky, the great Russian psychologist who lived from 1886 to 1934, brought a new theme into twentieth century psychology, that of how human thought is infused with socio-cultural thinking. This approach is considered internationally and universally as providing key concepts for the enhancement of thinking for all children. Its particular value for our Tier I purposes includes the following.

Vygotsky's work is like a deep theoretical base which underpins the work of a number of other key writers on the teaching of thinking. This is expressed in rather poetic style by the present writer in the following comment on Vygotsky's contribution:

> The teaching of thinking can be likened to a tree, deeply rooted in its theoretical beginnings and now leafing luxuriantly. The deepest substratum in which the roots are firmly embedded, and from which they draw their nourishment, is the work of Lev Vygotsky... Vygotsky stressed the culturally mediated nature of psychological processes. (Howie 2003a, p.24)

Central to Vygotsky's socio-cultural theory is that we see learning and thinking as based on social interaction, and so as embedded within each learner's unique historical and cultural existence. This is reflected in a key quotation from Vygotsky: 'Every function in the child's development appears twice: first *between* people (interpsychological) and then *inside* the child (intrapsychological)... All the higher functions originate as actual relations between human individuals' (Vygotsky 1978, p.57, italics his). We can consider this theory and approach as particularly suited to the affirmation of culturally unique ways of thinking, and for multicultural environments, as discussed by Wertsch (1979). Wertsch wants us to attend to the unique meanings which are being jointly constructed by the learner and the communicating individuals in the learner's culturally unique cultural context. These become internalised within the learner and regulate the learner's thinking and behaviour.

Vygotsky sees cultural tools as important in this meaning-making and regulation. Psychological tools, including the following, also have some important roles, according to Vygotsky (1978):

- *mastery of attention*: 'With the help of the indicative function of words, the child begins to master his attention.' (p.35)

- *overcoming impulsivity*: 'The system of signs restructures the whole psychological process and enables the child to master her movements.' (p.35)

- *planning*: 'Once children learn how to use the planning function of their language effectively, their psychological field changes rapidly.' (p.28)

- *purposeful action*: 'Basic alterations in the child's needs and motivations' (p.37) mean that the child wishes to engage in purposeful action.

These psychological skills are all central to learners' active engagement in new learning, and Vygotsky saw the role of the teacher or mediator as making these tools available to the child (Kozulin 1998). For example, a teacher could mediate a cultural tool, the drawing up of a table, with learners in the class, to decide collaboratively on a class visit. The various options or choices would be tabulated as a first column, and scored systematically against criteria such as relevance to the topic under study, access for all class members (e.g. cost), and interest to all class members. A further cultural tool, the computer, could be used to represent this decision making, and to gain any necessary information regarding the proposed choices.

Vygotsky's writing about the importance of the cultural tools used, through human mediation, to assist in mastering thinking (e.g. 'signs, symbols, texts, formulae, and graphic-symbolic devices') is emphasised by Kozulin (1998 p.1). He discusses the difficulties which populations of learners can experience in using symbolic tools (such as a table) effectively in problem solving, if these are not commonly used in their culture. Using a tabular approach to represent and organise data effectively needs mediation in order for it to be internalised and transformed into an inner psychological tool (Kozulin 2008, p.15).

Vygotsky emphasises the importance of studying the learning process, in terms of how learning comes about. He wants us to concentrate not so much on the outcome or product of the learning, but the process itself by which learning is developed (Vygotsky 1978, p.64.) This focus on the learning process underpins current interest in the metacognitive thinking processes whereby we think about our own thinking so as to manage our learning and thinking. It is useful to draw on Meichenbaum's (Meichenbaum *et al.* 1985) three main aspects of metacognition in thinking about this process, and what in the process needs to be managed by the thinker. Examples are given below of the sorts of questions which can be asked by the thinker while managing this process. These questions which thinkers could ask themselves are drawn from the writer's work in discussing their thinking process with young people involved in problem-solving tasks (Howie 2003a, p.124):

1. *Metacognitive knowledge of the task*
    - 'What do I have to do on this task?'
    - 'How difficult is this task?'

2. *Metacognitive knowledge of the self as learner and thinker*
    - 'What thoughts about myself will be helpful in this situation?'
    - 'How am I feeling in this situation?'

3. *Metacognitive knowledge of strategy*
    - 'When I am planning what to do in this situation, what do I need to think carefully about?'
    - 'What strategy is best for this problem, and why?'

An approach to learning enhancement or the teaching of thinking which addresses the learning process is called 'inquiry learning'. Hattie (2009) describes inquiry-based teaching as 'the art of developing challenging situations in which students are asked to observe and question phenomena; pose explanations of what they observe; devise and conduct experiments in which data are collected to support or contradict their theories; analyse data; draw conclusions from experimental data; design and build models; or any combination of these' (p.208). The link to Vygotsky's learning process can be seen in Hattie's comment that such activities 'involve the students more in the process of observing, posing questions', etc. (p.209). Further, this Vygotskian social interaction may have particular value for students who have had limited opportunity to think critically, a conclusion drawn by Hattie from a meta-analysis showing the largest effect sizes for this approach from studies with culturally different learners (Bangert-Drowns 1992).

Vygotsky places importance on the unrealised potential of each learner. His related concept of the 'zone of proximal development' (the difference between independent performance and assisted performance) has led not only to a more dynamic way of assessing intellectual abilities, but also to interest in the processes he outlines for assisting the learner within the zone of proximal development (e.g. human mediation with the cultural tools of speech and language, imitation and particularly peer modelling, the use of play, and 'scaffolding', meaning the provision of guided assistance appropriate to the learner in order to succeed on a task).

A very interesting perception of how the zone of proximal development can be used in the classroom to promote inclusion and foster a community of learners was shared by Professor Ann Brown, an early leading researcher on metacognition, and her colleagues (Brown *et al.* 1993). They state:

> Theoretically, we conceive of the classroom as composed of zones of proximal development (Vygotsky 1978) through which participants can navigate via different routes and at different rates... A zone of proximal development can include people, adults and children, with various degrees of expertise, but it can also include artifacts such as books, videos, wall displays, scientific equipment, and a computer environment intended to support intentional learning... (p.191)

Further, they note that the teacher must be 'sensitive to current overlapping zones of proximal development, where certain students are ripe for new learning. She must renegotiate zones of proximal development so that still other students might become ready for conceptual growth' (p.207).

Of particular interest to us, and also used in other approaches to the teaching of thinking, are Vygotsky's ideas on the development of speech and language (Vygotsky 1986). Vygotsky considered that the child progresses from *social* speech (regulated by external speakers), through *egocentric* speech (social speech spoken aloud to self, as externalised thinking), and finally to *inner speech*, as 'speech for oneself', that is, thinking (p.225). This has proved very valuable as a basis for using 'inner speech', the last phase in the development, to help control thinking, a metacognitive skill.

AN EXAMPLE FROM PRACTICE IN A SCHOOL SETTING

To give an example of a number of Vygotskian ideas in practice, a dissertation on the way children's self-talk, or 'inner speech' can be used to help them manage their use of strategies in the writing process, was completed by Joy Thompson in 2003, supervised by the present writer. Children in Thompson's class, an ordinary classroom of learners, were required to master a set of writing strategies detailed for their writing achievement in the UK Key Stage 2 literacy requirements.

The teacher, who was also the researcher, taught all children in the class, including through modelling, to use inner speech or 'self-talk' to control their use of writing strategies such as:

- use of punctuation

- segmenting polysyllabic words to aid spellings

- repeating words used

- spending more time scribing

- use of self-monitoring strategies, such as pausing and re-reading for editing.

The children provided with this metacognitive intervention showed a better than expected improvement in their writing scores over the year. Analysis of self-talk showed positive changes in the children's self-talk regarding their knowledge and use of specific strategies including the initially least able writers. It also indicated that self-instruction procedures had become embedded in the children's self-talk and in their use of the strategies at a metacognitive level.

Retrospective briefings indicated that the children had acquired metacognitive knowledge of their own thinking processes. For example, one initially able writer reported on his use of the strategy of 're-reading your work so that you can check the flow'. He thought that this was a good idea and '[does] it all the time now'. One less able writer reported that he 'now writes more slowly and takes one word at a time so that [he] can concentrate on the spellings'. Two able writers, when asked what they were thinking during long pauses, reported that they 'needed to refer back to a mental picture'(Thompson 2003, p.55).

A class questionnaire about the intervention revealed high levels of self-esteem with regard to both narrative and non-narrative writing, in association with the use of self-talk procedures. Even the least able group in the class, which contained children with statements of special educational needs with regard to literacy, recorded positive responses to their self-appraisal of their writing ability, especially in non-narrative writing. Joy Thompson, the teacher/researcher, links this to the way self-management enables children to become more active in their learning, and she states: 'I would suggest that this group perhaps benefited most from the heightened awareness of self-talk and its usefulness to their learning' (p.58).

2. Feuerstein's theory of mediated learning experience

Feuerstein's theory, and the tools he has developed from the theory, are used widely internationally, and with a wide variety of learners in terms of culture, age and learning needs. Human mediation of learning is central in Feuerstein's theory. It focuses on the essential role that the human mediator plays in learning, and thinking, by coming between the learner and the learner's world to organise and mediate that world to the learner. The theory outlines the criteria of human mediation which are important for enhancement of learning, and tools to both assess and enhance these criteria systematically have been developed. The particular values of Feuerstein's work for Tier 1 are as follows:

Feuerstein spells out the criteria or qualities of human mediation which are universally found and essential for both the enhancement of learning, and the development of cognitive modifiability. These are:

- mediation of intentionality/reciprocity (making clear the intention and the aim of the learning process and content, which should be shared with the learner)

- mediation of meaning (helping the learner to understand why the learning will be important and of value to him/her)

- mediation for transcendence (going beyond the immediate focus of the learning task, to apply the learning to other tasks and contexts).

These criteria should be applied by teachers and parents for any learners, in any learning context.

Later in this section an example is described of Feuerstein's criteria for mediation being used in an ordinary classroom, as this is the most likely use of Feuerstein's theory in a whole-school, systematic way.

An excellent example of the systemic use of Feuerstein's approach to the teaching of thinking is found in the Scottish Borders, where all teachers are trained in the use of Feuerstein's mediated learning experience criteria and are provided with a recently revised book by Mentis and colleagues (Mentis *et al.* 2009) which offers interesting examples of all the criteria, as a handbook (Anne-Theresa Lawrie (2009); Lawrie is the Scottish Borders Council Learning and Teaching Development Officer).

Feuerstein's criteria are listed as follows:

1. The universal criteria, found in every culture, are:

    • mediation of intentionality and reciprocity – sharing of the learning goal

    • mediation of meaning – giving a sense of the need for and value of the learning goal

    • mediation of transcendence – going beyond the immediate learning goal.

2. The non-universal criteria, which are found to differing extents in different cultures, are:

    • mediation of regulation and control

    • mediation of goal setting, planning and achievement

    • mediation of challenge, novelty and complexity

    • mediation of the human as a changing entity

    • mediation for sharing behaviour

    • mediation for individuation and psychological differentiation.

It is also important for us to recognise that there may be further criteria valued by a unique culture which need to be understood and utilised in the mediation of thinking with learners in that culture.

Also of interest to us at this Tier 1 level is the development of a tool to analyse the needs of the learner in terms of the learning process, which is a checklist of cognitive functions and dysfunctions. Feuerstein breaks the learning process into three phases, the *input, elaboration* and *output* phases, and identifies cognitive functions/dysfunctions that are found at each of these phases. The checklist allows the classroom teacher to analyse the learner's process, not just the end product of the learning. The key cognitive functions/dysfunctions at each of the three phases are as follows:

1. Input phase:

    • systematic (or impulsive) exploration of a learning situation

    • precise and accurate (or imprecise and inaccurate) understanding of words and meanings

    • ability (or lack of ability) to use information from more than one source.

2.   Elaboration phase:

- ability (or lack of ability) to define a problem
- ability (or lack of ability) to think about information stored in one's brain
- ability (or lack of ability) to make comparisons
- ability (or lack of ability) to select relevant cues
- ability (or lack of ability) to relate objects and events to previous and anticipated situations
- ability (or lack of ability) to summarise information
- ability (or lack of ability) to engage in planning behaviour.

3.   Output phase:

- controlled and planned (or poorly controlled and impulsive) expression of thoughts and actions
- precise and accurate (or imprecise and inaccurate) expression of words and concepts
- mature (or immature and egocentric) communication which takes (or does not take) into account the other person involved in the communication.

(adapted from Howie 2003a, p.36)

Any classroom teacher should be able to use this checklist developed by Feuerstein, to help in understanding a learner's process needs. It can also be used to help the learner gain insights into his/her own cognitive skills – important in reflective thinking and metacognition, as noted by Skuy and Mentis (1991).

A further tool, the 'cognitive map', for analysis of the teaching/ mediation requirements of any task, including real-life problem-solving tasks, helps us to break down the learning task into its key aspects, which can then each be modified to encourage learning. The key aspects of the cognitive map are the content of the learning task; the modality through which the task is taught; the phases (input, elaboration, and output) with their cognitive functions and operations which are involved in the task thinking process; and the levels of complexity, abstraction, and efficiency required of the task. An up-to-date description of the cognitive map, showing how it can be applied in the analysis and learning of a variety of tasks, of different levels of complexity, is detailed by Howie (2008).

For example, using a 'plan of search' task, a commonly experienced problem both academically and in real life, the following parameters of the cognitive map are required:

1. *Content*: searching for a lost wallet/purse in a field, a real-life problem-solving task.

2. *Modality*: pictorial/symbolic, in the form of a diamond-shaped field; lines have to be drawn by the problem solver to show the search process.

3. *Phase*: functions and operations.

    *   At the *input* phase, the problem solver has to perceive the task information precisely and define the task, taking in and understanding the instructions and the field depiction. The term 'show me' has to be appreciated as requiring the problem solver to 'represent' the search by drawing lines, with attention to the temporal sequence of the task. Several sources of information need to be considered, such as the size of the field and the shape of the field.

    *   At the *elaboration* phase, planning behaviour is the strongest cognitive function required, to overcome trial-and-error responding. The problem solver needs to orientate him- or herself in the field, infer that the wallet could be anywhere in the field (as no information is given about its locality), and deduce that the whole field needs to be covered systematically in the plan of search.

    *   At the *output* phase, the problem solver needs accuracy and precision in drawing the lines which symbolise the research plan. Trial-and-error responding, and impulsivity, need to be restrained in order to complete the task systematically. Any blocking and lack of flexibility in the final drawing of the plan needs to be overcome.

4. Level of complexity: the 'plan of search' task appears at the 13-year level of the Binet test, suggesting some complexity, although the units of information involved are limited.

5. Level of abstraction: the concrete–abstract–concrete linking is not at the highest abstract–abstract level (i.e. moving from a concrete depiction of a field to abstract planning, and back to representing this on the depiction of the field).

6. Level of efficiency: this is delineated by the scoring criteria outlined in the Binet manual for this task.

In response to the Instrumental Enrichment programme, which emphasises systematic problem-solving strategies, 13- to 14-year-old Maori learners made considerable shifts in their performance on this task (Howie, Richards and Pirihi 1993).

Feuerstein's best known tool for the enhancement of thinking is his Instrumental Enrichment programme (Feuerstein *et al.* 2006), which has been used in some countries (e.g. Israel, USA, UK, Venezuela, and Brazil) for the teaching of thinking to large populations of learners, on a whole-school basis. This is the way Feuerstein wants this tool to be used, for the systematic provision of mediated experiences (mediated through a variety of 'tools' or 'instruments' which address both cognitive and metacognitive thinking strategies). A meta-analysis of 40 studies on the use of Instrumental Enrichment, where learners were mainly in ordinary classrooms, and where effect sizes could be calculated, was presented by Romney and Samuels (2001). Significant effect sizes were found for cognitive ability, including both verbal and spatial ability (the main aim of the programme is for structural cognitive modification), achievement and adaptive functioning.

However, in order to ensure proper mediation with the instruments, including the addressing of both cognitive and emotional needs, and the complex bridging to academic and real-life problem solving, specialised training is required for delivery of this programme, and the tools cannot be acquired without this training. The quality of teacher mediation is central to the success of this programme. Excellent examples of mediation and bridging in the use of this programme, to meet the needs and interests of learners today, are given by Mentis *et al.* (2009).

Feuerstein's Instrumental Enrichment programme is discussed in more detail in Chapter 5.

A dynamic assessment tool for the individual assessment of cognitive abilities, the Learning Potential Assessment Device, has also been developed by Feuerstein and his team (Feuerstein, Rand and Hoffman 1979; Feuerstein *et al.* 2003). It is one of the internationally most widely used tools for dynamic assessment, allowing for the exploration of an individual's zone of proximal development. It is discussed in more detail in Chapter 6.

AN EXAMPLE FROM PRACTICE IN A SCHOOL SETTING

An example of the key mediation criteria in use in an ordinary school setting and classroom, in work led by the writer (Howie, Richards and Pirihi 1993), is now detailed. The work was carried out with a whole class in a New Zealand school where Maori learners formed the majority of the school population. The class, which was the lowest in a 'streamed' ordinary school system, did include learners with a variety of learning needs, including those associated with socio-economic disadvantage and ongoing school failure.

The project involved the writer and two of the regular Maori teachers of the class in delivering Feuerstein's cognitive enhancement tool (Instrumental Enrichment), but it also illustrates well how the Maori teachers mediated the thinking strategies using the various mediation criteria, and how these mediation criteria are important within any cultural context, using any means of communication which is culturally relevant.

An example of mediating *the criteria of intentionality and reciprocity* (that is, a shared intention), was given by Hone Pirihi, who taught the class for both maths and art. He decided to use Maori string games to enhance engagement in understanding and following instructions, as covered within the 'instructions' instrument of the programme, which he was teaching. This gave the opportunity to 'teach the skills of good listening, observing the steps carefully when demonstrated, following instructions step by step, self-monitoring in following the instructions, and self-reinforcement through successful completion' (Howie 2003a, p.15).

Not only were the string games used to mediate shared intention in working through the strategies taught in the instructions instrument; they were also used, after each set of instructions, to discuss with the learners their skills in following the instructions, and to help them to generalise their new learning to other activities, with the latter involving the mediation of transcendence.

An example of the mediation of *meaning* (a universal criterion in Feuerstein's criteria for mediation) was demonstrated by Ruhi Richards, who also taught these learners for social studies. She decided to relate the 'Orientation in space' instrument to the positioning of individuals according to the Maori protocol for formal occasions, which specifies where individuals should sit or stand (especially, for example, on the Maori meeting place, known as the *marae*). Ruhi Richards discussed with the learners how Maori valued the importance of left-side and right-side seating positions in relation to status, role (for example, visitor or speaker) and gender. This allowed her to discuss with the learners how their shared meanings about Maori protocol illustrated some of the key ideas in this tool about the orientation and organisation of people within systems.

Throughout the project, comments by the two Maori teachers which were shared with the writer as they jointly planned and reflected on each lesson were recorded and later analysed for key themes. Two of the main categories of responses involved the cultural relevance of the approach used, and the relevance which the teachers felt the approach had for meeting the needs of the learners (see Howie 2003a, p.57 for an overall table of analysis). This relevance, which related to the mediation of meaning, had particular impacts on motivation and the meeting of emotional needs. For example, the teachers made the following comments:

- 'Today X worked hard at communicating an idea verbally, whereas previously he would have given up and said "I don't know."'

- 'The kids are reacting differently – much more settled and responsive. Discipline is better.'

- 'They are thinking more carefully and trying things for themselves.'

- 'They are accepting and feel secure. They are part of it...everyone participates in one way or another.'

(Howie 2003a, p.58)

3. Robert Sternberg's problem-solving cycle and metacognition

This problem-solving cycle has arisen from early groundbreaking work which Professor Robert Sternberg carried out in delineating his theory of the nature of mental abilities (Sternberg 1979). In this paper he gives empirical evidence not only for the information-processing cognitive processes which make up thinking, but for the higher-level executive metacomponents used in thinking about thinking. For us at Tier 1 level, the value of this work in terms of approaches that can be used for all learners includes the following.

Sternberg gave us the first strong empirical validation of the key role which metacognition (thinking about thinking) plays in learning and thinking. Traditional problem-solving tasks such as an analogies task (e.g. 'teacher is to pupil as doctor is to...?') were selected by Sternberg in developing his model (Sternberg 1979). He divided the task into subtasks (the information-processing components) using a precuing procedure to identify key components for an analogies task: the learner would *encode* the terms of the analogy, *map* the higher order relationship that links 'teacher' to 'pupil', and *apply* the inferred relationship to 'patient', so that the learner can *respond* 'patient'. (The words in italics are the key information-processing components required in this analogies task.)

Using a componential process of data analysis, Sternberg identified that something else was going on while the tasks were being solved. He noted the use of higher-level information-processing 'metacomponents' in carrying out the task. Sternberg states that 'the level of metacomponents deals with…metacognition, or the control an individual has over his or her own cognitive processes' (Sternberg 1979, p.226). They are the processes which problem solvers use to decide what components to apply to a problem, how to represent the problem, what strategies to use to solve the problem, and the rates at which to carry out the component processes.

Sternberg showed us the value of the metacomponents, and how to use them. In a very accessible description of the metacomponents (metacognition) in his chapter entitled 'Metacomponents: The "white collar" processes of human intelligence' (Sternberg 1988), he gives guidance relevant to all class teachers on how the metacomponents can be enhanced in real-life problem solving. The seven metacomponents outlined are considered by him to be at the core of mental self-management, and are:

- recognising the existence of a problem
- defining the nature of the problem
- generating a series of steps needed to solve the problem
- combining these steps into a workable strategy for problem solution
- deciding how to represent information about the problem
- allocating mental and physical resources to solving the problem
- monitoring the solution to the problem.

These metacomponents have been operationalised in an assessment tool to measure metacognitive functioning (Clements and Nastasi 1990), and used in research projects for the enhancement of both academic

(Barry-Joyce 2001) and real-life (Fong and Howie 2007) problems. The detailed example given below for the use of this approach was carried out by Mary Barry-Joyce, using Sternberg's metacomponent processes in an ordinary classroom situation, and using this metacomponential measure.

Sternberg has also used these metacomponents to detail a problem-solving cycle which can be used extensively for the enhancement of problem solving in both academic (Barry-Joyce 2001) and real-life (Fong and Howie 2007) problem-solving tasks. (See Figure 4.2 below, drawn from Sternberg 1995, p.13.)

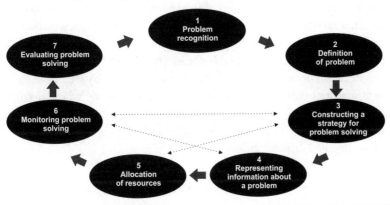

Figure 4.2 Sternberg's problem-solving cycle

The cycle involves, first, recognising the existence of a problem, followed by defining the nature of the problem, then allocating resources to problem solving, representing information about the problem, formulating a strategy for problem solution, and finally, monitoring the problem solving, and evaluating the solution. Sternberg (2005) states that although there is a risk of cultural imperialism in thinking about culture and intelligence, and that successful intelligence is the ability to succeed in life within one's own cultural context, he considers that his general problem-solving cycle is the same everywhere, although the problem-solving tasks are different. This problem-solving cycle could be used by any teacher to address problems themselves, and to teach learners how to address problems, and it is also very similar to key evaluation tools, such as the action research paradigm, which is used by teachers in evaluating interventions, including interventions in the teaching of thinking. The action research paradigm normally involves a cycle of information gathering about the problem, developing an action plan to solve the problem, implementation and monitoring of the implementation of the action plan, and evaluation of the solution. (See models of action research presented in Baumfield, Hall and Wall (2008).)

Sternberg (1985) has outlined his own intervention programme aimed at developing the metacomponents. He describes the early use of this programme, which seeks to train learners in three kinds of skills: the metacomponents (as outlined above); the performance components (encoding, inference, mapping, application, comparison, and justification – the basic cognitive processes involved in the thinking process); and finally the components of acquisition, retention, and transfer which are taught within the context of inferring the meanings of words, with training on use of textual and other cues (Sternberg 1985). His intervention programme may be more suitable for secondary-level learners.

Because of its strong information-processing nature, this meta-componential approach may be particularly useful when used in association with the learning of new computer technologies, which also take a strong information-processing approach. This is also demonstrated in the detailed example below.

AN EXAMPLE FROM PRACTICE IN A SCHOOL SETTING

This detailed example concerns the use of Sternberg's metacomponents in an ordinary rural school, involving learners in ordinary classrooms, in the Republic of Ireland, carried out as a doctoral study by Mary Barry-Joyce (2001) under the supervision of the writer. Barry-Joyce investigated the effects of metacognitive instruction using Sternberg's metacomponents as operationalised by Clements and Nastasi (1990). She used as a training context two alternative computer environments: the LOGO computer-programming environment, and the alternative spreadsheet computer environment. (LOGO is a computing environment which provides an interactive programming language. It is appropriate for mathematics education.) Within both environments, she provided metacomponential problem-solving training, using theoretical coverage of the metacomponent processes (explication), practical examples (both modelled and with exercises for the learners to work through), individual scaffolded instruction on the problem solving, and group reflection on metacomponent use. All of this used mathematical problem-solving tasks.

She used cartoon pictures of persons as a teaching tool to illustrate the key Sternberg metacomponents:

- a problem decider (for recognising and defining the nature of the problem)
- a representer (representing information about the problem)
- a strategy planner (generating a set of steps for problem solution and combining them into a strategy)
- a debugger (monitoring progress and utilising feedback).

She used a dynamic assessment metacomponential measure, as developed by Clements and Nastasi (1990) for looking at individual difference in problem solving. Further single-subject analysis was carried out to see how learners were responding to each part of the metacomponential training, using learners selected by their results on the Drumcondra Reasoning Test (a standardised Irish measure of both verbal and numerical reasoning), involving detailed analysis of their metacomponential measures.

A trend analysis of the data indicated that the metacognitive intervention was associated with greater use of, and increased problem-solving success with, the metacomponent on the nature of the task (i.e. recognising and defining the nature of the problem). In their 'think aloud' protocols, while solving the problem, students made comments such as, 'This is like the first one, I know how to do this now,' and 'Oh, yeah, that's easy. Now that you have showed me how to do the first one I know how to do them now' (Barry-Joyce 2001, p.241).

At post-intervention assessments, students were making good use of the metacomponent on representing the problem externally (e.g. by drawing key information on worksheets).

On the tests of generalisation to tasks involving problem solving, numeric reasoning and verbal reasoning, the post-test scores showed that many of the learners, and particularly the learners with high and medium-high ability, were applying many of the problem-solving metacomponents which they were taught in the intervention, such as planning and monitoring. Students with lower ability, while not demonstrating this so clearly, were nevertheless shown in the trend analysis to have profited from the training in their generalisation to the problem-solving and numeric reasoning tasks. These students with lower ability also revealed positive attitudes to the intervention programme. Mary Barry-Joyce, the researcher, notes 'perhaps on gaining familiarity with problem solving techniques these students were able to take greater responsibility for their own learning and improve their performance' (Barry-Joyce 2001, p.249).

4. Bandura and Walter's social learning theory

This theory addresses the role of imitation or modelling in learning. In imitative learning the observer imitates the model's behaviour, including cognitive, social and emotional behaviours. An extensive series of research studies with ordinary children which identified many of the key factors that enhance learning through imitation was carried out by Albert Bandura and Richard Walters (1963). External reinforcement can play a role, either rewarding the observer for such imitation, or rewarding the model for the behaviour, and thus making imitated behaviour more likely. Other aspects of the model are also important, such as status and power, while emotional arousal of the observer, such as moderate anxiety, may play an important role in increasing imitation.

The value of applying this theory for enhancement of learning by all learners is related to the following factors:

1. It explains how humans learn not only social behaviours and values, but also cognitive behaviours (which is why it is included in this section).

2. Imitative learning underpins two commonly used approaches for enhancing learning and thinking. The first is co-operative learning (Brown and Thomson 2000; Johnson, Johnson and Stanne 2000; Slavin 1991). One of the reasons why mixed ability group learning is so important in inclusive learning is that it enables imitative learning. The second is Meichenbaum's (1985) cognitive-behavioural approach, which is dealt with in detail in Chapter 5 (see p.182). The use of cognitive self-instructions is modelled to the learner, as part of the learning process.

3. Its particular value in the present context is that it is important and effective in learning new behaviours and skills. Bandura and Walters (1963) show how easily and effectively such new or novel responses are learnt through imitation. They contrast this to operant conditioning or behaviourism, an approach where reinforcement is applied to already existing behaviours, and new behaviours have to be learnt through a prolonged learning process requiring continual shaping of responses which approximate to the desired new response.

4. Imitative learning brings together emotional and cognitive factors within a wide range of learning, and can enhance not

only the performance of an observer, but also the learning of a feeling or behaviour that is not actually performed. (In testing for learning through imitation it is possible to distinguish between imitative *recall* and imitative *performance*. Learners may be able to recall learning they have observed, but which they may not be able, or may not wish, to perform. For example, Bandura and Walters (1963) carried out detailed experimental work regarding the learning of altruism, which is related to empathy – a key emotional skill for learners today. They used ingenious real-life situations in which a model gave to someone asking for money in the street, and the effect on observers was noted. An observer might well be able to recall the model's empathetic and giving behaviour (altruism) but in not every case was the model's behaviour repeated (i.e. performed) by the observer.

5.   The teacher can capitalise on imitative learning by focusing the learner on the task to be learnt, with specific instructions to observe and copy the modelled behaviours. This is called 'instrumental' imitative learning. Learners also often learn through 'incidental' imitative learning, including learning what might be seen as irrelevant behaviours of a model, outside of the intended focus of the learning task.

6.   There is considerable concern worldwide with the learning needs of children with social, emotional and behavioural difficulties. Often such children are present in the ordinary classroom. This theory can be used as a means to approach their learning needs.

7.   There is particular concern about the role of imitative learning in the learning of violence, both through peer modelling and through 'symbolic models' such as television models. Factors such as the status of the model, and identification with the model through shared emotions, which are important in imitation, were identified by Bandura, Ross and Ross (1963). Sporting bodies now recognise the impact that the status of the model has in imitation of violence, and take steps to ensure that such behaviour by sporting models is not seen to be rewarded.

There is a valuable framework for problem solving, called *Thinking Actively in a Social Context* (Wallace and Adams 1993) which builds both on Vygotsky's theory of the importance of social interaction in thought, and on Bandura and Walter's social learning theory. The approach aims at developing the thinking potential of children within disadvantaged communities. It takes a holistic approach, looking not only at tools for effective thinking, but also at learning experiences which could facilitate self-esteem and the ability of the learner to deal with problems in everyday life. It also emphasises the importance of thinking skills and the context in which they are embedded being culturally relevant. This framework is endorsed as important by Robson and Moseley (2005) at the Centre for Learning and Teaching at Newcastle University, UK, in their paper on an integrated framework for thinking about learning.

AN EXAMPLE FROM PRACTICE IN A SCHOOL SETTING

As an example of enhancing learning through imitation, the writer carried out her doctoral research (Howie 1969) on imitative learning both by ordinary schoolchildren of various ages, and by children with severe learning difficulties, with these two main groups of children matched on both chronological age and 'mental age'. The study looked at a variety of a more cognitive type of 'instrumental' learning tasks, such as completing a maze puzzle, in which first, through instruction, the learners' attention was focused on the adult model completing the maze correctly, and learners were then asked to imitate the solution. This modelling assisted learners both with and without learning difficulties to succeed with the task. There was also exploration of the extent to which the learners would also imitate behaviours carried out by the adult model which were quite incidental to completing the instrumental task. There was a high level both of recall of these incidental behaviours, and of performance (imitation) of them, by both groups of learners. Novelty of the presentation was also found to be important, for both groups of learners.

There were several results of the studies which the writer considers indicate a particular challenge regarding the use of imitative learning as an approach for enhancing learning. The first is the considerable range of individual differences (within both groups of learners) in their willingness to imitate. There is probably a continuum of such difference, with, at one extreme, a small percentage of learners who will *always* imitate, no matter what the characteristics of the task, the model, or the reinforcement involved. (Some work suggests to us that children who are 'outer-directed' in this way when involved in problem solving may be affected by past failures, and also by possible deprivation in their social histories (Turnure and Zigler 1964).) At the other extreme of the continuum could be a small percentage of learners who *rarely* imitate, resisting the power of a model. Most learners will probably come somewhere between these extremes, and be influenced by characteristics of the imitative task, availability of the task requirements in their already existing cognitive repertoire, their level of attention to the task, and emotional and motivational aspects (such as anxiety and emotional relationship to the model, including a wish for 'approval', and emotional 'dependency' (Ross 1966)). Bandura (1977) has also given us a theory of 'self efficacy', and it is probable that low feelings of self-efficacy could be associated with willingness to imitate for approval.

Maximising the positive use of imitative learning requires not only sound knowledge of how this learning is enhanced, and of the wide variety of ways in which such learning enhancement can be utilised, but also willingness to consider individual variation in response to an imitative opportunity, even in an ordinary classroom.

The second challenge concerns the power of incidental imitation in more long-term social learning, including learning of less desirable (such as aggressive) behaviours, for all learners, no matter what their cognitive abilities. One of the studies carried out by the writer, incorporating an instrumental imitative learning task (plan of search), also introduced incidental imitative learning of novel behaviours towards a 'bad doll', using a peer filmed model, in a way similar to that used in studies by Bandura and Walters. Some time after conclusion of the research, the writer took one of the least able learners with her to demonstrate instrumental and incidental modelling procedures to students training to be teachers. Immediately on entering the car and sighting the 'bad doll', the learner carried out some of the novel, incidental behaviours towards the doll, quite spontaneously.

The power of imitative learning needs to be used to enhance positive social behaviours such as empathy (also studied by Bandura and Walters), sharing, and tolerance, by drawing attention to, and rewarding high-status peers who model such behaviours.

Approaches which include creative thinking

5. Robert Sternberg's triarchic theory of intelligence

A theory of intelligence which outlines not one traditionally conceived unitary intelligence, but three abilities – hence 'triarchic' – is presented by Robert Sternberg (1997a, 1997b, 2000). He sees these three abilities as having equal importance and value, while constituting a form of thinking in its own right, with its own procedures or processes for using it. The three abilities are:

- analytical ability, including critical thinking and problem solving, normally measured by traditional tests of intelligence. It is used when learners are asked to analyse, compare and contrast, critique, judge, explain, etc.

- practical thinking, when learners apply what they know to everyday events. It is used when learners are asked to apply, show how they can use, implement, demonstrate in the real world, etc.

- creative thinking, when learners think about a problem in a new way. It is used when learners are asked to imagine, design, say what would happen if, suppose that, etc.

The value of applying this theory for enhancing thinking for all learners is related to the following factors:

1. It recognises considerable individual differences in each person's profile of abilities. In one of his research studies Sternberg was able to identify a great variety of unique patterns of individual differences in learners (Sternberg 2000). For example, he identified learners who were very high in analytical abilities, very high in creative abilities, or very high in practical abilities, as well as learners who were relatively high or relatively low in all three abilities. He recognises that there is a much wider range of ways for learners to 'be able', than is indicated by the traditional idea of intelligence. So it is a very inclusive notion of 'being able'. Further, he comments that learners in the very high creative groups and very high practical groups were not predominantly white and of middle to upper-middle-class background. He states that 'when you expand the range of abilities considered, the range of students identified as gifted increases as well' (Sternberg 2000, p.66).

2. The triarchic intelligences (the three abilities) can be trained or developed, according to Sternberg. He believes that analytic, creative and practical abilities need to be developed equally if learners are to reach their full potential. Of practical use to us is his book outlining the characteristics of a creative classroom, including suggestions such as 'encouraging students to question

assumptions' and 'more encouragement of sensible risk taking' (Sternberg and Williams 1996). Such ideas would require a whole-school ethos which shared control of learning with students, and rewarded creativity in all of its forms.

3.   A further unique contribution is the idea that learners should be both taught and evaluated using the three intelligences. Sternberg's own research (2000) indicated that learners do better when the teaching approaches match their patterns of abilities. He also lists assessment approaches best suited to each type of intelligence (Sternberg 2000). His research across different school settings also supported the effectiveness of teaching with the three abilities, for raising achievement (Grigorenko, Jarvin and Sternberg 2002).

4.   Sternberg has devised a Triarchic Abilities Test which measures each of the three abilities on three different scales.

5.   The personality and motivational approaches that enable creative learners to 'invest in creativity' have also been considered by Sternberg. He argues that 'creative insight' requires not just a cognitive ability, but an attitude of 'searching for the unexpected, the novel, and even for what others might label as bizarre. The creatively insightful person seeks the paths that others avoid or even fear: he or she is willing to take risks and stray from the conventional' (Sternberg and Lubart 1995, p.353). These motivational approaches are needed not only for lifelong success, or for adapting to the world of the future, but for contributing to its future change.

There can be confusion in relation to the two different versions of the triarchic theory of intelligence put forward by Sternberg. Sternberg first presented a triarchic theory in an early book, *Beyond IQ: A Triarchic Theory of Human Intelligence* (1985) with the following subtheories (later linked by the present author to the three abilities):

•   componential subtheory (as outlined in Section 3 of this chapter), involving *analytical* abilities or thinking

•   experiential subtheory (including ability to deal with novelty), involving *creative* abilities or thinking

•   contextual subtheory (including adaptation, selection and shaping), involving *practical* abilities or thinking

In his paper 'Practical intelligence for successful schools' (Sternberg, Okagaki and Jackson 1990), Sternberg himself makes the connection between the early triarchic intelligence subtheories and the three abilities.

A model of a Triarchic Instruction and Assessment Unit (TIA), with triarchic characteristics of teaching and assessment, has been outlined by Sternberg and Grigorenko (2000). These characteristics help us to understand what an ordinary school and classroom might look like, following this approach. Some of the characteristics are:

- sharing with students the value of diversity in thinking, and that all three characteristics are important

- developing students' individual ability profiles through a variety of strategies such as reflection time, journal writing, discussions, preferred activities, and self-reported strengths and weaknesses

- consideration by the teacher of what content needs to be taught, leading to creation of a list of analytical, creative and practical activities appropriate to that content, and covered in a systematic and logical way which allows all learners to capitalise on their ability strengths and strengthen their ability weaknesses

- use by teachers of various assessment methods to assess learning following triarchic teaching, including 'essays, short answer exams, projects, performances, portfolios' (Sternberg and Grigorenko 2000, p.144). Each topic should provide for assessment questions using analytical, creative and practical intelligences.

In our concern for preparing learners for future independent learning and real-life success, it is important to note Sternberg's emphasis on the value of the three abilities for future success. He presents this aspect of his theory in workshops on 'Successful intelligence' and states (in Cianciolo and Sternberg 2004) that an important feature of the triarchic theory for successful intelligence is adaptability, not only within the individual, but also within the individual's own sociocultural context.

In relation to unique individual profiles of ability, Sternberg points out that even though people may not be equal in all three abilities, most of those who are 'successfully intelligent' find ways to make the three abilities work together harmoniously (thanks to the individual adaptability mentioned above) (Sternberg 2008).

A particular curriculum to enhance adaptation to the environment is spelled out by Sternberg as the *Practical Intelligence for Schools (PIFS) Curriculum* (Sternberg 2008). This curriculum addresses the skills and knowledge required for adaptability within the individual's own socio-cultural context, including how to manage oneself, manage tasks, and work with (managing) others.

AN EXAMPLE FROM PRACTICE IN A SCHOOL SETTING

The present writer has not had personal experience in a school using this approach, but an example of a school in the United States which, with some collaboration with Sternberg himself, has put in place in a whole-school way of using his triarchic theory, is the Hunter Elementary Talented and Gifted Magnet School, set in an urban multiracial community in North Carolina. This transition, reported by Lynn English (1998; see internet reference), aimed to address the needs of the diverse school population by applying Sternberg's theory in a whole-school way. The principal states:

> When our North Carolina, inner-city, magnet elementary school applied Robert Sternberg's triarchic theory of intelligence to curriculum, instruction and assessments, teachers began to reconsider the ways their students were 'smart' in ways unacknowledged by conventional school standards... Narrowing the gap between majority and minority students has been our greatest achievement. (Cited in English 2008)

The school 'teaches to a student's often-hidden strengths' and this has required teachers both to have patience and to apply their own analytical, creative and practical intelligences. The principal notes that 'staff development was key to the process. During in-service programs, teachers experienced creative, practical and analytical activities', and looked in particular at how homework tasks reflected these, as a model for teachers to consider what is asked of the students in the three ability areas.

Then, in their classroom teaching, teachers provided 'balanced experiences for the students' – and 'as a result of teaching to all three intelligences, students are experiencing a time to shine in their dominant intelligence as well as developing skills in the other areas'. Teachers and students also developed sample rubrics that assessed the outcome of instruction with practical applications, in addition to traditional analytical assessments. This working together 'provided consistency and common understandings about assessment across classrooms', along with students' self-evaluation.

The school was involved with Sternberg in a research project which found that in social studies projects that highlighted the different intelligences in a balanced way, Third Grade students retained information at a higher level. The principal also states that teachers noted that 'students were surprisingly enthusiastic about the activities'.

Finally, the principal stresses the importance of understanding that 'learning ways of new teaching and valuing students' strengths comes as a gradual process', requiring time to uncover prejudices and beliefs that undermine high expectations.

6. Howard Gardner's theory of Multiple Intelligences

Gardner's theory is included in this section because, like Sternberg's triarchic theory, it offers a multiple rather than a unitary view of intelligence, and a number of the intelligences identified by Gardner (1983), such as bodily-kinaesthetic intelligence, musical intelligence, and visual-spatial intelligence, are usually thought of as creative abilities.

Gardner's theory is important to us for the enhancement of thinking of all learners for the following reasons.

It provides a view of Multiple Intelligences that function autonomously, including not only the three already mentioned, but *logical/ mathematical* intelligence, *linguistic* intelligence (these two are normally tested in traditional tests of intelligence); *intrapersonal* intelligence – akin to metacognition (Gardner 1999), *interpersonal* intelligence (the personal intelligences, later expanded by Goleman as 'emotional intelligence'); *naturalist* intelligence, and possibly *existentialist* intelligence.

Each individual has a unique profile of intelligences that combine relatively stronger and relatively weaker intelligences, and 'these relative strengths and weaknesses help to account for individual differences in learning' (Gardner, Kornhaber and Wake 1996, p.211). It is therefore an important approach in relation to personalised learning, and indeed, the UK government has been advocating the use of Gardner's Multiple Intelligences for some time.

Gardner's theory presents a more holistic view of intelligence, compared to a traditional unitary view, with intellectual capacities being understood in terms of their cultural value (Gardner 1999). For Gardner the intelligences are modifiable, and he sees the purpose of schools as being to modify them, by playing from strengths and boosting weaknesses. This reminds us to see intelligences not as static, but as all open to enhancement.

One of the aspects of his theory most strongly advocated by Gardner himself, concerns the importance of assessing these intelligences in authentic and contextualised ways, that is, using multiple measures of thinking in real-life contexts that require problem solving. (He would not be happy with the assessment of Multiple Intelligences using simplistic checklists that lead to 'labelling' learners, with the labels acting as barriers to more complex and abstract learning, and to enhancement of all of the intelligences.) Gardner contrasts, on the one hand, his authentic approach to assessment of the Multiple Intelligences with, on the other hand, traditional assessment of individual intelligence. The chapter by Hatch and Gardner entitled 'If Binet had looked beyond the classroom: The assessment of Multiple Intelligences' (2001) makes the case for 'contextualised' assessment of the Multiple Intelligences (p.415). Guidance and a number of tools for such a contextualised approach are given to us by Lazear (2004).

Gardner advocates one way of teaching based on the theory of Multiple Intelligences, which is to take a topic or 'domain' and provide 'entry points' to it via a number of Multiple Intelligences, to help learners easily grasp new materials according to their particular strengths (Gardner 1991). Examples of how to use such entry points in the teaching of history and the social sciences are given by Gardner in his books *The Unschooled Mind* (1991) and *Intelligence Reframed* (1999). He advocates an in-depth approach to a topic. The link between Gardner's theory of Multiple Intelligences and a typical, generic approach to a knowledge-based curriculum, as in the recent review of the UK Primary Curriculum core skills (Rose 2009), is pointed out by the Cambridge Primary Review team (Alexander 2009). The knowledge areas covered in the knowledge-based curriculum are considered to match closely with Gardner's different types of intelligences. Gardner's theory could strengthen the argument for a curriculum grounded in the different ways of knowing and understanding the world.

A useful guide on teaching and learning through Multiple Intelligences is provided by Campbell, Campbell and Dickinson (2004) – a broadly based guide to the use of Gardner's theory not only for classroom practices (for example, team teaching), but more widely (as in community involvement). It also includes material on model Multiple Intelligence school programmes.

Gardner also advocates applying Multiple Intelligences to assessment of knowledge and understanding. Alternative approaches to assessment from a Multiple Intelligences perspective, such that learners can demonstrate both their strengths and interests in their mastery of a topic, are helpfully provided by Chen and Gardner (2001).

Gardner has expressed in his more recent works his concern for the moral qualities needed by thinkers in the future. For example, he identifies the following cognitive abilities that will be sought and cultivated by leaders in the future, in his book *Five Minds of the Future* (2006): the *disciplinary* mind, the *synthesising* mind, the *creating* mind, the *respectful* mind, and the *ethical* mind.

An Irish sociological study carried out by Marie Flynn (2000) looked at teaching and learning with Multiple Intelligences in order to overcome inequality. This rich qualitative study has clear implications for inclusion.

There are parallels between Gardner's Multiple Intelligences theory and Sternberg's triarchic theory of three abilities. Sternberg attempts to combine his own triarchic theory and Gardner's theory of Multiple Intelligences, particularly in terms of practical examples, in his paper 'Practical intelligence for success in schools' (Sternberg, Okagaki and Jackson 1990). In another paper, Sternberg discusses how his and Gardner's theories can work together, and be integrated into a joint intervention programme (Sternberg and Spear-Swerling 1996).

There is a need for more rigorous evaluation of the use of Gardner's Multiple Intelligences approach, even though it has already been applied and evaluated in a wide variety of ways. Shearer (2004) provides useful discussion of a number of ways in which it has been applied and evaluated over the past 20 years.

AN EXAMPLE FROM PRACTICE IN A SCHOOL SETTING

An excellent example of the use of Gardner's theory of Multiple Intelligences in an ordinary school and classroom context is provided by a research project carried out by Rhys Davies, then a history teacher in a UK secondary school, supervised by the writer (Davies 2004). As well as using a rigorous, quasi-experimental research design, he looked at individual differences through case studies, with extensive interviewing of the case study learners.

The intervention itself had a number of phases, each representing a different way of applying Multiple Intelligences theory.

1.   The first main phase of intervention involved the learners in choosing the form of assessment, guided by some understanding of Multiple Intelligences, to demonstrate their understanding of a topic, following teaching of that topic.

2. The second main phase involved enrichment of whole-class topic teaching, using whole-class Multiple Intelligences approaches, plotted across the scheme of work. (This is consistent with Gardner's advice to teach a topic in depth, using a variety of Multiple Intelligences.) This second phase appeared to have the greatest positive effects on the intervention class.

3. The final phase involved the grouping of learners according to their Multiple Intelligences profiles, with work pitched to these profiles, and some encouragement to learners to explore and strengthen their areas of weakness as well as utilise their strengths.

Rhys Davies interviewed six selected case study learners at depth. They were 11 years of age. They were selected to represent initial history attainment (high, medium and low) prior to the Multiple Intelligences intervention. Responses from two case study learners are discussed here.

Case study 1

This initially high history achiever had strengths in interpersonal, kinaesthetic and logical intelligences. He commented in the interview that the Multiple Intelligences approach helped him in general: 'It was better and I found it easier with the others, working with the other people.' This learner enjoyed the video choice assessment option he chose in the first phase, and on the second phase, with use of Multiple Intelligences across a scheme of work, commented: 'I found the acting and the computers quite fun. I didn't really like the writing.' This learner also appreciated the third phase (involving grouping of students by Multiple Intelligences but with choice of activities) with the comment: 'I think I have the choice to do things in my own way.' He made it clear throughout the interview that he preferred working with others doing group work, rather than working on his own, and this is in line with his strong interpersonal intelligence. He was also aware of the importance of working on his weaker intelligences and commented that: 'you could have a go at one of your weaknesses,' in relation to the third phase intervention work.

Case study 2

This initially low history achiever had strengths in interpersonal, visual and kinaesthetic intelligences. Her middle intelligences were intrapersonal and linguistic, and her lowest were logical and musical intelligences. This learner also reported finding the work easier because she liked working with a group. She decided in the first phase of work to choose a tape approach for the assessment 'so that I didn't have to do any writing, and I think I talk a lot, so it was better for me'. She also noted that she used this choice to develop her weaknesses, quoting one of her lower intelligences, music, as an example. To a question concerning whether such choice is a good thing, she responded: 'I think it is a good thing because you can work hard on your weaknesses. You still work hard on your strengths but you know to work harder if you are working with a weakness.' She found the third phase work interesting, 'but especially the court case because I was one of the judges'. (Here she was able to use her strong interpersonal intelligence within that group placement, but also had a chance to develop her logical intelligence, an area of weakness, in her role as judge.) She also felt that the third phase 'taught me about my strengths and weaknesses'.

7. Edward de Bono's methods for teaching creative thinking

These methods, the Cognitive Research Trust (CoRT) and 'Six Hats' methods, are tools for the practice of thinking based on an information-processing model of thinking. They bring together the logical and the lateral thinking processes needed for creativity.

The CoRT programme involves 60 lessons based on material that is free of academic content, which address key aspects of thinking, including both critical and creative thinking, as follows:

1. CoRT 1 – breadth – to broaden perceptions

2. CoRT 2 – organisation – basic thinking operations such as 'recognise, analyse, compare, select' and how to organise them

3. CoRT 3 – interaction – involvement in interactive, constructive argument

4. CoRT 4 – creativity – to develop effective new ideas and engender fun

5. CoRT 5 – information and feeling – eliciting and assessing practical information, including beliefs and feelings

6. CoRT 6 – action – to fulfil the purpose of thinking, which is action.

The 'Six Hats' method also addresses critical and creative thinking, and can be used flexibly in any classroom situation. The different aspects of thinking covered by the 'Six Hats' are:

- **White Hat**: information – focus on information, disputed information, what information is available, what information would we like to have, what information do we need, what information is missing, how are we going to get the missing information?

- **Red Hat**: signal, no explanation, validity, decision, feelings right now, range of feelings, qualifications, (short) time allowed

- **Black Hat**: negative attitudes, does not fit, faults, potential problems, the future, devil's advocate, errors of logic, assessment, thoroughness, honesty

- **Yellow Hat**: judgement, logical thinking, feasibility, benefits, values, savings, competitive advantage, potential, concepts (underlying idea)

- **Green Hat**: time and place for creativity, creative effort, attitude, alternatives, modification, problem solving, possibilities, 'po' for provocation, specific lateral thinking techniques

- **The Blue Hat**: Thinking about thinking (i.e. metacognition).

These methods are of value for the teaching of thinking for all children for the following reasons:

1. They are based in information-processing theory, therefore address how we process information in our thinking and problem solving, and address both critical and creative thinking.

2. They can be applied systematically on a whole-school basis. Although de Bono states that the flexibility of the CoRT thinking programme allows it to be incorporated into the curriculum in any way that best suits the school and teacher (de Bono 1991) he does outline an order for teaching of the CoRT tools, with the CoRT unit on 'breadth' taught first. The whole-school purpose of the CoRT programme is reflected in de Bono's assertion that the CoRT lessons 'are designed to teach students of all abilities to effectively apply their intelligence to any academic, personal or social situation. The CoRT materials can be used with students of all ages, from elementary school to

the college level' (de Bono 1991, p.3) The example detailed at the end of this section describes an exemplary, systematic and whole-school approach using both CoRT and the 'Six Hats' methods.

As these methods aim to address creative as well as critical thinking, they should be evaluated for creative thinking outcomes. de Bono states that 'through the learning of CoRT thinking, students become lateral thinkers' (de Bono 1991, p.3). As an example of possible assessment tools for such creative thinking, the Torrance Tests of Creative Thinking (Torrance 1990) which provide three measures of creativity, fluency and flexibility, would be a good choice, and have been used by Professor John Edwards in his series of research evaluations of the CoRT programme (Edwards 1998; Ritchie and Edwards 1994).

de Bono asserts that learners acquire a set of transferable thinking tools that work well in all situations and all areas of the curriculum (de Bono 1991). He encourages teaching for generalisation to other areas of his programmes, wanting learners to acquire a set of transferable skills which they can apply to other situations (de Bono 1993). However, a key issue in the teaching of CoRT is the quality of the bridging, or generalisation to academic and real-life problem solving. When well taught, there is evidence of such generalisation (e.g. in an early New Zealand study reported by Walters (1978)). However, a study where there was inadequate teacher training and teacher commitment to teaching the CoRT method, carried out in the UK, suggests the effect that inadequate teaching for generalisation can have in limited outcomes from the use of this method (a Cambridgeshire study, carried out by Hunter-Grundin (1985), and critiqued by Adey and Shayer (1994)).

It is important, when we utilise the 'Six Hats' method, that we understand the underlying theory, and apply it in a systematic and well-informed way, with the benefit of de Bono's authorised training, and such structured de Bono provision as the two-day certificate course which was utilised in the example given below.

de Bono asserts that learners using the CoRT programme 'come to regard themselves as thinkers' (de Bono 1991, p.3). It would therefore be appropriate to utilise a measure of learners' self-perception of themselves as thinkers, such as that developed by Costa (1991), to evaluate the effectiveness of this programme.

AN EXAMPLE FROM PRACTICE IN A SCHOOL SETTING

The present writer was involved in the evaluation phase of a whole-school, systematic use of de Bono's thinking programmes at a high-achieving secondary school in Auckland, New Zealand. The school had implemented the programmes systematically and extensively, with its third and fourth formers (ages 13 and 14) all completing the 60 CoRT lessons, and with the sixth formers completing the two-day certificate 'Six Hats' course. The programmes were led by a staff member, Philip Coombe, who is a trained and registered de Bono instructor.

The teaching of the CoRT lessons allowed for the teaching of the ten thinking 'tools' in the programme, as follows:

1. treatment of ideas (plus, minus and interesting points in an idea are identified)

2. factors involved (considering all factors in a situation)

3. rules (considering the basic purposes and principles of rules)

4. consequences (considering immediate, short, medium and long-term consequences)

5. objectives (considering aims, goals and objectives)

6. planning (considering basic features and processes)

7. priorities (ordering priorities)

8. alternatives (generating new alternatives, priorities and choices)

9. decisions (making a decision, and the processes/operations involved)

10. viewpoint (considering the points of view of all others involved in the situation).

Group work is a central feature of the approach, where learners discuss a problem example given to them, using the thinking tool presented in that lesson.

The evaluation included a before-and-after implementation of the Costa rating scale of 'Characteristics of intelligent behaviour', which allows for a 10-point self-rating by learners themselves. This allowed the writer to identify whether the thinking characteristics which the learners considered themselves to have developed matched those covered in each of the components of the CoRT programme completed up to that point: these were CoRT 1, covering breadth of thinking; CoRT 2, covering organisation of thinking; and CoRT 3, covering interaction in thinking. (See Howie, Coombe and Lonergan 1998, for a detailed report of the outcomes.)

Some individual case study interviews were also carried out, with regard to the CoRT programme, with learners from different classroom levels. Some of the comments are reported here:

- One learner in a higher ability level class felt that the CoRT thinking skill programme could help her in a challenging situation such as that relating to a school change, where she could ask herself, 'What is my interest?' and 'Which one is best for me?'

- Another learner in a mixed ability class felt that the CoRT thinking skill programme helped her by 'giving me things to think about' and that 'I should think of everything'.

- One learner in a lower ability class who considered that he was placed in this class 'because I'm not bright' responded to the interview questions with considerable thought and detail. He stated, in relation to the way in which the CoRT programme was taught, that 'I'm not really into it…I don't like it. It's just things that I think come to you naturally, like I don't think you use it much.' He felt it could be improved, for example, that 'things could have been done to help you to use it more on your own initiative'. However, he did confide that one of the ways in which he did use learning from the programme was as follows: 'When I think I am going to do something stupid I think about it rather than going straight ahead with it.' He also reported that he was using the thinking skills in class to work out a problem and he was 'taking a bit more time to think about problems, rather than writing down any old answer'. Further on in the interview, in the section about responding to a school conflict issue, he said: 'I could say all I had to say, but I don't think the teacher would take into consideration much of it'. However, he concluded, regarding the way in which the CoRT thinking skills work helped, with: 'Before, I let loose and told them what I thought. I keep my mouth shut because I'd probably end up with more punishment' (i.e. he was thinking about consequences).

These responses are of interest to us in relation to a whole-school ethos requirement in developing thinking skills, as they remind us that it is important for the aims of a thinking approach chosen by a school to match the overall school ethos.

8. Tony Buzan's mind mapping method and 'ten creativity characteristics'

Tony Buzan has provided us with a series of publications on mind mapping techniques which are very accessible, including his 1991 Penguin publication, *Use Both Sides of Your Brain*. This approach can be used by any teacher, without special training. In a video available on the internet Buzan appears, spelling out the 'rules of mind mapping', which can be used with any information, to enhance the thinking process (www.iMindMap.com). These can be summarised as follows:

1. There is one word for each 'branch' of the map. There is freedom to branch out, which gives more clarity and freedom in thinking.

2. The word and the branch are connected, with the links made by colour and image to enhance the learning. This 'alights' the brain.

3. Key words and key images should be underlined and in colour. Use of imagery is fundamental to the way humans communicate.

4. The image should be clear and the structure beautifully organised, to clarify the ideas.

Although these methods and ideas can be utilised in any classroom, for all learners, in an infused way, they are discussed here as a particular contribution to the teaching of creative thinking for all. They also bring together logical thinking and creative thinking, as with mind mapping the learner develops an idea along its conceptual 'branch' in a logical way, but extends that conceptual train of thought with new creative thinking.

In writing about his ten creativity characteristics, Buzan suggests that new ideas can be developed from old ideas by using colour and shape, magnifying reality, viewing things from an alternative perspective, responding emotionally, and expressing a connection with energy.

These approaches are important to us for the teaching of thinking for all of the following reasons:

1. They bring together logical and lateral thinking, for creative thinking. In mind mapping an idea can be organised and expanded in a conceptually meaningful and organised way – for example, in developing ideas using the ten creativity characteristics, we might think logically about the key dimensions of that object or idea (e.g. for an object, its use, its shape, its colour, its size, etc.),

and then for each of these key dimensions or characteristics, we could provide alternative possibilities in a creative way.

2.   They can be useful for all school subjects, particularly where planning, learning facts, and generating written work are involved, according to Bridget Watts, a Special Educational Needs Coordinator in a primary school in Kent, UK. She states: 'Mind mapping provides a visual key to unlocking sequencing skills, and aids memory and the retrieval of information in a written format. These are essential skills required during work and group task activities in the literacy hour' (Watts 1999, p.32). She describes how a teacher can model the planning and development of a story, showing the organising and sequencing of ideas, using colour coding, numbering, or through pictures, which could be fun and helpful to all learners, and she considers that it is also particularly helpful to learners with specific learning difficulties, who may have difficulty in the sequencing of ideas and lack confidence in their writing abilities.

3.   It is a holistic approach, giving access for all learners to an integrated way of thinking which is strong on the visual access to thinking. Mind mapping makes use of Sternberg's metacomponent of representation in enhancing thinking, and allows for the use of Gardner's visual intelligence.

4.   It can be used at all levels of school and with a wide range of ages, with pictures for the youngest learners and detailed abstract conceptual linking at secondary level.

AN EXAMPLE FROM PRACTICE IN A SCHOOL SETTING

An example of the mind mapping approach in planning and developing a research project in the field of the teaching of thinking occurred in the writer's own planning of her doctoral project on imitative learning (Howie 1969), which had as a central aim a study of the imitative learning of children with very severe learning difficulties. Through a wide range of reading on this topic she was able to track the following 'branches' of key factors which linked to, or 'branched out' from this topic, as follows:

•   a branch for factors relating to what enhanced imitation (e.g. type of imitative task (instrumental or incidental); type of model (adult or peer); reinforcement of the model; anxiety in the observer; type of outcome (recall or performance))

- a branch for factors relating to attention to the model (e.g. novelty; complexity; the aggressive nature of the modelled task; the motor/verbal nature of the modelled task)

- a branch for factors relating to the learners' characteristics, to be taken into account in the design (e.g. mental age; chronological age; intelligence quotient; gender).

The writer, as well as having a 'whole topic' visual map to cover the topic and all of its branches, which was put up as a separate big sheet pinned to her wall, also developed a separate visual map for each key conceptual branch as she developed her reading on them. This allowed her to organise her review of the literature in a systematic way, seeing at a glance how any new reading 'fitted in'. It was also useful in planning and developing the three main research phases of her project.

Baumfield *et al.* (2008), in discussing action research in the classroom, give an example of how mind mapping was used 'as a mind-friendly way of collecting data regarding students' understanding of Learning to Learn, before and on the completion of the project...it was also the opportunity to explore the potential of using mind maps to analyse student understanding' (p.37).

These are just two examples of teachers and researchers using mind mapping as a research tool, when working in the field of the teaching of thinking.

Approaches that are more related to, or infused with, classroom learning

9. The Lipman 'Philosophy for Children' programme

The 'Philosophy for Children' programme developed by Professor Matthew Lipman (1976; Lipman and Gazzard 1998) helps teachers to convert their classrooms into 'communities of enquiry', using specially constructed texts for the teaching of thinking skills by carefully trained teachers. The programme consists of specifically designed early childhood programmes, which develop through to later ones, covering skills such as:

- clarifying concepts

- making appropriate generalisations

- formulating cause-and-effect relationships

- drawing syllogistic relationships

- identifying consistencies and contradictions
- identifying underlying assumptions
- working with analogies
- formulating problems
- applying principles to real-life problem solving.

Although the original programme does have some subject-specific texts with a school subject-specific focus (e.g. reasoning in science, reasoning in language arts, reasoning in social studies), the programme is not a fully infused programme, as it uses separate lessons, usually one per week, to lay down the basics of thinking and problem solving in general.

Robert Fisher, who was originally a teacher of Philosophy for Children, and then a UK leader in its use, has written guidance on how to develop a 'community of enquiry' when using this approach (Fisher 2000). A 'thinking circle' is created, in which a 'shared stimulus' (which could involve a wide range of sources, such as a book, work of art, video, or experiences) is used to invite reflections and discussion. All members of the circle are invited to raise their own questions about the 'shared stimulus', and one question is chosen to facilitate more in-depth discussion.

Further, the book gives a useful demonstration of how the teachers' manuals can guide discussion plans. Fisher outlines how the philosophical discussion plan consists of a group of questions around a central idea or problem. The questions can either build on each other to extend the discussion, or circle around the idea or problem, seeing it from different angles. (This is a sustained and systematic kind of questioning that Socrates used, and so the approach is considered 'Socratic'.) An example of such questioning is given by Fisher (2000, p.32).

Some of the values of this approach at Tier 1 level, for teaching thinking to all children, are as follows:

1.   It is aimed at developing the potential for reasoning and making judgements (or choices), for all children. Philosophy for Children is defined as 'philosophy applied to education for the purpose of producing students with improved proficiency in reasoning and judgement' (Lipman 1991, p.112). It has a main focus upon the quality of discussion among learners, so in this 'community of enquiry' the learner has to externalise the reasoning being used so that it can be scrutinised not only by other learners, but by the learner himself/herself, in a metacognitive (thinking about

thinking) way. Robert Fisher, interviewed by Winyard (2004), states of his experience in teaching with it: 'What surprised me was the quality of the questioning and dialogue provided by Mat's simple but philosophically charged stories. It transformed my ideas about what children could do, think and become through the practice of philosophical discussion' (p.42).

2. It recognises the long-term nature of the development of these thinking skills, with lessons taught over a long time-span, using materials of growing complexity. It is therefore suited to a whole-school approach.

3. It encourages a partnership and collaborative approach to enhancing thinking. Lipman, in his interview with Winyard, stated: 'In the community of enquiry children can be creative and sociable with ideas. It is an environment where they don't just converse like volleying before a tennis game! They start to develop roles within the community...an interdependency developing' (Winyard 2004, p.204). It is important that this partnership is recognised and understood by the whole-school community, including the parents. The use of community of enquiry techniques in a UK school Year 1 class are reported by Baumfield *et al.* (2008). They recount that in informal parent interviews as part of the whole-school work, some parents expressed concern about children using expressions such as 'I disagree with that because...' (a typical element of Philosophy for Children discourse). Baumfield *et al.* (2008) advocate close parental partnership in using such a programme.

There have been a number of studies with the programme. Some writers, including Sternberg (1984), consider the programme not well suited to poor readers with a less than middle-class background. However, research by Lipman himself with white and black learners from high and low socio-economic status groups showed, after only nine weeks of intervention, a substantially significant advantage to the experimental group on a test of reasoning ability (Lipman and Gazzard 1987). A review of ten rigorously evaluated studies with Philosophy for Children reported that all studies had positive effect sizes for outcomes including reasoning, reading and self-esteem (Trickey and Topping 2004).

The use of this programme is international, with materials being developed internationally which are appropriate to the various cultural needs of learners. In the UK, as part of SAPERE, the UK organisation for Philosophy for Children (www.sapere.org.uk), Robert Fisher has made available *Stories for Thinking* (1996) and *Poems for Thinking* (1997), which are philosophically charged materials. Also available from SAPERE are Muris' (2001) picture books and William and Sutcliffe's (2000) news stories. In his interview with Winyard (2004), Lipman spoke about developing new materials with teachers from Taiwan, Korea, the Ukraine and Iceland. In New Zealand, as reported by Howie (2003), a New Zealand Philosophy for Children Association has been formed, and the programme is used with learners having a range of ages, abilities, and socio-economic backgrounds. They are using culturally appropriate materials, including picture books, newspaper articles, films, and the internet. This all indicates the use of the approach internationally with a wide range of materials, including more visual materials which facilitate the overlap with Gardner's Multiple Intelligences, and foster inclusivity.

Lipman is also concerned about the moral aspects of thinking. He has engaged in research on what he calls 'caring thinking' (Lipman 2003), which involves understanding and thinking about both one's own and another person's feelings and emotions. In his chapter called 'Community of Enquiry: Creating Contexts for Moral Education' Fisher (1998) states:

> For some teachers philosophy undertaken in a community of enquiry is not so much about developing language and thinking skills, its value lies in its contribution to personal and social education. A community of enquiry can help children develop the skills and dispositions that will enable them to play their full part in a pluralistic and democratic society. It boosts self-esteem… (p.55)

Fisher states that it achieves this by creating a caring classroom characterised by children learning to explore issues of personal concern such as love, friendship, death, bullying and fairness; where they develop their own views and explore and challenge the views of others; make thoughtful judgements based on reason; listen to and respect each other; and experience quiet moments of thinking and reflection (Fisher 1998). This is all clearly inclusive.

Ideas for evaluating and assessing growth within a community of enquiry are shared in Fisher's (1998) detailed discussion of what characterises a community of enquiry, and in the East Riding guide (see below).

The writer has a professional colleague, Nicola O'Riordan, whom she supervised for a masters dissertation, who now takes a strong role in teacher development in inclusion in the School Improvement Service of the East Riding of Yorkshire Council, and who is also currently engaged in doctoral research on the Philosophy for Children approach (supervised by another colleague).

Nicola O'Riordan has written an excellent practical guide on Philosophy for Children (East Riding for Yorkshire Council, undated) which mirrors the Philosophy for Children model used in the UK. In this manual she states: 'Engaging with our primary tools for thinking, language and discourse, P4C encourages children and young people to search for meaning in their experiences, question, clarify and extend their understanding' (p.4). It is therefore of interest that O'Riordan has chosen to research the use of this approach in schools where many children come from homes experiencing socio-economic disadvantage, and their own unique experiences and meaning-making relating to that disadvantage.

O'Riordan's work is of particular relevance in relation to including all children, and there is a section in the manual on inclusion. Also, she argues in the guide that Philosophy for Children has a positive impact on children's social, emotional and behavioural development, a key issue for inclusion. In support of this, she quotes learners' own statements as follows:

- 'Philosophy relaxes me. If I'm worried, how can I learn anything? Because the class will respect my opinion, I can be myself and even change my mind without being laughed at.'

- 'I like being able to express myself and argue without getting into trouble.'

- 'It has helped me quite well with my growing up, and to release my bad and good feelings.'

(Ord 2006, SAPERE, p.15, cited in East Riding of Yorkshire Council undated, p.21)

AN EXAMPLE FROM PRACTICE IN A SCHOOL SETTING

In interim reports by Nicola O'Riordan (2009) of her research with Philosophy for Children the following comments are of particular interest regarding use of the programme in an inclusive way.

First, in one school serving a social context which is below the UK national average in deprivation, there were indications in early classroom lessons with Philosophy for Children that challenges included enhancing listening skills, taking turns without shouting or shocking, and providing support in asking philosophical questions. However, in one debriefing session the children themselves felt that they had built on the ideas of others during the enquiry, and the researcher comments that this was evident on several occasions as the children referred to previous comments of friends.

In another school from an area which is considered one of the most socially and economically deprived areas in the county, the teachers considered that their pupils had shown improvements in reasoning and personal and interpersonal skills through the regular Philosophy for Children lessons.

In one 'challenging' Year 6 class in this school, in commenting on Philosophy for Children the teacher made particular note of the way the class appeared to enjoy the lessons; that the children profited by having the language of debate, including new phrases to use, displayed on the interactive whiteboard (e.g. 'Can you clarify your last point?'), and that there were positive effects on behaviour associated with ground rules for the enquiry. Those learners in the class considered to have special educational needs appeared to benefit from the lessons not requiring written work, and they were treated as equals by the class; they made as many contributions as the other children, and they 'blossomed as individuals'.

Their teacher reported of this challenging class engaging in Philosophy for Children: 'General behaviour improved, which made them more receptive in all lessons. They have become a settled and responsible Year 6 class who are a good role model for the rest of the school' (O'Riordan 2009, p.2). At the end of the year, 78 per cent of this Year 6 class achieved Level 4 in the end of Key Stage 2 SATs for English in 2008, which compared with a similar year group achieving 60.7 per cent in 2007, and 63.3 per cent in 2006.

10. Philip Adey and Michael Shayer's CAME and CASE programmes

The cognitive acceleration programmes Cognitive Acceleration through Maths (CAME) and Cognitive Acceleration through Science (CASE), were first developed in the UK by Adey and Shayer (1994) to address the cognitive processing abilities underpinning the more abstract thinking needed for achievement at secondary school level.

More recently, the cognitive acceleration approach has been developed for technology education and for the development of arts and reasoning skills. It has also been developed for younger children. (See McGregor 2007, p.69 for a summary of these developments.)

The original lessons were carried out separately from normal curriculum lessons, over a period of two years. They involve the careful interweaving of the 'six pillars' of the programme:

1. concrete preparation (like scaffolding)

2. cognitive conflict (introducing 'dissonance', a Piagetian notion, to lead to cognitive growth)

3. construction (development through social exchange in the zone of proximal development (a Vygotskian idea))

4. metacognition (thinking about one's thinking)

5. bridging (to academic and real-life problem solving)

6. the schemata, or reasoning pattern, which is involved in the content and context of the lesson.

The CASE and CAME programmes are included in this section because Adey and Shayer initially saw the choice of science as an opening through which to explore the development of general thinking (Adey and Shayer 2002). In more recent work with the programmes there is closer linking with the curriculum subject areas (e.g. science for 14- and 15-year-olds in the work of Gunter, McGregor and Twist (publication forthcoming)).

In the development of CASE at Key Stage 1 (abbreviated as Case@ KS1), the CASE programme described above and adapted for Key Stage 1 use, each activity is linked to a curriculum area of science or numeracy. Also, each intervention activity addresses one of Piaget's schemata of concrete operations: seriation, classification, time sequencing, spatial perceptions, causality, and 'rules of the game'. The activities are designed to provide intellectual challenges through cognitive conflict, delivered to groups of six children in a way which maximises their shared 'social construction' and metacognition (thinking about their thinking). Within such shared activities the children are expected to express ideas about problem solving, give explanations, ask questions, offer suggestions, agree or disagree with peers, and reflect on the learning process. The activities require no reading or writing and groups are arranged with children of mixed abilities, to enhance sharing of problem solutions (a very Vygotskian idea).

The value of this approach for the teaching of thinking for all learners includes the following:

1. The strong base in theory, including Piaget's theory, Vygotskian socio-cultural theory, and Feuerstein's theory of mediated learning experience. (Shayer is also an important researcher with Feuerstein's cognitive enhancement approach.)

2. The programme's focus on the shared construction of meanings, in relation not only to the science or maths concepts being learnt, but also to metacognitive beliefs about thinking, and the learners themselves as thinkers. Larkin (2006) reports on the CASE@KS1 study carried out in ten primary schools in London (the full study was initially reported by Adey 2002), and notes the metacognitive development of two five-year-old children involved in the study. She carried out observations of these two children using Flavell's (1979) metacognitive model of cognitive monitoring, which includes person, task and strategy variables, to code the children's learning interactions. For each child a particular theme emerged: for one, 'the need to explain' her thinking processes to the group, and for the other, 'planning, evaluating and predicting'.

3. The learners develop in both their cognitive and emotional understandings. Larkin notes at the end of her paper on the metacognitive development of the two closely observed learners mentioned above:

    > Through collaborative group work the children are able to experience the emotional aspects of collaborative and productive thinking, they not only learn from each other, but also learn about each other. The tasks provide metacognitive experiences for the children that engage them on an emotional level as well as a cognitive level. (Larkin 2006, p.29)

    New evidence for CASE@KS1 is that there may be positive motivational as well as cognitive and academic impacts of the approach (Cattle and Howie 2007). (Adey and Shayer's evaluation of urban CASE@KS1 projects did not include a motivational measure.) There may be differential motivational impacts for male and female learners. Leo and Galloway (1996) in their critique of Adey and Shayer's findings up to that time, drew attention to the need to understand motivational aspects to 'understand better why the CASE programme appears to succeed for some children and not for others' (p.35).

Of interest to us are the ways in which classrooms are organised and used in the approach, so as to maximise the Vygotskian focus on social interaction. First there is the whole-class, concrete preparation, then smaller group work, where construction can arise while working on problems, followed by whole-class reflection on the solutions arrived at, and the nature of the thinking needed for them, and finally, the bridging to thinking in other contexts (including suggestions from the learners themselves – a partnership process).

The original CASE and CAME evaluations (Adey and Shayer 1994) showed positive effect sizes for science and mathematics, fulfilling the aims of the two-year programmes. The key role played in this by professional development of the teachers associated with the programmes was identified by Adey (2004).

There is growing evidence of the value of this approach in a variety of school contexts, including urban schools with a range of learners from lower socio-economic backgrounds (Adey 2002), and learners from a rural area, with a higher socio-economic status background (Cattle and Howie 2007).

This approach, developed in the UK, is also increasingly in use in other countries, including the USA, Finland, Australia, Germany, Holland, and Korea (Adey 2004).

AN EXAMPLE FROM PRACTICE IN A SCHOOL SETTING

As an example of ordinary school and classroom use of this approach for all learners, Julie Cattle, under supervision by the writer, evaluated a school programme for the development of thinking skills using the CASE@KS1 approach. This has been published by the *International Journal of Science Education* (Cattle and Howie 2007).

The study was carried out in a small, rural UK school, and used cognitive measures to duplicate those used in the urban evaluation by Adey and Shayer (Adey 2002), including Raven's Colored Progressive Matrices, a 'drawing' test, and the Boehm-R Test of Basic Concepts. Raven's Colored Progressive Matrices are a culturally reduced measure of general problem-solving ability (Raven 1963), the 'drawing' test is a test based on original Piagetian protocols and was developed as a group version by Shayer *et al.* (1978), and the Boehm-R Test of Basic Concepts measures development of concepts including those of importance within a Piagetian framework (Boehm 1986).

Julie Cattle developed a motivational self-concept measure suitable for the young age of the learners (it had a pictorial format), which drew on the domain-specific aspects of academic self-concept identified by Marsh and Yeung (1987). The measure looked both at self-concept more generally, and at maths and science self-concept (involving motivation in relation to those subjects).

Julie Cattle (the coordinator for science in the school) and the ordinary classroom teacher, both well trained in the CASE@KS1 approach, taught the programme to the Year 1 learners. This group was compared to a comparison group within another similar school, which was not receiving CASE@KS1. The programme was delivered, as required by Adey, 'in a way which maximised opportunities for social construction, metacognition and bridging' (Adey 2002, p.23).

The group with the CASE@KS1 programme did not differ from the comparison group in the gains made on the Raven and the Boehm-R Test, but scored higher on the 'drawing' test. In the motivation measure, the group with CASE@KS1 made gains on the 'All about me: school' part of the questionnaire, while the comparison group made a loss, and the same pattern was found for motivation towards science. (It was difficult to support both findings statistically because of the low ceiling effect of the measure, and the small class numbers involved.)

There is a suggestion in the results that girls responded more negatively than boys in the 'Myself' and 'School' parts of the motivational measure, in both the CASE@KS1 and the comparison groups, this being particularly so for the CASE@KS1 girls. These CASE@KS1 girls also showed noticeably lower gains on the cognitive measures associated with the programme than the gains made by the boys. It would have been useful to have carried out individual interviews, which might have thrown light on these differences in motivation. (Leo and Galloway (1996) in discussing motivation in relation to earlier CASE findings, suggest that 'the initial non-effects on girls of CASE lessons might have resulted from their tendency towards learned helplessness which was exacerbated by a lack of experience in the scientific setting' (p.42).) More time than the one-year CASE@KS1 programme was probably needed to move the girls to greater mastery of the new learning.

11. Swartz and Parks' approach to infuse critical and creative thinking into content instruction

Professor Carol McGuinness, a leader in the use of an infusion approach, describes a fully infused approach as follows:

> Infusion approaches contextualize thinking directly within a curricular area so that the goals of topic understanding and developing thinking are simultaneously and – in the long term – are seamlessly pursued... In the context of teaching thinking, it means that the teaching of curricular content is infused with explicit instruction in thinking, with developing understandings of the kinds of thinking that might be required and with being strategic and self-regulatory about one's own thinking. (McGuinness 2005a, p.115)

An American approach to infusion which is now widely used internationally is that of Swartz (2001a, 2001b) and Swartz and Parks (1994a, 1994b). As described by them, infusion lessons bring into subject content lessons an explicit emphasis on skilful thinking, so that time is spent not only on content, but on the thinking skill or process involved. The thinking skills or processes addressed are:

- comparing/contrasting
- classifying
- parts/whole
- sequencing
- uncovering assumptions
- reliable resources/accurate observations
- reasons/conclusions
- causal explanation
- prediction
- reasoning by analogy
- generalisation
- generating possibilities
- generating metaphors
- decision making
- problem solving.

It is expected that these skills or processes will be integrated across key curricular subjects, using opportunities where the content area and the skill can be taught in a complementary manner. These skills and processes are considered as 'powerful examples' of the type of thinking involved, and as important in the following types of tasks:

- generating ideas
- clarifying ideas
- assessing the reasonableness of ideas
- complex thinking tasks such as decision making and problem solving.

Swartz and Parks (1994a) provide a wide range of graphic organisers (called 'thinking diagrams' by McGuinness) to guide the nature of the thinking involved in the content learning task. For example, the 'Open compare and contrast' graphic organiser has, first, a space for detailing how aspects of the learning task are alike, then a place for systematic detailing of how they are different 'with regard to' (i.e. delineating the aspects or dimensions on which they are different). Finally, there is a section in which patterns of significant similarities and differences are noted, and then a space for the conclusion or interpretation.

Graphic organisers are used as prompts which scaffold support in this thinking process (McGregor 2007). With the 'Skillful problem solving' graphic organiser, the problem is first defined: 'How I might…' Possible solutions are then listed. The main portion of the organiser card is allocated to 'solutions considered', and each solution is to be described systematically under its criteria (the solution), consequences, pro and con, and value. Finally, the new solution is noted. A similar graphic organiser for 'Skillful decision making' lists the options, and then considers the options systematically in terms of 'consequences', 'support' and 'value'. (We can note that in the 1997 evaluation by McGuinness concerning the Northern Ireland work mentioned below, 'there were mixed views on the benefits of the thinking diagrams. While all of the teachers recognised their importance in terms of providing a guide to clear thinking, many commented that they needed modification in one way or another' (p.5).)

Within infused lessons, a four-step strategy is suggested as follows:

1. First, the teacher introduces the thinking skill or process involved and demonstrates its importance.

2. Next, the learners are guided with the graphic organiser to engage in the thinking as they learn the content of the lesson.

3. Then the teacher asks the learners reflective questions about their thinking.

4. Finally, additional opportunities are offered to engage in using the thinking skill more independently.

An excellent example of how such an approach can be used in a systematic and not only whole-school, but whole-country way, is provided by Professor Carol McGuinness (2005b). She has built on this approach to develop her infusion programme for learners in Northern Ireland, called 'Activating Children's Thinking' (ACTS I) and 'Activating Children's Thinking in Sustainable Thinking Classrooms' (ACTS II). She also reports on the use of ACTS in Wales, in two languages (McGuinness 2002).

McGuinness describes the programmes as follows:

> ACTS adopted an infusion methodology where the goals of enhancing thinking and subject/topic understanding were simultaneously pursued. The theoretical perspective with regard to children's learning focused on the development of their metacognitive capacities – on their ability to become proactive about their learning in terms of planning, monitoring and appraising. (McGuinness *et al.* 2005, p.2)

The ACTS framework for thinking involves metacognition at the centre, with five different kinds of thinking feeding into that:

1. Search for meaning (sequencing, ordering, ranking, sorting, grouping, classifying, analysing, identifying parts and wholes, noting similarities and differences, finding patterns and relationships, comparing and contrasting).

2. Critical thinking (making predictions and formulating hypotheses, drawing conclusions, giving reasons, distinguishing fact from opinion, determining bias, reliability of evidence, relating causes and effects, designing a fair test).

3. Decision making (identifying why a decision is necessary, generating options, predicting the likely consequences, weighing up the pros and cons, deciding on a course of action, reviewing the consequences).

4. Problem solving (identifying and clarifying situations, generating alternative solutions, selecting and implementing a solution strategy, evaluating and checking how well a solution solves problems).

5. Creative thinking (generating ideas and possibilities, building and combining ideas, formulating own points of view, taking multiple perspectives and seeing other points of view).

(McGuinness et al. *2005)*

For the teaching of thinking for all learners, this infusion approach is of value for the following reasons:

1. It is meant to be used over time across the curriculum as teachers proceed through a unit of study. Habits of thinking can therefore be built up over time, in a whole-school way.

2. Because ordinary classroom teachers teach this approach, and are also expected to be good models of these types of thinking, there is the possibility of strongly generalising the thinking skill to curriculum subject content. (However, there may well be some difficulty for teachers in adequately teaching both the thinking skill involved and the content, in one lesson, with some risk of the latter stages of the four-step strategy (reflection and wider generalisation) being rushed, or even missed owing to classroom time pressures. For example, McGuinness, reporting on teacher feedback in her 1997 evaluation, notes: 'Without doubt, teachers identified time as the main constraint…teachers also commented that thinking skills lessons went on longer than initially planned' (1997, p.23).)

3. The wide range of thinking skills involved suggests that it is suitable in a variety of contexts. (However, users need to consider what adaptations might be required to ensure that the approach is used in a culturally appropriate way. It is also important to make sure that this content-based approach will meet the cognitive and emotional needs of learners who have previously experienced failure with content learning, and so careful evaluation for individual difference in response to this approach is important.)

EXAMPLES FROM PRACTICE IN A SCHOOL SETTING

The present writer has not been involved personally with the use of an infusion approach, but did participate in an international seminar on 'Thinking Skills in the Classroom' in Belfast in 2002, led by Professor Carol McGuinness and hosted by the British Council. It allowed her to read the research reports on the ACTS project and view videos of classroom teaching using the approach. The writer was also present when Professor Carol McGuinness presented a paper called 'Metacognition in classrooms' to a Harrogate International Conference on Thinking in 2002, where McGuinness presented transcripts from videos of metacognitive dialogue by learners involved in the ACTS programme.

The research and development work of Professor McGuinness on ACTS I and ACTS II, supported by the Teaching and Learning Research Programme, is exemplary. It is a model of system-wide training in, supported use of, and rigorous evaluation of, a programme for the teaching of thinking. For example, under her leadership, the ACTS II project, which aimed at developing 'Sustainable Thinking' classrooms, had three strands:

1. construction of a professional development programme to enable teachers to use ACTS pedagogy in their classroom lessons

2. video recording of thinking lessons to identify features of classroom dialogue that might help the development of metacognition

3. tracking of the learning progress of 8- to 11-year-old children who participated in the ACTS project over a three-year period, and comparison of them with a similar group of children who did not participate.

(McGuinness 2006)

McGuinness reports that:

> participating in the ACTS intervention for three years had a positive effect on children's ratings of their use of cognitive and metacognitive strategies, in the sense that it moderated decreases that were evident in the control group. By the end of three years, the ACTS children reported more frequent use of the cognitive and metacognitive strategies than do the controls. (McGuinness *et al.* 2005, p.8)

However, with a concern for the progress of all learners, which is important for our consideration at Tier 1 level, McGuinness does note that the positive effects were not the same for all children, with moderate to high ability children (80% of the sample) benefiting most. There were no positive outcomes identified for the low ability learners (p.8).

In another report, McGuinness notes:

> developing children's capacity to learn and become more skilful thinkers takes time. It needs careful support if children are to become autonomous and self-regulating. When scaling up, particular attention should be paid to children with poorer cognitive and social resources. (McGuinness 2006, p.1)

The evaluation found no individual difference for gender outcomes in terms of pattern of change over the intervention, although girls initially rated themselves on the use of cognitive and metacognitive strategies more positively. The positive changes made by learners in terms of their metacognitive strategies were related to effort. McGuinness reports some items from the learners' responses which reflect this:

- 'I spend some time thinking about how to do my work before I begin it.' (self-monitoring)
- 'I ask myself questions when I do my work to make sure I understand.' (self-monitoring)
- 'When I make mistakes I try to figure out why.' (evaluating)
- 'When we have difficult work to do in the class, I try to figure out the hard parts on my own.' (independence)

(McGuinness 2006, p.3)

A key contribution of the project concerns sustainability, a very important issue in use of cognitive enhancement programmes. McGuinness reports that:

> teachers involved in the project participated in a Continuing Professional Development (CPD) programme. They reported changes in their classroom practices, in their perceptions of children's thinking, and in their images of themselves as thinkers... Sustained teacher development needs to focus not only on classroom practices but on teachers' beliefs about, and images of, learners and learning. (McGuinness 2006, p.1)

For example, in her 1997 report McGuinness noted, in terms of benefits for teachers:

> teachers noted that it had sharpened their concept of thinking skills, enabled them to review their schemes of work from this perspective and encouraged more effective planning. Several teachers mentioned the degree to which their expectations within the classroom had changed and that they now seek out opportunities to extend and challenge children's thinking. They also noted changes in their questioning strategies, even those who had previously believed that their questioning was good. (McGuinness 1997, p.23)

A key argument for using an infusion approach, according to McGuinness, is that 'teaching for thoughtfulness is directly supported across the curriculum' and 'transfer of learning can be more easily promoted in other areas of the curriculum and reinforced at later stages' (McGuinness 1997, p.4). She reports in her early 1997 evaluation that 'Some teachers emphasised the across-the-curriculum effects. They said that thinking skills had general applicability across the curriculum and that they can be transferred from one subject to another' (McGuinness 1997, p.23). They saw it as tying in well with the underpinning principles of the Northern Ireland curriculum.

Approaches with a strong emotional or motivational focus

12. Goleman's emotional intelligence

The concept of emotional intelligence is included here because key researchers on emotional intelligence give evidence for it as an intelligence, that is, about thinking. Mayer, Caruso and Salovey (2000), who have done considerable scholarly work on this concept, define emotional intelligence as follows:

> Emotional intelligence refers to the ability to recognise the meanings of emotions and their relationships, and to reason and problem solve on the basis of them. Emotional intelligence is involved in the capacity to perceive emotions, assimilate emotion-related feelings, understand the information of those emotions, and manage them. (p.267)

Mayer *et al.* (2000) present their solid research evidence for the abilities called 'emotional intelligence' being 'intelligences'.

The concept of emotional intelligence has been popularised by Goleman, who described programmes which have been developed to enhance it. He identifies the different aspects of emotional intelligence as follows:

1. knowing one's emotions (self-awareness and recognition of an emotion when it happens)

2. managing emotions

3. motivating oneself

4. recognising emotions in others (and especially being able to empathise)

5. handling relationships (largely managing emotions in others).

(Goleman 1995/6)

These abilities emerge from the work of Mayer, Caruso and Salovey (2000).

A model for the teaching of emotional intelligence, in the 'self science' curriculum, is presented by Goleman in his first book (1995/6). He states:

> The topics taught include self-awareness, in the sense of recognising feelings and building a vocabulary for them, and seeing the links between thoughts, feelings, and reactions; knowing if thoughts or feelings are ruling a decision; seeing the consequences of alternative choices; and applying these insights to decisions about such issues as drugs, smoking and sex. Self-awareness also takes the form of recognising your strengths and weaknesses, and seeing yourself in a positive but realistic light... Another emphasis is on managing emotions... Still another emphasis is on taking responsibility for decisions and actions... A key social ability is empathy, understanding others' feelings and taking their perspective, and respecting differences in how people feel about things. Relationships are a major focus, including learning to be a good listener and question-asker. (p.268)

He also gives an example of a classroom lesson on 'identifying feelings' which used pictures of faces brought in by the children from magazines, with class discussion on naming the feelings being expressed and explaining how to tell the person had those feelings. Children in the class imitate the pictures and follow the facial-muscle recipes for each emotion (Goleman 1995/6).

Emotional intelligence is of importance for the teaching of thinking for all children for the following reasons:

1. It brings together cognition (information and problem solving) with affect/emotions.

2. It includes a range of abilities covered by other key theorists in this discussion of approaches for Tier 1. For example, the following components, which link to approaches we are familiar with, feature in Goleman's description of the emotional abilities addressed by the W. T. Consortium programme to enhance 'emotional literacy' (Goleman 1995/6):

   • 'self-talk' – conducting an inner dialogue as a way to cope with a topic or challenge or reinforce one's own behaviour (see the section on Vygotsky's approach earlier in this chapter)

   • using steps for problem solving and decision making – e.g. controlling impulses, setting goals, identifying alternative actions, anticipating consequences (see the section on Sternberg's problem-solving cycle earlier in this chapter)

   • understanding the perspectives of others (Feuerstein's Instrumental Enrichment cognitive enhancement programme has an instrument called 'orientation in space' which has this ability as a key focus).

3. It has a self-management or metacognitive aspect. Goleman quotes Salovey and Mayer in 'defining intelligence in terms of being able to monitor and regulate one's own and others' feelings, and to use feelings to guide thought and action' (Goleman 1998, p.317).

4. It adds to a broader and more inclusive notion of intelligence, and builds on Gardner's interpersonal and intrapersonal intelligences. (However, Goleman considers that Gardner focused more on cognition (thinking) about feelings, and not enough on the feelings involved (Goleman 1995/6).

5. It is important in real life and future life experiences. Goleman makes a case for this in his book *Emotional Intelligence: Why it Matters More Than IQ* (Goleman 1995/6). He states: 'No one can yet say exactly how much of the variability from person to

person in life's course it accounts for. But what data exist suggest it can be powerful, and at times more powerful, than IQ' (p.34).

6. It addresses key emotional, social and behavioural needs which are of such importance and concern to all classroom teachers today, and are important in inclusion.

Learning for emotional intelligence should begin as early as possible, according to Goleman. It is argued that 'children's readiness to learn depends to a large extent on acquiring some of these emotional skills' (Goleman 1995/6, p.273), so he advocates their teaching in preschool programmes. He wants the teaching of the emotions to match the emotional timetable for their development. For example, he sees emotional capacities like empathy and emotional self-regulation as developing from infancy, while the more social emotions that relate to comparing oneself with others, such as pride and confidence, peak in their development at kindergarten stage.

In terms of teaching emotions in relation to an ordinary school curriculum, Goleman advocates that 'the teacher should not create a new class but blend lessons on feelings, and emotional lessons can merge naturally into reading and writing, health, science, social studies' (Goleman 1995/6, p.276).

Emotional intelligence covers a very broad range of emotional, social and behavioural skills, making it an obvious choice for a whole-school community approach. This concept of emotional intelligence is widely embraced internationally, and the UK government has used it to underpin their documentation to address social and emotional needs in their policy document on social and emotional aspects of learning (SEAL) (DfES 2005) in a whole-school approach.

AN EXAMPLE FROM PRACTICE IN A SCHOOL SETTING

An example of the possible use of emotional intelligence in a whole-school way can be seen in the work of one of the writer's Masters students undertaking the Inclusive Education programme at the University of Hull. She was interested in looking at the SEAL programme of the UK to see how well it would address whole-school needs in meeting an inclusion agenda. The student, Cheri Pattison, holds a role within her local education authority that involves responsibility for developing the use of the SEAL programme by schools. She sought to explore how a school which was emotionally literate (i.e. using Goleman's emotional intelligence through SEAL) manifested progress towards inclusion.

The DfES policy document *Excellence and Enjoyment: Social and Emotional Aspects of Learning (SEAL)* (DfES 2005), which is based on Goleman's ideas about emotional intelligence, states that in initial piloting of the SEAL programme they found that 'for the resource to work well, it is important that the whole school community engage with the materials. For maximum impact, all the classes in the school will be thinking about the same idea, and using a shared language over the same period of time' (DfES 2005, p.19).

The document presents on the same page an outline of a full school year planning timetable, covering seven themes comprised by the programme and showing how they link to key social and emotional aspects of learning, which in turn relate directly to the five aspects of emotional intelligence identified by Goleman (listed above).

Cheri selected two key indicators from each of the three dimensions of the *Index for Inclusion* (Booth and Ainscow 2002), a tool to study a school's progress towards inclusion, for her analysis. She sought to explore the links between these indicators and the SEAL programme, as follows:

Dimension 1: Creating inclusive cultures; *Indicator A:1:2 Students help each other.*

Cheri notes that the SEAL theme 'Getting on and falling out', which discusses how pupils feel in different situations and how best to deal with disagreements, goes some way in addressing this indicator.

Dimension 2: Creating inclusive cultures; *Indicator A:1:4 Staff and students treat each other with respect.*

Cheri notes that the 'Relationships' theme in SEAL considers what pupils can do to help establish good relationships with others and understand the need to respect others' feelings and opinions, even if they differ from their own.

Dimension 3: Producing inclusive policies; *Indicator B:2:6 Pastoral and behaviour support policies are linked to curriculum development and learning support policies.*

Cheri notes that SEAL should underpin the entire curriculum, and in her view it is entirely possible to establish firm cross-curricular links for effective delivery. She also points out that in each theme overview, links are made with initiatives such as the emotional and well-being strand within the Healthy Schools Standard. The Healthy Schools Standard is a UK National Standard launched in 1999 as a framework of quality standards to support the development of the Government's Healthy Schools Programme (see Sinkler and Toft 2000).

Dimension 4: Producing inclusive policies; *Indicator B:2:9 Bullying is minimised.*

Cheri notes that this links to the SEAL theme 'Say no to bullying'. She considers that work on this theme should help pupils to understand the context (feelings and circumstances) that relate to bullying, understand the different roles in a bullying situation (including that of an onlooker), develop assertiveness and the skills to manage a bullying situation, value diversity, nurture empathy and understand the responsibilities of being part of the school community.

Dimension 5: Evolving inclusive practices; *Indicator C:1:2 Lessons encourage the participation of all pupils.*

Cheri links this indicator to the SEAL theme of 'Going for goals' which should give pupils the opportunity to explore motivation and self-awareness.

Dimension 6: Evolving inclusive practices; *Indicator C:1:4 Classroom discipline is based on mutual respect.*

Cheri considers that if pupils and staff develop the skills involved in SEAL, including understanding and managing ourselves and our emotions, thoughts and behaviours, then pupils and staff will be able to understand and respond respectfully to the emotions and behaviours of others.

13. Approaches involving learning style

Learning style theories are concerned with learning preferences, so they have a strong personality/motivational component. Riding, defining learning style (cognitive style), states: 'Cognitive style is an individual's preferred and habitual approach to organising and representing information' (Riding 2002, p.22).

There are a great number of theories on learning style, and these can be organised in terms of those which are more personality/motivation based, as compared to those which are more educationally based. An example of this kind of organisation of learning styles is given by Sternberg and Grigorenko (1997).

A more 'personality centred' approach is illustrated by Myers' (Myers and Myers 1980) 16 types of cognitive style, with dimensions such as sensing vs. intuition, thinking vs. feeling, and introversion vs. extroversion.

A more 'cognitive centred' approach is Riding and Rayner's (1995) two-dimensional approach involving analytic vs. holistic and verbaliser vs. imager styles.

A more 'activity centred' approach is provided by Dunn, Dunn and Price's inventory of learning preferences relating to how the individual responds to a number of stimuli, including environmental, emotional, sociological, physical (comprising auditory, visual, tactile and kinaesthetic), and psychological (comprising global vs. analytic, impulsive vs. reflective, and cerebral dominance) (Dunn, Dunn and Price 1989).

An extensive review of learning style theories and their effectiveness, which groups theories in terms of how modifiable they are, has been carried out by Coffield and his team at Newcastle University (Coffield *et al.* 2004a, 2004b). For example, they consider Sternberg's 'thinking styles' (1999) much less 'fixed' (i.e. more open to modification) than either Riding and Rayner's 'cognitive styles' (1998a) or Dunn and Dunn's 'visual, auditory and kinaesthetic' learning style approach (Dunn, Dunn and Price 1989).

Sternberg, taking a less 'fixed' approach, states: 'if styles are indeed socialized, even in part, then they are almost certainly modifiable to at least some degree' (Sternberg 1993, p.32). In contrast, Riding states that 'style is inbuilt, habitual in use and fairly fixed, while learning strategies may be developed by the pupil to help in situations where their style does not suit the task being done' (Riding 2002, p.22).

In the UK solid research evidence is provided by Riding and Rayner for their theory of cognitive style, which has two main dimensions: holistic vs. analytical and verbaliser vs. imager (Riding 2002; Riding and Rayner 1998a). These learning style dimensions may complement or intensify each other, and individuals encountering a task where their style is not appropriate are seen as employing other dimensions where possible, as alternatives (Riding 2002). Also, the style of the learner interacts with the materials being presented. For example, presentation mode is important in relation to the verbal vs. imagery dimension, with learners at the imaging end tending to learn better from pictorial presentation and learners at the verbalising end learning better from verbal presentations. For the analytic vs. holistic dimension the amount of working memory required for the task has more effect for learners at the analytic end of the dimension than for learners at the holistic end of the dimension (Riding 2002). A computer programme is available for analysis of a learner's cognitive style, in a school context (Riding and Rayner 1998b).

A learning style approach which has strong educational implications, and which links well to the metacognitive aspects of thinking, is Sternberg and Grigorenko's mental self-government approach (Sternberg 1993, 1999; Sternberg and Grigorenko 1997). Their theory of thinking style utilises government as a metaphor in the mental self-management style framework they outline, where the style dimensions on which people differ consist of:

- *functions* of mental self-government (legislative, executive and judicial styles)
- *forms* of mental self-government (monarchic, hierarchic, oligarchic and anarchic styles)
- *levels* of mental self-government (local and global styles)
- *scope* of mental self-government (internal and external styles)
- *leanings* (attitudes) of self-government (liberal and conservative styles).

Work with learning style for the teaching of thinking for all learners is valuable for the following reasons:

1. the bringing together of motivation (emotion) and cognition in the concept of preferred learning style, with motivation playing a strong role

2. the understanding that individual learners differ in their learning preferences, and that it is important for us to individualise teaching in order to enhance access to understanding, and engagement in learning, through these preferred learning styles

3. appropriate use of learning style preferences is considered important not only for school success but for later real-life success, as argued by Sternberg and Grigorenko (1997).

It is important to distinguish between a theory of learning styles, which is about *learning preferences*, and Gardner's theory of Multiple Intelligences, which is about *intelligences* (i.e. cognitive abilities). These different ideas can be confused, because they seem similar. However, they belong to two very different theoretical approaches, and research has shown that cognitive style (learning style) is independent of cognitive ability or intelligence. Riding states: 'Cognitive style, as assessed by the *Cognitive Styles Analysis*, appears to be independent of intelligence' (Riding 2002, p.29).

There is danger that learning preferences will be viewed as 'fixed' and unmodifiable, and that if this restricts teaching and assessment in a simplistic way, there may be both under-expectation and unfulfilling of abstract learning potential by both learners and their teachers.

A caution against labelling learners too readily with a preferred learning style, and then limiting learning opportunities to these styles, is given by Coffield *et al.* (2004b). In the experience of the present writer, we need to be aware of the dangers inherent in a simplistic view of learning style when adopting the visual, auditory and kinaesthetic (VAK) approach (Dunn, Dunn and Price 1989) that has been developed and researched widely in the USA. If schools label learners as visual, auditory or kinaesthetic learners, and use teaching styles which mainly match these learning preferences, learners may well not be stimulated to develop the more abstract reasoning skills needed for higher-level thinking and achievement.

A critique of the way a VAK approach has been used in the UK is presented by Sharp, Bowker and Bryne (2008). They also point out that Dunn and Dunn's Learning Style Inventory has been criticised for containing many variables which *affect* learning styles rather than *define* them, and that it has never been made clear how the components were chosen.

In the UK, the VAK approach is sometimes used as a component of the Accelerated Learning in Primary Schools (ALPS) approach (Smith and Call 2000). If the value of the VAK approach is being evaluated within this context, then the evaluation design needs to be able to explore each separate component of the ALPS programme.

An interesting relationship between the teacher's cognitive style and his or her relationships with pupils is discussed by Riding (2002). He states that the cognitive style of the teacher may affect both the type of relationship with pupils, and expectations about their behaviour. For example: 'If the teacher is analytic–bimodal, analytic–imager, intermediate–bimodal or intermediate–imager then the natural relationship with pupils may be more distant, and these teachers may need to make a positive effort to be more outwardly encouraging' (Riding 2002, p.61.)

We are exhorted to utilise the concept of learning style in both teaching and assessment, particularly by Sternberg (1999). He presents an interesting analysis of how different types of assessment link to different preferred cognitive styles, within his own theory of cognitive style. A learning style approach could therefore inform and shift assessment practices in a whole-school context.

New Zealand researchers (Hattie 1999; Hattie, Biggs and Purdie 1996) in their meta-analysis of learning style studies found only limited effect sizes with explicit teacher–student style-matching approaches. In commenting on these findings, Joyce (2008) suggests that applying learning style theory in a broader way, as 'repertoire enhancement' (including a broader range of learning styles than just the teacher's preferences) may be useful.

AN EXAMPLE FROM PRACTICE IN A SCHOOL SETTING

An example is now given of work in the UK with the UK-based Riding and Rayner's cognitive style approach. The present writer is familiar with Robert Bolton's dissertation research (supervised by a colleague) on Riding's cognitive style (Bolton 2005), through his sharing of this work with students on a postgraduate module which she taught.

Robert Bolton applied the *Cognitive Styles Assessment and Information Processing Index* instruments developed by Riding (1991) in his science teaching for all 53 pupils in Year 10 of his secondary school, following guidance given by Riding (1998). A simple explanation of their results was given to the learners.

They had been told at the beginning of the study that the work they would do (in the assessment process and the topic) related to their learning styles and working memories, and that they would be asked for their opinions about the tests and the activities later.

The Science Teaching Group 1 was chosen as the particular focus for investigating the effect of teaching in relation to cognitive style. Following assessment for cognitive style, these learners were taught a science topic in which particular care was taken to ensure that information was presented in a variety of modes, including interactive whiteboard for presentation in text, pictures and diagrams; supplementary 'handouts' and book references; and video and multimedia formats where appropriate.

During one teaching session of teaching the topic, pupils were divided into groups based on their cognitive styles. The groups were given a common task, but were given resources chosen to complement their styles (combinations of the dimensions holistic–analytic; and verbaliser–imager).

In another session groups were formed by selecting pupils with different styles, and the groups were asked to carry out a co-operative exercise using a variety of written resources.

Throughout the study, both formal and informal opportunities were created to encourage learners to think about how they learn and develop as independent learners, and to seek their opinions.

Coffield *et al.* (2004b) raise a question concerning the reliability of the cognitive style assessment procedure. Robert Bolton attempted to check its reliability by retesting six pupils, and this indicated that the test results for this small number were reproducible, by the third assessment.

Bolton also had measures of cognitive ability on each pupil (using the Cognitive Abilities Test which is carried out by a number of UK secondary schools). He states: 'The data supports Riding's finding that Cognitive style is independent of ability. A spread of cognitive style was found in each of the ability groups' (Bolton 2005, p.88).

In the session which grouped learners according to cognitive style all except the holistic–imager group worked productively. Bolton notes of this particular group that the observer and himself

> agreed that placing the holistic imagers [learners who have a holistic imager learning style] together is not likely to be a productive combination. These three pupils all have a tendency to exhibit challenging behaviour and to allow themselves to be distracted. It may be that the best approach is to separate them into groups at the complementary end of the scale, providing additional support where needed. (Bolton 2005, p.93)

Bolton also comments that overall the session grouped by learning style, evaluated through a homework task, showed that

> In the homework exercise, most pupils in the class demonstrated that they had acquired understanding. Most of those spoken to said that they had appreciated the presentation of the material and that they were comfortable working with it... Some said that they would not want to work in those groups all the time because they liked to sit in friendship groups, a reminder that other aspects of learning such as the 'affective domain' must be taken into consideration. (Bolton 2005, p.93)

In the session where learners were placed in groups with a mix of cognitive styles, the results were inconclusive –

> possibly because there were confounding variables, the role of the pupil in the team vs. the pupil's cognitive style vs. the cognitive demands of the task... If I were to repeat the exercise I would choose a situation with clearly defined roles and allocate the pupils to the appropriate tasks, based on their cognitive styles. (Bolton 2005, p.94)

Overall, Robert Bolton felt that a valuable outcome of the study was that the cognitive style assessment had 'given a framework to discuss preferred learning style and to offer strategies that the pupils might use to improve their understanding of information' (Bolton 2005, p.95). He felt that the two group situations provided an excellent format for discussing pupils' learning with them. He sees this all as metacognition, 'thinking about thinking', which he considers 'fundamental in terms of developing pupils' abilities to become independent learners and in enabling them to take an active part in the target setting process' (Bolton 2005, p.96).

14. Perkins' thinking dispositions

Perkins has come to his theory of thinking dispositions after involvement with, and writing about, a number of approaches for the teaching of thinking. In this theory, he brings together the importance of providing learners with worthwhile, authentic, open-ended tasks (this links to his writing about 'smart schools') and the development of positive patterns of intellectual behaviour, called 'dispositions'.

He defines a disposition as follows: 'in our sense it is a psychological element with three components: inclination, sensitivity, and ability' (Perkins, Jay and Tishman 1993, p.4). As an example, inclination could relate to a person with an inclination to be open-minded, and sensitivity to alertness, where 'a person sensitive to the need to be open-minded will notice occasions where narrow thinking and prejudice and bias are likely and open-mindedness called for', and 'a person with ability to be open-minded knows how to go about it: resisting the impulse to decide quickly, listening to evidence for rival points of view' (Perkins *et al.* 1993, p.4).

In Perkins' discussion of sensitivity, the affinity between this idea and the identification of a problem in the first stage of Sternberg's problem-solving cycle become clear. Perkins gives an example of sensitivity in recognising an occasion for problem solving, as follows:

> For an example from some of our work on the cognition in computer programming: A student may be able to apply a construct like a FOR-NEXT loop effectively (ability), may want to solve the problem by using whatever means (inclination to use whatever constructs are needed), but may not recognize a problem as an occasion for FOR-NEXT loops (sensitivity to FOR-NEXT occasions...' (Perkins 1993, p.5)

These three components of *inclination, sensitivity* and *ability* are the foundations for Perkins' seven key dispositions for good thinking. Perkins believes that 'good thinking' can be characterised as reflecting seven broad thinking dispositions, as follows:

1. To be broad and adventurous.

2. Towards sustained intellectual curiosity.

3. To clarify and seek understanding.

4. To make plans and be strategic.

5. To be intellectually careful.

6. To seek and evaluate reasons.

7. To be metacognitive.

For each of these broad thinking dispositions, he outlines their related components of inclination, sensitivity and ability (Perkins *et al.* 1993).

It is emphasised that these seven dispositions are chosen because they specifically benefit good thinking. They are seen as each individually being necessary for good thinking practice, and complementing each other to foster good thinking.

The importance of this theory for the teaching of thinking for all learners is as follows:

1. It focuses on some of the more motivational/emotional aspects of critical and creative thinking, such as passions, attitudes, and values of mind. Perkins believes that dispositions are important because abilities are not sufficient to ensure intelligent behaviour. For example, people may know how to think better about something, 'but are not disposed to do so for one reason or another (for instance, bias, prejudice, impatience, overconfidence,

or simply a failure to notice that the situation invites broader and/or more careful thinking)' (Perkins *et al.* 1993, p.2).

2. Because of this focus, there is room for the inclusion of cultural meanings and attitudes relating to ways of thinking and learning. The seven dispositions are seen as 'fitting with strong cultural intuitions' (Perkins *et al.* 1993, p.9). He also states: 'Because dispositions are grounded in belief systems, values and attitudes as much as in cognitive structures, we need a culturally based account of their development' (p.16). This means that when we use this approach we should ensure that the identification of dispositions to work with and enhance should involve dispositions which are culturally relevant to the learner, and they should be enhanced in culturally relevant ways.

3. The theory emphasises the key role played by the choice of learning tasks or content, to engage the learner in meaningful tasks which will foster the habits of critical and creative thinking.

4. It is seen by Perkins to have important implications for classroom practices in general, as is clear in the book by Tishman, Perkins and Jay (1995), *The Thinking Classroom: Learning and Teaching in a Culture of Thinking.* It is therefore important for ordinary classroom practice related to the needs of *all* learners.

5. The thinking dispositions are developed from a very early age, when children interact socially with experienced members of society, and learn the dispositions through modelling and guided learning. Perkins refers to the role of such Vygotskian ideas as 'expert scaffolding' in such learning (Perkins *et al.* 1993, p.17).

6. Perkins also notes the importance of opportunities and challenges in the use of dispositions – for example, in the social demands for rigorous thinking in co-operative learning situations: 'to cultivate the right inclination, one must provide learners with frequent opportunities to set goals and make plans for themselves in meaningful contexts' (Perkins *et al.* 1993, p.17).

7. A similar focus on the dispositions or habits of thinking is made by Art Costa (Costa and Kallick 2000). Costa includes

persistence, managing impulsivity, listening to others with understanding and empathy, thinking flexibly, thinking about our thinking (metacognition), questioning and posing problems, applying past knowledge to new situations, gathering data through all senses, creating, imagining and innovating, responding with wonderment and awe, taking responsible risks, finding humour, thinking interdependently, and learning continuously. Costa offers a wider ranging list than Perkins, going beyond the focus on more attitudinal and motivational aspects. However, he does list the following (which are similar to Perkins' dispositions): taking responsible risks (being broad and adventurous); persistence (towards sustained intellectual curiosity); questioning and posing problems (clarifying and seeking understanding); and managing impulsivity (being intellectually careful). Both include being metacognitive in their lists.

The present writer was present at a working seminar on 'Thinking Skills in the Classroom', run by the British Council in Belfast in 2002, where Professor David Perkins presented a working session on dispositions, called 'The Tame and the Wild'. The following comments are taken from the writer's copy of the overheads David Perkins used in that session. They are chosen as examples of how to incorporate work on dispositions into classroom topics. 'Wilding the tame' involves:

1. from teaching thinking to teaching thinking dispositions

2. from teaching knowledge to teaching understanding

3. from teaching the topic to teaching for transfer

4. from small-scale miracles to large-scale progress

5. from simply implementation to include knowledge capture and sharing.

(Overhead 6)

Perkins identified some of the key opportunities and questions which might be useful in teaching dispositions – for example, 'in the wild' of everyday family and professional life, how people think is as much a matter of proactive attitudes and alertness to situations as it is ability to follow through. Questions could include 'Yeah, you know, there's another way to look at that'; 'Wait a minute, but what if that does happen? Then what?' 'I know that seems sensible, but…?' (Overhead 8).

Using dispositions involves talking about it – conceptual exploration, with such questions as 'Sometimes it's hard to know…?' 'When its hard to know, what can you do about it'? 'When is it worth…?' (Overhead 10).

It also involves teaching for understanding, which is thinking with what you know to extend it further, as in explaining, predicting, justifying, analysing and evaluating (Overhead 17).

Also important is a move to teaching for transfer, including both talking about how the idea can be transferred, and doing the transferring, with questions like 'How does this relate to me?' 'How can I use it?' and by spotting learners who find occasions for transfer and investing in them (Overhead 24).

It is of interest for UK teachers to know that Anne de A'Echevarria, who has recently co-authored the *Teaching Thinking Pocketbook* (de A'Echevarria, Patience and Hailstone 2008), has developed support materials (2009) for implementing the UK Qualification and Curriculum Authority (QCA) framework for personal, learning and thinking skills (PLTS), including what she calls 'disposition cards', which she states are drawn from the framework itself. In the example that she gives, she depicts, like a mind map, the 'concept star' where one of the six skill areas is chosen, and then the disposition cards are placed either close to the central skill, or more distant from it. The concept star of 'Creative Thinkers' as a skill area has the related disposition cards of 'takes action', 'curious' 'risk-taking' and 'open-minded', so there does seem to be a link here to the dispositions outlined by Perkins.

15. Locus of control and attribution theory

Locus of Control and Attribution Theory are separate but similar, and are covered here because they focus on key emotional/motivational perceptions of the learner which have an important link with the learner's explanations to himself/herself about his/her learning. (Metacognitive knowledge of the self as learner is part of metacognition in general.)

The 'Locus of control' concept comes originally from Rotter (1972). It links together the idea of control of reinforcement (internal or external control) and the learner's 'expectancy' concerning the effect of their own behaviour or attributes on the reinforcement they receive. *Internal locus of control* is when the learner believes he/she has control over a desired goal (e.g. a learning goal) or reinforcement, and that what happens in terms of achieving that goal, depends on his/her own behaviours (such as effort). *External locus of control* is when a learner believes that successful attainment of a desired goal or reinforcement is beyond his/her own control, and is primarily controlled by forces such as luck or powerful others.

Attribution theory is about causal attribution. It looks at how learners' understanding of the causes of their own and others' behaviours, determines their expectations concerning future events and the extent of their own control over them. An attribution theory of achievement motivation has been developed by Weiner (1986). Its core idea is that a learner evaluates his/her achievement as either a success or failure, and attributes this to his/her own ability, effort, luck, and task difficulty as the key causal factors.

There are some important other concepts relating to these theories. The idea of 'learned helplessness' (a cycle of motivational failure to act because of perceived expectations of failure, leading to passive acceptance of a negative outcome) was originally developed by Seligman (1975).

The term 'learned helplessness' for the characteristic of learners who attribute only their failures, and not their successes, to their own ability, was developed by Diener and Dweck (1980). Learners with 'learned helplessness' consider themselves inadequate and unable to overcome any obstacle to success. This leads to a vicious cycle of escalating failure as feelings of lack of control lead to poor performance, which confirms through experience the learner's failure-related explanation (i.e. 'inadequate ability').

These concepts are important for the teaching of thinking for all learners for the following reasons:

1. They link emotion and cognition, combining appraisals of the self and feelings toward the self.

2. Metacognitive knowledge of the self is a key part of metacognition. We need to use the ideas of locus of control and attribution to ensure that learners have a positive self-view, and have positive control over their own self-regulated learning. Borkowski, Carr, Rellinger and Pressley (1990) outline the important connections between metacognition, attributions and self-esteem.

3.   Effort attribution has been shown to have an important effect in terms of individual difference in applying newly learnt thinking strategies, and in transfer and generalisation of them to other tasks. Borkowski *et al.* (1990) state:

> Attributional beliefs are of particular importance for metacognitive development because children must first believe in the utility of their strategy-related effort...before they will apply those efforts in situations which demand strategic behaviour. Effort is actualized in the form of well-chosen strategies that are carefully and thoughtfully applied to difficult tasks. It follows that children with positive self-systems are more likely to acquire specific strategy knowledge, and to apply this knowledge on new tasks because they have a general belief in the utility of strategies and effort. (Borkowski *et al.* 1990, p.16)

An 'instructional approach' to attributions is presented by Borkowski *et al.* (1990). In one of their studies, underachieving children in a strategy-plus-attribution condition were given direct instructional training in reading comprehension strategies, as well as attributional training. This strategy-plus-attribution condition promoted the maintenance of the trained strategies, and embedding attributional training within strategy instruction appeared to facilitate generalisation of the strategies in the classroom. The authors state: 'It was the addition of the attributional component that bridged the gap between knowledge about reading and actual reading performance' (p.31). They also point out that:

> Retraining of attributional beliefs may be necessary to alter dysfunctional attributions, since intensive strategic training alone did not modify attributional beliefs about the utility of effort. This is probably because attributional beliefs are deeply embedded within cultural and familial contexts...and are often reinforced by parents' and teachers' attributions about the causes of success and failure. (p.31)

Research shows that positive patterns of locus of control and attributions are important for both classroom achievement and social skills. An example of the use of effort attribution in the classroom is given in a study by Gipps and Tunstall (1998). They outline the suggestion by Ames (1992) that classrooms which enhance children's commitment to effort and use effort-based strategies involve teachers with a focus on the following individual improvements:

- progress and mastery
- making evaluations private, not public
- recognising children's efforts
- providing opportunities for improvement
- encouraging a view of mistakes as part of learning.

(Gipps and Tunstall 1998, p.161)

They show in their example that a teacher's emphasis on effort attributions in a classroom of young learners was associated with effort as the most commonly cited reason for success or failure.

There has been considerable development and use of measures of both locus of control, and attributions, in a variety of cultural contexts. However, as mentioned by Tam (2003), who has been researching with these concepts in Hong Kong, locus of control is likely to be culturally specific. We therefore need to give careful attention to the culturally sensitive use of these tools and approaches.

Another issue is the need to be sensitive to the emotional responses of learners when we use these tools and approaches. The present writer sought to use a simplified version of a locus of control measure which she created for learners with mild learning difficulties in an intermediate school (ages of learners 11 and 12) in New Zealand (Howie *et al.* 1985). Both internal and external locus of control were explored in relation to success or failure in a school maths test, and in playground friendships. The distress of some learners when engaged in the assessment caused the writer to abandon the use of this tool. (See Howie (1999) for a discussion of this issue.)

Further, if individuals are placed at points along this dimension of internal–external locus of control, it is possible that learners who are unsure where they fall on this continuum, and to what extent their internal control is responsible for their achievement, will experience difficulties in attribution, leading to poor achievement.

What is called a 'process model' of perceived control and children's engagement and achievement in schools has been presented by Skinner, Wellborn and Connell (1990). The title of their paper, 'What it takes to do well in school and whether I've got it?, reminds us that in looking at locus of control we are looking at learner characteristics, and there is a danger of focusing only on problems within the learner, without taking into account any problem with the task itself, or in mediation of learning. The work by Tam (2003) outlined below demonstrates the school community-wide factors associated with patterns of locus of control and attribution.

In the writer's experience, negative self-attributions by adolescents are not easy to shift, and require a multi-pronged approach to address all aspects involved. For example, the wider school environment needs to be inclusive, valuing all learners. Tasks need to be chosen and taught in ways which meet the learners' needs, with appropriate mediation to the learners of reasons for success. Learners need to learn to self instruct to apply effort in the use of learning strategies taught, and to attribute their consequent success to positive internal causes.

AN EXAMPLE FROM PRACTICE IN A SCHOOL SETTING

As an example of work with locus of control and attribution within an ordinary school system, Tony Tam (2003) carried out, under the writer's supervision, a doctoral study of the locus of control and attributional style in low-achieving adolescents who were truanting in less advantaged schools in Hong Kong. He had two main groups of learners: truants and non-truants.

When he explored their locus of control and attributional style, using the most culturally relevant and up-to-date tools available, he found that the non-truant learners exhibited a 'self-serving pattern of attributions', that is, internal attributions for success (having control) and external attributions for failure (outside their control). This was not so of the truants, who attributed bad events (e.g. failure) to internal, stable and global causes (within themselves, unable to be changed, and pervasive), and good events (e.g. success) to external, unstable and specific causes. Tam considered that these findings were similar to the attribution pattern displayed by low-status children in three other studies he cites, including one by Goetz and Dweck (1980).

Tam notes:

> The truants have difficulties not only in dealing with bad events, but good events as well. When confronted with success or other positive events, the truants are likely to believe that the causes lie outside themselves, and that they had nothing to do with that outcome. As a result of believing that positive events are due to or controlled by external forces, the truants have a lower expectancy for future success. (Tam 2003, p.225)

He also notes that 'If the school is seen as one where controllability is absent, it is highly likely that the truants are experiencing depression and feelings of helplessness' (Tam 2003, p.226).

In terms of locus of control the truants and non-truants did not differ significantly on the measure used, but the difference was only a little short of significance. It would seem that both groups in this Hong Kong setting were externally oriented, which 'echoes the general observation that the Chinese adolescents in Hong Kong are external in locus of control [studies cited]... As repeatedly pointed out by these investigators, this belief orientation has its roots in the Chinese belief in fatalism... and the traditional emphasis on the maintenance of group goals and affiliation' (Tam 2003, p.228). Although not statistically different, the learners who were truanting appeared more externally oriented than non-truants, feeling less control over their fate. Tam writes:

> Given the fact that the truants find themselves in a school environment in which they experience relatively little reinforcement both in terms of academic achievement and interpersonal relationships, it is not surprising that they tend to feel that the environment is not under their control. (Tam 2003, p.229)

Self-reflective questions

☐ Within your own school community, what are the key issues for the teaching of thinking at Tier 1 level?

☐ Which of the approaches at Tier 1 level might best meet the learning needs of all learners in your school community, and why?

☐ How would those approaches need to be implemented and evaluated in order to meet the specific contextual and cultural needs of all learners in your school community?

References

Introduction

Costa, A.L. (ed.) (2001) *Developing Minds: A Resource Book for Teaching Thinking* (3rd edition). Melbourne: Hawker Brownlow.

Costa, A.L. (ed.) (2003) *Developing Minds: A Resource Book for Teaching Thinking* (3rd edition). Alexandria, VA: Association for Supervision and Curriculum.

Howie, D.R. (2001) 'The systematic teaching of thinking: Ways forward, informed by our New Zealand research.' Paper presented to the 9th International Conference on Thinking, Auckland.

Howie, D.R. (2003a) *Thinking about the Teaching of Thinking.* Wellington: New Zealand Council for Educational Research.

Howie, D.R. (2003b) 'Crossing boundaries: The cultural imperative.' Paper presented to the 9th International Conference of the International Association for Cognitive Education and Psychology, Seattle, WA.

Hattie, J. (2009) *Visible Learning: A Synthesis of over 800 Meta-analyses Relating to Achievement.* London: Routledge.

Ministry of Education (New Zealand) (2007) *National Curriculum.* Wellington: New Zealand Government.

QCA (2007) *The Big Picture of the Curriculum.* London: Mike Waters, Qualification and Curriculum Authority.

Rose, J. (2009) *The Independent Review of the Primary Curriculum.* London: BCSK.

Sternberg, R.J. (1983) 'Criteria for intellectual skills training.' *Educational Researcher 12,* 2, 6–12, 26.

Sternberg, R.J. (1987) 'Questions and Answers about the Nature and Teaching of Thinking Skills.' In J.R. Baron and R.J. Sternberg (eds) *Teaching Thinking Skills: Theory and Practice.* New York: Freeman and Company.

Vygotsky

Bangert-Drowns, R.L. (1992) 'Meta-analysis of the effects of inquiry-based instruction on critical thinking.' Paper presented at the Annual meeting of the American Educational Research Association, Boston, MA.

Brown, A.L., Ash, D., Rutherford, M., Nakagawa, K., Gordon, A. and Campione, J. (1993) 'Distributed Expertise in the Classroom.' In G. Salomon (ed.) *Distributed Cognitions: Psychological and Educational Consideration.* Cambridge: Cambridge University Press.

Howie, D.R. (2003a) *Thinking About the Teaching of Thinking.* Wellington: New Zealand Council for Educational Research.

Kozulin, A. (1998) *Psychological Tools: A Socio-cultural Approach to Education.* Cambridge, MA: Harvard University Press.

Kozulin, A. (2008) 'Sociocultural Paradigm.' In J.W. Clegg (ed.) *The Observation of Human Systems: Lessons from the History of Anti-Reductionistic Empirical Psychology.* London: Transaction Publishers.

Meichenbaum, D., Burland, S., Gruson, L. and Cameron, R. (1985) 'Metacognitive Assessment.' In S.R. Yussen (ed.) *The Growth of Reflection in Children.* London: Academic Press.

Thompson, J.E.M. (2003) 'Children's self-talk and writing: How can self-instruction be used to raise attainment in writing in Key Stage Two pupils?' Unpublished M.Ed. dissertation, University of Hull.

Vygotsky, L. (1978) *Mind in Society.* Cambridge, MA: Harvard University Press.

Vygotsky, L. (1986) *Thought and Language* (revised by Kozulin). Cambridge, MA: Harvard University Press.

Wertsch, J.V. (1979) 'From social interaction to higher psychological processes: A clarification and application of Vygotsky's theory.' *Human Development 22*, 1, 1–22.

Feuerstein

Feuerstein, R., Rand, Y. and Hoffman, M.B. (1979) *The Dynamic Assessment of Retarded Performers: The Learning Potential Assessment Device: Theory, Instruments and Techniques.* Baltimore, MD: University Park Press.

Feuerstein, R., Feuerstein, Ra.S., Falik, L.H. and Rand, Y. (2003) *The Dynamic Assessment of Cognitive Functions: The Learning Propensity Assessment Device, Theory, Instruments, Techniques.* Jerusalem: International Centre for the Enhancement of Learning Potential.

Feuerstein, R., Feuerstein, Ra.S., Falik, L.H. and Rand, Y. (2006) *The Feuerstein Instrumental Enrichment Program.* Jerusalem: International Centre for the Enhancement of Learning Potential.

Howie, D.R. (2003a) *Thinking about the Teaching of Thinking.* Wellington: New Zealand Council for Educational Research.

Howie, D.R. (2008) 'The Cognitive Map and Real-life Problem Solving.' In O. Tan and A.S. Seng (eds) *Cognitive Modifiability in Learning and Assessment: International Perspectives.* Singapore: Cengage Learning.

Howie, D.R., Richards, R. and Pirihi, H. (1993) 'Teaching thinking skills to Maori adolescents.' *International Journal of Cognitive Education and Mediated Learning 3*, 2, 70–91.

Lawrie, A.-T. (2009) Personal communication.

Mentis, M., Dunn-Bernstein, M.J., Mentis, M. and Skuy, M. (2009) *Bridging Learning: Unlocking Cognitive Potential In and Out of the Classroom.* London: Corwin Press.

Romney, D.M. and Samuels, M.T. (2001) 'A meta-analytic evaluation of Feuerstein's Instrumental Enrichment program.' *Educational and Child Psychology 18*, 4, 19–34.

Skuy, M. and Mentis, M. (1991) 'Applications and Adaptations of Feuerstein's Instrumental Enrichment Programme in South Africa.' In H.C. Van Niekerk (ed.) *Cognitive Development in the Southern African Context.* Papers of a seminar on cognitive development. Human Sciences Research Council, Pretoria, South Africa.

Sternberg's metacomponents

Barry-Joyce, M. (2001) 'The effects of a LOGO environment on the metacognitive functioning of Irish students.' Unpublished PhD thesis, University of Hull.

Baumfield, V., Hall, E. and Wall, K. (2008) *Action Research in the Classroom.* London: Sage.

Clements, D.H. and Nastasi, B.K. (1990) 'Dynamic approach to the measurement of children's metacomponential functioning.' *Intelligence 14*, 1, 109–125.

Fong, K. and Howie, D. (2007) 'Metacomponential assessment and training in real-life problem solving.' *Journal of Cognitive Education and Psychology 6*, 2, 165–193.

Sternberg, R.J. (1979) 'The nature of mental abilities.' *American Psychologist 34*, 3, 214–230.

Sternberg, R.J. (1985) 'Instrumental and Componential Approaches to the Nature and Training of Intelligence.' In S.F. Chipman, J.W. Segal and R. Glaser (eds) *Thinking and Learning Skills Vol. 2: Research and Open Questions.* Hillsdale, NJ: Lawrence Erlbaum.

Sternberg, R.J. (1988) *The Triarchic Mind: A New Theory of Human Intelligence.* New York: Viking.

Sternberg, R.J. (1995) *In Search of the Human Mind.* Orlando, FL: Harcourt Brace.

Sternberg, R.J. (2005) 'Culture and Intelligence.' Keynote Address to the 10th International Conference of the International Association for Cognitive Education and Psychology, Durham, July 2005.

Bandura and Walters

Bandura, A. (1977) 'Self-efficacy: Toward a unifying theory of behavioural change.' *Psychological Review 84*, 2, 181–215.

Bandura, A. and Walters, R.H. (1963) *Social Learning and Personality Development.* New York: Holt, Rinehart and Winston.

Bandura, A., Ross, D. and Ross, S.A. (1963) 'Imitation of film-mediated aggressive models.' *Journal of Abnormal and Social Psychology 66*, 1, 191–215.

Brown, D. and Thomson, C. (2000) *Co-operative Learning in New Zealand Schools.* Palmerston North: Dunmore Press.

Howie, D.R. (1969) 'Imitative learning of the mentally retarded child.' Unpublished PhD thesis, University of Auckland.

Johnson, D.W., Johnson, R.T. and Stanne, M.B. (2000) *Co-operative Learning Methods: A Meta- analysis.* Minneapolis, MN: Co-operative Learning Center, University of Minneapolis.

Meichenbaum, D. (1985) 'Teaching Thinking: A Cognitive Behavioural Perspective.' In S.F. Chipman, J.W. Segal and R. Glaser (eds) *Thinking and Learning Skills Vol.2: Research and Open Questions.* Hillsdale, NJ: Lawrence Erlbaum.

Robson, S. and Moseley, D. (2005) 'An integrated framework for thinking about learning.' *Gifted Education International 16*, 3, 203–213.

Ross, D. (1966) 'Relationship between dependency, intentional learning, and incidental learning in preschool children.' *Journal of Personality and Social Psychology 4*, 4, 374–381.

Slavin, R.E. (1991) *Student Team Learning: A Practical Guide to Co-operative Learning.* Washington, DC: National Education Association.

Turnure, J. and Zigler, E. (1964) 'Outerdirectedness in the problem solving of normal and retarded children.' *Journal of Abnormal and Social Psychology 69*, 4, 427–436.

Wallace, B. and Adams, H. (1993) *The 'Thinking Actively in a Social Context' TASK Project: Developing the Potential of Children in Disadvantaged Communities.* Oxford: AB Academic Publishers.

Sternberg's triarchic theory

Cianciolo, A.T. and Sternberg, R.J. (2004) *Intelligence: A Brief History.* Oxford: Blackwell Publishing.

English, L. (1998) *Uncovering Students' Analytical, Practical and Creative Intelligences: One School's Application of Sternberg's Triarchic Theory.* Available at http://findarticles.com/p/articles/mi_m0JSD/is_1_55/ai_77195567, accessed on 16 June 2011.

Grigorenko, E.L., Jarvin, L. and Sternberg, R.J. (2002) 'School-based tests of the triarchic theory of intelligence: Three settings, three samples, three syllabi.' *Contemporary Educational Psychology 27*, 2, 167–208.

Sternberg, R.J. (1985) *Beyond IQ: A Triarchic Theory of Human Intelligence.* New York: Cambridge University Press.

Sternberg, R.J. (1993) *Sternberg Triarchic Abilities Test.* New Haven, CT: Yale University.

Sternberg, R.J. (1997a) *Successful Intelligence.* New York: Plume.

Sternberg, R.J. (1997b) 'The concept of intelligence and its role in lifelong learning and success.' *American Psychologist 52*, 10, 1030–1037.

Sternberg, R.J. (2000) 'Group and Individual Differences in Intelligence: What Can and Should We Do about Them?' In A. Kozulin and Y. Rand (eds) *Experience of Mediated Learning.* Oxford: Pergamon.

Sternberg, R.J. (2008) 'Applying psychological theories to educational practice.' *American Educational Research Journal 45*, 1, 150–165.

Sternberg, R.J. and Grigorenko, E.L. (2000) *Teaching for Successful Intelligence: To Increase Student Learning and Achievement.* Arlington Heights, IL: IRI Skylight Training and Publishing Inc.

Sternberg, R.J. and Lubart, T.I. (1995) 'An Investment Perspective on Creative Insight.' In R.J. Sternberg and J.E. Davidson (eds) *The Nature of Insight.* Cambridge, MA: Bradford Books.

Sternberg, R.J., Okagaki, L. and Jackson, A.C. (1990) 'Practical intelligence for success in school.' *Educational Leadership 48*, 1, 35–39.

Sternberg, R.J. and Williams, W.M. (1996) *How to Develop Student Creativity.* Alexandria, VA: Association for Supervision and Curriculum Development.

Gardner's Multiple Intelligences

Alexander, R.J. (2009) *Toward a New Primary Curriculum: A Report from the Cambridge Primary Review. Part 2: The Future.* Cambridge: University of Cambridge Faculty of Education.

Campbell, L., Campbell, B. and Dickinson, D. (2004) *Teaching and Learning Through Multiple Intelligences.* Boston, MA: Pearson Education/Allyn and Bacon.

Chen, J. and Gardner, H. (2001) 'Alternative Assessment from a Multiple Intelligences Perspective.' In B. Torff (ed.) *Multiple Intelligences and Assessment.* Palatine, IL: IRI Skylight.

Davies, R.W. (2004) 'What is the effectiveness of using Multiple Intelligences (MI) theory in the teaching and learning of history in an English secondary school?' Unpublished M.Ed. thesis, University of Hull.

Flynn, M.A. (2000) *Extending the Limits: The Possibilities of Multiple Intelligences Practices for Equality.* Unpublished PhD thesis, Education Department, National University of Ireland/University College Cork.

Gardner, H. (1983) *Frames of Mind: The Theory of Multiple Intelligences.* New York: Basic Books.

Gardner, H. (1991) *The Unschooled Mind: How Children Think and How Schools Should Teach.* New York: Basic Books.

Gardner, H. (1999) *Intelligence Reframed: Multiple Intelligences for the 21st Century.* New York: Basic Books.

Gardner, H. (2006) *Five Minds for the Future.* Cambridge, MA: Harvard University Press.

Gardner, H., Kornhaber, M. and Wake, E. (1996) *Intelligence: Multiple Perspectives.* Orlando, FL: Harcourt Brace.

Hatch, T. and Gardner, H. (2001) 'If Binet had Looked Beyond the Classroom: The Assessment of Multiple Intelligences.' In B. Torff (ed.) *Multiple Intelligences and Assessment.* Palatine, IL: IRI Skylight.

Lazear, D.G. (2004) *Multiple Intelligences: Approaches to Assessment.* Carmarthen: Crown House Publishing.

Rose, J. (2009) *Independent Review of the Primary Curriculum: Final Report.* Nottingham: Department of Children, Schools and Families (DCSF).

Shearer, B. (2004) 'Multiple Intelligences theory after 20 years.' *Teachers College Record 106*, 1, 2–16. (Special issue on Multiple Intelligences.)

Sternberg, R.J., Okagaki, L. and Jackson, A.C. (1990) 'Practical intelligence for success in school.' *Educational Leadership 48*, 1, 35–39.

Sternberg, R.J. and Spear-Swerling, L. (1996) *Teaching for Thinking.* Washington, DC: American Psychological Association.

de Bono

Adey, P. and Shayer, M. (1994) *Really Raising Standards: Cognitive Intervention and Academic Achievement.* London: Routledge.

Costa, A.L. (1991) Personal communication. 'The intelligent behaviour rating scale.' (Based on his 14 characteristics of intelligent behaviour.)

de Bono, E. (1991) *The CoRT Thinking Programme.* Columbus, OH: SRA Division Macmillan/McGraw Hill.

de Bono, E. (2003) *Teach Your Child How to Think.* London: Penguin.

Edwards, J. (1998) 'The direct teaching of thinking skills: CoRT-1, an evaluative case study.' Unpublished PhD thesis, James Cook University, Queensland, Australia.

Howie, D.R., Coombe, P. and Lonergan, J. (1998) 'Using single subject research design in an Auckland study of the CoRT thinking skill programme.' Paper presented to the Conference on Teaching for Successful Intelligence, Auckland.

Hunter-Grundin, E. (1985) *Teaching Thinking: An Evaluation of Edward de Bono's Classroom Materials.* London: The Schools Council.

Ritchie, S.M. and Edwards, J. (1994) 'Promoting Classroom Thinking of Urban Aboriginal Children.' In J. Edwards (ed.) *Thinking: International Interdisciplinary Perspectives.* Melbourne: Hawker Brownlow.

Torrance, E.P. (1990) *Manual for Scoring and Interpreting Results. Torrance Tests of Creative Thinking– Verbal, Forms A and B.* Bensenville, IL: Scholastic Testing Service.

Walters, S. (1978) 'Thinking Lessons.' In J. Shallcrass (ed.) *Forward to Basics.* Wellington: New Zealand Educational Institute.

Buzan's mind mapping

Baumfield, V., Hall, E. and Wall, K. (2008) *Action Research in the Classroom.* London: Sage.

Buzan, T. (1991) *Use Both Sides of Your Brain: New Mind-Mapping Techniques* (3rd edition). New York: Penguin.

Buzan, T. (undated) 'The Rules of Mind Mapping.' [Video] Available at www.imindmap.com/videos/rules%20of%20MM.aspx, accessed on 13 June 2011.

Howie, D.R. (1969) 'Imitative learning of the mentally retarded child.' Unpublished PhD thesis, University of Auckland, New Zealand.

Watts, B. (1999) 'Map of the hour.' *Special Children*, 32–33.

Philosophy for Children

Baumfield, V., Hall, E. and Wall, K. (2008) *Action Research in the Classroom.* London: Sage.

East Riding of Yorkshire Council (undated) *Philosophy for Children: A Guide.* Beverley: East Riding of Yorkshire Council.

Fisher, R. (1996) *Stories for Thinking.* Oxford: Nash Pollock.

Fisher, R. (1997) *Poems for Thinking*. Oxford: Nash Pollock.

Fisher, R. (1998) *Teaching Thinking: Philosophical Enquiry in the Classroom*. London: Cassell.

Fisher, R. (2000) *Teaching Thinking: Philosophical Enquiry in the Classroom*. London: Continuum.

Howie, D.R. (2003) *Thinking about the Teaching of Thinking*. Wellington: New Zealand Council for Educational Research.

Lipman, M. (1976) 'Philosophy for Children.' *Metaphilosophy 7*, 1, 17–33.

Lipman, M. (1991) *Thinking in Education*. Cambridge: Cambridge University Press.

Lipman, M. (2003) *Thinking in Education* (2nd edition). Cambridge: Cambridge University Press.

Lipman, M. and Gazzard, A. (1987) *Philosophy for Children: Where are We Now?* Montclair, NJ: Institute for Advancement of Philosophy for Children.

Lipman, M. and Gazzard, A. (1998) *Getting our Thoughts Together: Instructional Manual to Philosophy for Children*. Montclair, NJ: Institute for the Advancement of Philosophy for Children.

Muris, P. (2001) *Picture Book Pack*. London: Ladybird Books.

Ord, W. (2006) *SAPERE Report to DfES*. Cambridge: DfES.

O'Riordan, N. (2009) Personal communication. 'Philosophy for Children 2007–2008.'

Sternberg, R.J. (1984) 'How can we teach intelligence?' *Educational Leadership 42*, 1, 38–48.

Trickey S. and Topping, K.J. (2004) 'Philosophy for Children: A systematic review.' *Research Papers in Education 19*, 3, 363–378.

Williams, S. and Sutcliffe, R. (2000) *The Newswise Almanac 2000: Thinking through News Stories*. London: DialogueWorks.

Winyard, J. (2004) 'Simple gifts.' (An interview with Professor Matthew Lipman, founder of the Philosophy for Children movement.) *Teaching Thinking and Creativity*, Winter 2004, 42–47.

CAME and CASE

Adey, P. (2002) 'Cognitive Acceleration with Five-year-olds.' In M. Shayer and P. Adey (eds) *Learning Intelligence: Cognitive Acceleration Across the Curriculum for 5 to 15 Years*. Buckingham: Open University Press.

Adey, P. (2004) *The Professional Development of Teachers: Practice and Theory*. Dordrecht: Kluwer.

Adey, P. and Shayer, M. (1994) *Really Raising Standards: Cognitive Intervention and Academic Achievement*. London: Routledge.

Adey, P. and Shayer, M. (eds) (2002) *Learning Intelligence: Cognitive Acceleration across the Curriculum from 5 Years*. Buckingham: Open University Press.

Boehm, A.E. (1986) *Boehm-R: Boehm Test of Basic Concepts*. New York: The Psychological Corporation.

Cattle, J. and Howie, D.R. (2007) 'An evaluation of a school programme for the development of thinking skills through the CASE@KS1 approach.' *International Journal of Science Education 3*, 2, 1–18.

Flavell, J.H. (1979) 'Metacognition and cognitive monitoring.' *American Psychologist 34*, 10, 906–911.

Gunter, B., McGregor, D. and Twist, J. (2007) *Reflective Science: A KS4 Series of Activities (On DVD) Designed to Promote Higher Order Skills*. Material available from: barrygunter@thinkingandlearning. co.uk.

Larkin, S. (2006) 'Collaborative group work and individual development of metacognition in the early years.' *Research in Science Education 36*, 1/2, 7–27.

Leo, E.L. and Galloway, D. (1996) 'Conceptual links between cognitive acceleration through science education and motivational style: A critique of Adey and Shayer.' *International Journal of Science Education 18*, 1, 35–49.

Marsh, H.W. and Yeung, A.S. (1987) 'Causal effects of academic self-concept on academic achievement: Structural equation models of longitudinal data.' *Journal of Educational Psychology* 89, 41–54.

McGregor, D. (2007) *Developing Thinking, Developing Learning: A Guide to Thinking Skills in Education.* Maidenhead: McGraw Hill/Open University Press.

Raven, J.C. (1963) *Colored Progressive Matrices.* London: H.K. Lewis and Co. Ltd.

Shayer, M., Wylam, H., Kuchemann, D. and Adey, P. (1978) *Science and Reasoning Tasks.* Slough: National Foundation for Educational Research.

Swartz and Parks' infused approach

McGregor, D. (2007) *Developing Thinking, Developing Learning: A Guide to Thinking Skills in Education.* Maidenhead: McGraw Hill/Open University Press.

McGuinness, C. (1997) *ACTS: Activating Children's Thinking Skills: Final Report Phase 2.* Belfast: Queen's University.

McGuinness, C. (2002) 'Metacognition in classrooms.' Paper presented to the International Conference on Thinking, Harrogate.

McGuinness, C. (2005a) 'Teaching thinking: Theory and practice.' *British Journal of Educational Psychology,* Special Monograph Series, Pedagogy–Learning for Teaching, 107–127.

McGuinness, C. (2005b) *Thinking Lessons for Thinking Classrooms: Tools for Teachers.* Abingdon: Routledge.

McGuinness, C. (2006) 'Building Thinking Skills in Thinking Classrooms: ACTS (Activating Children's Thinking Skills) in Northern Ireland.' *Teaching and Learning Research Programme 18,* September 2006, 1–4. Available at www.tlrp.org/pub/documents/McGuinness_RB_18.pdf, accessed on 25 March 2011.

McGuinness, C., Curry, C., Eakin, A. and Sheehy, N. (2005) 'Metacognition in primary classrooms: A pro-ACTive learning effect for children.' Paper to TLRP Annual Conference, Warwick, 2005.

Swartz, R.J. (2001a) 'Infusing Critical and Creative Thinking into Content Instruction.' In A.L. Costa (ed.) *Developing Minds: A Resource Book for Teaching Thinking* (3rd edition). Melbourne: Hawker Brownlow.

Swartz, R.J. (2001b) 'Thinking about Decisions.' In A.L. Costa (ed.) *Developing Minds: A Resource Book for Teaching Thinking* (3rd edition). Melbourne: Hawker Brownlow.

Swartz, R.J. and Parks, S. (1994a) *Infusing the Teaching of Critical and Creative Thinking into Content Instruction: A Lesson Design Handbook for the Elementary Grades.* Pacific Grove, CA: Critical Thinking Press and Software.

Swartz, R.J. and Parks, S. (1994b) *Infusing the Teaching of Critical and Creative Thinking into Content Instruction.* Pacific Grove, CA: Critical Thinking Books and Software.

Goleman's emotional intelligence

Booth, T. and Ainscow, M. (2002) *Index for Inclusion.* Bristol: Centre for Studies on Inclusive Education.

Department for Education and Skills (DfES) (2005) *Excellence and Enjoyment: Social and Emotional Aspects of Learning (SEAL).* Nottingham: DfES.

Goleman, D. (1995/6) *Emotional Intelligence: Why it Matters More Than IQ.* London: Bloomsbury.

Goleman, D. (1998) *Working with Emotional Intelligence.* London: Bloomsbury.

Mayer, J.D., Caruso, D.R. and Salovey, P. (2000) 'Emotional intelligence meets traditional standards for an intelligence.' *Intelligence 27*, 4, 267–298.

Sinkler, P. and Toft, P. (2000). 'Raising the National Healthy School Standard (NHSS) together.' *Health Education 100*, 2, 68 – 73.

Learning styles

Bolton, R.W. (2005) 'Cognitive styles and learning–A case study of the application of Riding's Cognitive Styles analysis.' Unpublished master's dissertation, University of Hull.

Coffield, F., Moseley, D., Hall, E. and Ecclestone, K. (2004a) *Learning Styles and Pedagogy in Post-16 Learning: A Systematic and Critical Review.* London: Learning and Skills Research Centre.

Coffield, F., Moseley, D., Hall, E. and Ecclestone, K. (2004b) *Should We Be Using Learning Styles? What Research Has to Say to Practice.* London: Learning and Skills Research Centre.

Dunn, R., Dunn, K. and Price, G.E. (1989) *Learning Styles Inventory.* Lawrence, KS: Price System.

Hattie, J.A. (1999) 'Influence on students' learning.' Inaugural lecture, University of Auckland.

Hattie, J., Biggs, J. and Purdie, N. (1996) 'Effects of learning skills interventions on student learning: A meta-analysis.' *Review of Educational Research 66*, 2, 99–136.

Joyce, D. (2008) 'Cognitive Interventions, Enrichment Strategies and Temperament-Based Learning Styles.' In O. Tan and A. Seng (eds) *Cognitive Modifiability in Learning and Assessment: International Perspectives.* Singapore: Cengage Learning.

Myers, I.B. and Myers, P.B. (1980) *Gifts Differing: Understanding Personality Type.* Palo Alto, CA: Consulting Psychologists Press.

Riding, R.J. (1991) *Cognitive Styles Analysis.* Birmingham: Learning and Training Technology.

Riding, R.J. (1998) *Cognitive Styles Analysis–CSA Administration.* Birmingham: Learning and Training Technology.

Riding, R.J. (2002) *School Learning and Cognitive Style.* London: David Fulton.

Riding, R. and Rayner, S. (1995) *Personal Style and Effective Teaching.* Birmingham: Learning and Training Technology.

Riding, R.J. and Rayner, S. (1998a) *Cognitive Styles and Learning Strategies: Understanding Style Differences in Learning and Behaviour.* London: David Fulton.

Riding, R.J. and Rayner, S. (1998b) *Assessment of Cognitive Style. The Computer-presented Cognitive Styles Analysis 2.* Birmingham: Learning and Training Technology.

Sharp, J.G., Bowker, R. and Byrne, J. (2008) 'VAK or VAK-uous? Towards the trivialisation of learning and the death of scholarship.' *Research Papers in Education 23*, 3, 293–314.

Smith, A. and Call, N. (2000) *The ALPS Approach: Accelerated Learning in Primary Schools* (revised edition). Stafford: Network Educational Press.

Sternberg, R.J. (1993) 'Intellectual Styles: Theory and Classroom Implications.' In B.Z. Presseisen, R.J. Sternberg, K.W. Fischer, C.C. Knight and R. Feuerstein (eds) *Learning and Thinking Styles: Classroom Interaction.* Washington, DC: National Educational Association.

Sternberg, R.J. (1999) *Thinking Styles.* Cambridge: Cambridge University Press.

Sternberg, R.J. and Grigorenko, E.L. (1997) 'Are cognitive styles still in style?' *American Psychologist 52*, 7, 700–712.

Perkins' dispositions

Costa, A. and Kallick, B. (2000) (eds) *Discovering and Exploring Habits of Mind.* Alexandria, VA: Association for Supervision and Curriculum Development.

de A'Echevarria, A. (2009) 'Implementing QCA's framework for (PLTS) personal, learning and thinking skills.' Available at www.teachingexpertise.com/e-bulletins/implementing-qcas-framework-for-plts-personal-learning-and-thinking-skills-3087, accessed on 10 April 2011.

de A'Echevarria, A., Patience, I. and Hailstone, P. (2008) *Teaching Thinking Pocketbook.* Alresford: Teachers' Pocketbooks.

Perkins, D.N. (2002) 'The Tame and the Wild.' Presentation to British Council Seminar 'Thinking Skills in the Classroom', Belfast.

Perkins, D.N., Jay, E. and Tishman, S. (1993) 'Beyond abilities: A Dispositional Theory of Thinking.' *Merrill-Palmer Quarterly 39*, 1, 1–21.

Tishman, S., Perkins, D.N. and Jay, E. (1995) *The Thinking Classroom: Learning and Teaching a Culture of Thinking.* Boston, MA: Allyn and Bacon.

Locus of control and attributions

Ames, C. (1992) 'Classrooms: Goals, structures and student motivation.' *Journal of Educational Psychology 84*, 3, 261–271.

Borkowski, J.G., Carr, M., Rellinger, F. and Pressley, M. (1990) 'Self-regulated Cognition: Interdependence of Metacognition, Attributions and Self-Esteem.' In B.F. Jones and L. Idol (eds) *Dimensions of Thinking and Cognitive Instruction.* Hillsdale, NJ: Lawrence Erlbaum.

Diener, C.I. and Dweck, C.S. (1980) 'An analysis of learned helplessness: The processing of success.' *Journal of Personality and Social Psychology 39*, 5, 940–952.

Gipps, C. and Tunstall, P. (1998) 'Effort, ability and the teacher: Young children's explanations for success and failure.' *Oxford Review of Education 24*, 2, 149–165.

Goetz, T.W. and Dweck, C.S. (1980) 'Learned helplessness in social situations.' *Journal of Personality and Social Psychology 39*, 2, 246–255.

Howie, D.R. (1999) 'Models and morals: Meanings underpinning the scientific study of Special Educational Needs.' *International Journal of Disability, Development and Education 46*, 9–24.

Howie, D.R., Thickpenny, J.P., Leaf, C.A. and Absolum, M.A. (1985) 'The piloting of 'Instrumental Enrichment' in New Zealand with eight mildly retarded children.' *Australia and New Zealand Journal of Developmental Disabilities 11*, 1, 3–16.

Rotter, J.B. (1972) *Social Learning and Clinical Psychology.* Englewood Cliffs, NJ: Prentice Hall.

Seligman, M.E.P. (1975) *Helplessness: On Depression, Development and Death.* San Francisco, CA: Freeman.

Skinner, E.A., Wellborn, J.G. and Connell, J.P. (1990) 'What it takes to do well in school and whether I've got it: A process model of perceived control and children's engagement and achievement in schools.' *Journal of Educational Psychology 82*, 1, 22–30.

Tam, S.K.T. (2003) 'Locus of control, attributional style, and school truancy: The case of Hong Kong.' PhD thesis, University of Hull.

Weiner, B. (1986) *An Attributional Theory of Motivation and Emotion.* New York: Springer-Verlag.

CHAPTER 5

Tier 2 – Working with Small Groups for Learners Needing Particular Attention to the Teaching of Thinking

Introduction

It is important that we support Tier 1 work on teaching of thinking for all learners with small group work that gives extra support with more intensive intervention, focused on the particular 'exceptional' learning needs of the group. Figure 5.1 depicts this Tier 2 level of work in the teaching of thinking.

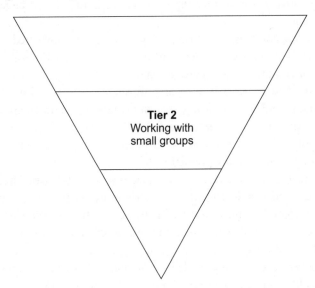

Tier 2
Working with
small groups

Figure 5.1 Tier 2 – Small group work

There may be a variety of needs which we view as exceptional for this Tier 2 work. These needs may be exceptional in terms of the cognitive ability of the group, such as high ability or particular learning difficulties. They may be exceptional in terms of barriers to learning which the learner has to overcome, such as sensory difficulties. There may be barriers to learning which have built up through difficulties in engagement in the school curriculum, relating to a wide range of complex factors such as socio-economic disadvantage, emotional difficulties, and prolonged failure with the school curriculum. Learners who have the challenge of bridging their own and a different school cultural context may find group work focused on their own cultural values helpful.

Small group work allows us to place more focus on the needs of all individuals in the group. One of the criticisms of a number of programmes for the teaching of thinking used in a lock-step fashion for whole classes of learners is that they may not address equally the needs of all learners in the large group. Most of the research evaluations of the programmes covered in the Tier 1 outline use only experimental and control group comparisons, making it difficult to know how individuals are responding to the approach used. It is important to look at individual responses to the programme, and to ensure that it is being applied in a way which meets the needs of all learners in the group. Also, there are ethical and equity issues in using a programme that gives further advantage to the most cognitively able learners in a group, but holds limited benefit for the less able.

However, ensuring that the teaching of thinking is delivered in ways that cater for groups of learners with shared exceptional needs raises a number of complex issues, which are discussed below.

We need to consider how to identify shared exceptional needs on a systematic school basis, in a way that ensures that all children are valued and have the highest expectations for their learning. There is a strong critique of traditional cognitive assessment which often labels learners and, through self-fulfilling prediction, leads to low expectations for future academic success. One such critique is made by Feuerstein (see Chapter 4, Section 2) who has developed approaches to assessment, including the listing of cognitive functions/dysfunctions, and his Learning Potential Assessment Device (Feuerstein, Rand and Hoffmann 1979; Feuerstein et al. 2002), which can explore the learning process used by the learner, and discover how best to provide intervention and assistance in response to difficulties in this process. Gardner (Hatch and Gardner 2001) and Sternberg (1985)both critique traditional methods of assessing intelligence, and suggest alternatives, including Gardner's advice of more authentic assessment in real-life contexts and the building of portfolios, leading to a multi-pronged assessment of each individual's unique profile of intelligences. We may find the Framework for Educational Assessment by Gipps (2005) helpful here, with its criteria of curriculum fidelity, comparability, dependability, public credibility, context description, and equity.

It is important to organise the grouping in a way that maximises learning within a range of abilities, so that peers within the group can still provide models of good thinking. Pertinent here are the key roles played by social interaction and speech/language for the development of more abstract cognitive functioning, through guided assistance, within the zone of proximal development (Vygotsky 1978, 1986), and peer modelling is a key tool for doing this. We need to be particularly careful, when organising learners into groups (whether that be by cognitive ability, Multiple Intelligences profiles, or learning styles), to ensure that all strengths are recognised, and that all groups have opportunity to develop adequately the more abstract conceptual abilities that they will need to master curriculum challenges at secondary school level.

We need to give careful thought to the interfacing of the smaller group work and work within the wider classroom environment. It is extremely important that a range of such extra group support work is given, in a way that minimises negative labelling, or group members' negative perceptions of the purpose of the group. The ways in which the group is identified, and the work introduced to them, are extremely important, so that there is ownership, partnership, and pride in the work. The writer found in her project at Kowhai Intermediate, in a special class for children with learning difficulties, that sharing their work with parents, including a well-attended parents' event, fostered pride in their accomplishments.

It is important to ensure that the strengths and the needs of the groups targeted in Tier 2 are clearly identified and understood, so that the approach to the teaching of thinking for them can address these characteristics appropriately. (A number of examples later in this chapter show how this matching is achieved.)

For learners who have a history of disadvantage or school failure, it is obvious not only that there will be a need for more intensive teaching of thinking, but that it needs to be linked to high-quality teaching in key subject areas, to which the thinking skills can be applied. The importance of providing both the prerequisite cognitive and metacognitive skills, and opportunities to generalise them to appropriate intensive basic skills programmes such as reading, was shown in a study carried out by the present writer with learners with a mild learning disability and ongoing school failure (Howie *et al.* 1985). The learners in the study, who had received a two-year Feuerstein Instrumental Enrichment intervention, made considerably greater gains in reading on subsequent exposure to a tailored reading intervention, than did learners from classes in other schools which had not received this cognitive intervention.

The needs of learners with behavioural, emotional and social difficulties is a particular challenge at Tier 2, and a number of the approaches covered in this chapter address this. No matter what shared group needs are being worked with at Tier 2 level, particular attention needs to be paid to motivation, self-esteem and attribution needs of the individuals concerned. Some relevant approaches to this have already been covered in relation to Tier 1 in the previous chapter.

Any work at Tier 2 level should ensure that we understand these emotional and motivational needs as fully as possible, both prior to, and throughout the work on the teaching of thinking. Perhaps the most authentic way of gaining this understanding is an interview with each learner (more realistic for smaller group work) prior to the intervention, careful observation throughout the intervention, ongoing action through the intervention to adapt to the motivational, social and emotional needs identified, and interview afterwards to evaluate and reflect on the success of the intervention in terms of meeting these needs. An example of how such an interview could be constructed, to take into account 'metacognitive' knowledge such as person (including attribution), task and strategy aspects, would include questions like: 'What did you have to do on this task?' (task knowledge); 'How did you feel you did in this problem-solving situation?' (self-knowledge); and 'When you are planning what to do in that situation, what do you need to think carefully about?' (strategy knowledge) (Howie 2003, p.124).

When teaching thinking to groups of learners who are from a culturally different group within the main school, it is essential to ensure that the aims of the intervention, the processes used throughout the intervention, and evaluation of the intervention, are appropriate and sensitive to the cultural differences of learners involved in such groups. The role of dynamic assessment with learners who are culturally diverse has been identified by Lidz and Macrine (2001). This chapter will devote particular attention to approaches to the teaching of thinking which are appropriate for groups of learners from culturally unique backgrounds.

Approaches which have a strong theoretical base, and have been shown to be of value for groups of exceptional learners

1. Vygotsky's socio-cultural approach

The collaborative, participatory and co-constructive nature of the learning enhancement process are stressed by Vygotsky (1978, 1986) and other key theorists taking a Vygotskian approach, such as Rogoff (1990, 2003). This approach already underpins the wide use of co-operative group work in the classroom. Its collaborative nature makes it particularly important for more intensive teaching of thinking with smaller groups of learners sharing common learning needs.

Another very exciting and important idea given to us by Vygotsky (1978) is that of the 'zone of proximal development'. It encourages us to ensure that appropriate mediation and guided assistance, including modelling by more capable peers, is given to move the learner to the 'proximal' or 'next' level of development.

The 'zone of proximal development' is

> the distance between the actual developmental level as determined by independent problem solving and the level of potential development as determined through problem solving under adult guidance or in collaboration with more capable peers. (Vygotsky 1978, p.86)

These are important contributions by Vygotsky to the teaching of thinking in this tier, and encourage us to provide input to the learner that is not merely limited to where they are in their present learning, but which assists and challenges them to move within their zone of proximal development, onto the next level of development, and to higher levels of abstraction. Within the zone of proximal development there are a number of mediation or assistance approaches which can enhance learning, discussed by Vygotsky (1978) as follows:

1. **Use of imitation**

    The human ability to learn through the specific social interaction involved in imitation, 'by which children grow through the intellectual lives of those around them', was stressed by Vygotsky. He states:

    > Children can imitate a variety of actions that go well beyond the limits of their own capabilities. Using imitation, children are capable of doing much more in collective activity or under the guidance of adults. (Vygotsky 1978, p.88)

In line with co-operative learning, he states: 'What the child can do in co-operation he can do alone tomorrow' (1978, p.188).

2. **Understanding of the role of speech and language in fostering learning within the zone of proximal development**
    Vygotsky states:

    > Language arises initially as a means of communication between the child and the people in his environment. Only subsequently, upon conversion to internal speech, does it come to organise the child's thought, that is, become an internal mental function. (1978, p.89)

    The role that the mediator can play, through language, to bridge between the learner's present knowledge and new knowledge, to provide a structure to support new learning, and to help shift the responsibility of learning from the mediator to the learner is highlighted in Rogoff's important book *Apprenticeship in Thinking – Cognitive Development in Social Context* (1990).

3. **Use of play as a leading factor in development**
    This means play with the focus on enhancing meanings and the use of rules for increased self-regulation, rather than just the imaginary situation. Vygotsky states:

    > Play creates a zone of proximal development of the child. In play a child always behaves beyond his average age, above his daily behaviour...play contains all the developmental tendencies in a condensed form and is itself a major source of development. (1978, p.102)

    It is also a means of developing more abstract and symbolic thought. It allows us to develop new relations between situations in thought and real situations.

4. **'Scaffolding'**
    One type of provision of guidance and collaboration needed by the learner is called 'scaffolding', a process which allows for appropriate guided assistance within the zone of proximal development. This has been explored by many writers. Wood and Bruner, two important experts on Vygotsky, proposed the idea of 'scaffolding' to describe the teaching process where an adult or expert (it could be a more expert peer) provides

'a kind of "scaffolding" process that enables a child or novice to solve a problem, carry out a task, or achieve a goal which would be beyond his unassisted efforts' (Wood, Bruner and Ross 1976, p.90). A teacher can offer more help and instruction than ordinarily given, if a learner is seen to get into difficulty, and then 'fade' that help progressively, providing the learner with minimal help needed to succeed. In this way, control is passed to the learner (Wood and Wood 1996).

5. **The role of emotion**

    Attention should be given to the important role of emotion in creating meaning for the child within the zone of proximal development. Thinking must not be separated from 'the fullness of life, from the personal needs and interests, the inclinations, and impulses, of the thinker' (Vygotsky 1986, p.10).

Let us now turn to teaching in Tier 2 in relation to groups of learners with shared exceptional needs. The following pertinent points are made in a recent chapter by Kozulin and Gindis (2007), 'Sociocultural Theory and Education of Children with Special Needs'.

Vygotsky makes a very important link between a learning difficulty or disability and the social implications of that difficulty. He wants the difficulty or disability to be compensated for through the acquisition of cultural tools (in particular, through social mediation and the acquisition of symbolic tools). This reminds us not to impose social barriers, such a low expectations, when working with groups of learners with special needs. Vygotsky wants us to search for positive capacities in the learner, and provide educational opportunities to ensure that the learner has a future high quality of life. An example of a supportive social environment and an appropriate compensatory programme which can bypass the initial disabilities a child is born with is given by Kozulin and Gindis (2007): a child with a neurological difficulty affecting the right side of his body, and putting him at a disadvantage in communicative speech, peer interaction, role play and writing skills, can through such compensation, reach full mastery of the higher psychological functions. They state, in relation to a child with such a pattern of disabilities:

> Vygotsky emphasised the role of social mediation and the acquisition of symbolic tools. Vygotsky would probably have suggested compensating for a child's motor problem by cultivating his verbal functions, teaching him to use a typewriter at a relatively early age,

> organising peer interaction around nonmotor activities, and in general by substituting higher cognitive and verbal functions for the impaired motor skills. What the child cannot do by hand, he should be able to do by word. (Kozulin and Gindis 2007, p.432–433)

Kozulin and Gindis consider that it is important to gain understanding of the learner's unique disability by developing a 'disability-specific profile' of the discrepancy between the 'natural' and 'social' aspects of the development of the learner with a disability. The latter should include the forms of socialisation which the learner engages in, mastery of psychological tools (including speech and language), and use of compensatory strategies. Compensatory strategies should be designed to meet the individual child's needs for overcoming the barrier to learning presented by the initial 'natural' disability (e.g. visual disability), and provide the best possible cultural tools to meet the highest possible goal of cultural development. (See other key works on speech and language as cultural tools: Vygotsky 1986; Kozulin 1998.)

A particular version of a disability profile in which there are 'three strata or components of disability' (by Venger, in a Russian paper) is described by Kozulin and Gindis: the first is stratum composed of individual characteristics of the child; the second consists of those characteristics which are disability-specific or disability-dependent; the third includes parameters of social interactions determined by the child's individual and disability-specific characteristics. Social and cultural interactions influence the processes not only in the third stratum, but in the two previous strata as well (Kozulin and Gindis 2007).

Dynamic assessment (considered to have been founded by Vygotsky, with his idea of the zone of proximal development) is a key approach for assessment of learners with disabilities. Dynamic assessment tools have also been developed for learners from culturally different groups (Gupta and Coxhead 1998). Vygotsky considered that a learner's ability to learn (cognitive ability) is best assessed through a collaborative process, and that the zone of proximal development is not a fixed entity but constantly changing with appropriate assistance/guidance. Dynamic assessment usually involves:

1. conventional assessment of unassisted performance (testing)

2. a teaching phase to explore the best means of developing skills within the zone of proximal development (teaching)

3. retesting without assistance to explore the extent of the enhanced learning.

Addressing not only cognitive but also motivational aspects is central to such an approach. The wide use of these procedures with learners with a variety of needs is demonstrated in an important book by Haywood and Lidz (2007), called *Dynamic Assessment in Practice: Clinical and Educational Applications*. Carol Lidz, one of the leading international writers on dynamic assessment, developed the Application of Cognitive Functions Scale (Lidz 2000) to address the specific assessment needs of young learners, in relation to the typical cognitive processes involved in the US preschool curricula:

* classification
* auditory memory
* visual memory
* sequential pattern completion
* verbal planning
* perspective taking.

It involves first, administering the tasks without assistance (*testing*), then providing mediation needed by the child in strategies and task solution (*teaching*), and finally post testing without assistance (*testing*) – a typical dynamic assessment procedure. Although developed for a particular cultural situation, it does demonstrate an approach to dynamic assessment which could be developed in any cultural situation, and there is no reason why such a tool could not be developed to explore learning needs on a small group basis.

There are a number of specific programmes in the West which are compatible with these concerns of Vygotsky, as noted by Kozulin and Gindis. These include Feuerstein's Learning Potential Assessment Device, and his Instrumental Enrichment cognitive enhancement programme, which will be dealt with in the next section. There is also another group of programmes which combine a Vygotskian approach with information processing and other approaches; this includes the work of Das and Kendrick, and Haywood, Brooks and Burns:

* The Das and Kendrick (1997) programme for a 'high incidence' specific reading disability uses two key ideas of Vygotsky, gaining of psychological tools, and social-cultural mediation, delivered first through a global cognitive process training unit for internalisation of cognitive strategies, and then through a 'bridge unit' for training in the specific strategies relevant to reading and writing.

- Haywood, Brooks and Burns' 'Bright Start' cognitive enhancement programme (1992) is designed for young children who are at high risk of failure, especially because of disadvantage.

Finally, let us consider in some depth the particular implications of Vygotsky's socio-cultural theory for work with learners who are culturally different. Vygotsky's attention to the cultural embeddedness of learning reminds us of the key cultural meanings and values that learners bring to their learning situation (Sutton 1988). Vygotsky wanted this to be a positive understanding, revealing the positive characteristics of the thinking of such learners (Sutton 1988). Such a study would do away with the old methods and traditional tests of intelligence, which were inappropriate, and the new study would:

- make understanding of the unique cultural and social environment itself, with its structures and dynamics, central to the study

- show how the unique environment forms and shapes all of the higher forms of behaviour and thinking

- show the unique characteristics which impact on the learner's development

- place on society itself the responsibility for ensuring the child's fullest cognitive development, thus shifting the focus away from the supposed properties of, or failures of, the learner.

Of particular interest is one example of an attempt to obtain such understanding within a programme for the teaching of thinking carried out with young people with learning disabilities, within the contextual developments of China (Robson and Lin 2002). It used both a Vygotskian and a Feuerstein approach. One of the components of the enhancement work concerned the ability to use the language of thinking, a Vygotskian idea of language as a cultural tool for higher-level thinking. The project evaluation utilised a number of approaches, including a more grounded theory, qualitative approach (identifying themes from a variety of process-type information including teacher diaries and verbal and written communication by teachers), to tap into culturally sensitive meanings. Some of the issues arising from the study, and relating to these cultural meanings, involved understanding of the unique characteristics of the Chinese culture which impacted on the teaching process, such as uniformity and rigidity of input, teachers making their valued and moral judgements evident in classroom discussions, and a strong competitive motivation.

A DETAILED EXAMPLE

There follows here a detailed example of the use of Vygotskian social construction and a 'scaffolding' approach in a study of real-life problem solving (Howie 2003a, 2003b). The work was with learners who were considered to have shared learning disabilities as well as some motivational and emotional difficulties, attending the Auckland Sheltered Workshop training organisation to prepare for work in the wider community. Particular attention will be given to one of these learners who, among several in the group, came from a minority cultural (Pacific Island) background. He was a young man who had been born in New Zealand, although his parents had emigrated from a Pacific Island to New Zealand, and who had recently left school, where he had experienced some failure.

The needs of the learners were assessed through a dynamic assessment process similar to the kind Vygotsky suggests in order to explore the zone of proximal development.

It was given both prior to and following the full problem-solving intervention work. Using two tasks, a Raven's matrices problem-solving task, and a real-life problem-solving task (self-advocacy), scaffolding or prompting was applied as needed by the learners. The scale of prompts, from the most minimal to complete assistance, was as follows:

- Level 1: the request to 'do it again' (many learners know how to solve the problem but make mistakes)

- Level 2: visual focusing, with the assessor drawing the learner's attention to key aspects of the task through pointing/visual tracing

- Level 3: verbal description of the key dimensions to be attended to

- Level 4: verbal description of the strategy needed to solve the problem

- Level 5: modelling the solution, with the strategy explained.

The full intervention consisted of both small group work and individual work as needed on the problem-solving skills involved in self-advocacy, carried out over six months on a once-weekly basis. This work focused on skills which were identified as needed in the pre-intervention scaffolding assessment. This included the need for systematic and thorough information gathering. As part of this collaborative learning, learners were asked to gather and document in a regular way the problem-solving and self-advocacy opportunities they were experiencing in real life, for guided practice in the skills being learnt, and to ensure meaningful examples. They also had mediated to them the broad content of human rights relating to self-advocacy. Solution planning for the self-advocacy problems was taught, along with teaching of appropriate communication of decisions, using modelling.

In terms of responses to the initial scaffolded assessment process (see Figure 5.2), on the Raven problem-solving task (the five Raven tasks are labelled AB, AI, AJN, CI and EI, and the performance is indicated by the □ symbol in Figure 5.2) the young man in our example responded immediately and clearly to the third-level prompts and required no further prompts on the first set of tasks. More prompting was needed in the second, third and fifth set of tasks, which were at increasingly difficult levels. Less prompting was required on the fourth set of tasks. This ability to profit from scaffolded mediation was reflected in his considerable upward shift on the Raven's matrices following the full intervention.

This young man, from a background which was limited in its use of English language, also responded very positively to scaffolding on the real-life problem-solving tasks. (Figure 5.2 shows this pattern with the O symbol.) On the first set of tasks ('Asking for help') he initially required the highest level of prompting, but by the third task ('Representation') in this set level, he succeeded independently. On the second set of tasks ('Asking for skills'), the fourth set ('Equal opportunity') and the fifth set ('Asking for confidentiality') he required minimal prompting, showing independence in this skill development and generalisation to later skills (as a result of learning on earlier scaffolding of self-advocacy skills). It was no surprise to the writer when this young man moved successfully to open employment while she was still researching at the Sheltered Workshop.

2. Feuerstein's theory of mediated learning experience, and related tools

This approach is of particular importance to us because a number of tools which are particularly relevant when working with learners with exceptional needs have been developed by Feuerstein and his team. A very important early paper by Kaniel and Feuerstein (1989), which focused on his work in relation to learners with special needs was presented in *Oxford Review of Education*. He also takes a particular approach towards conceptualising cultural difference and cultural disadvantage, which

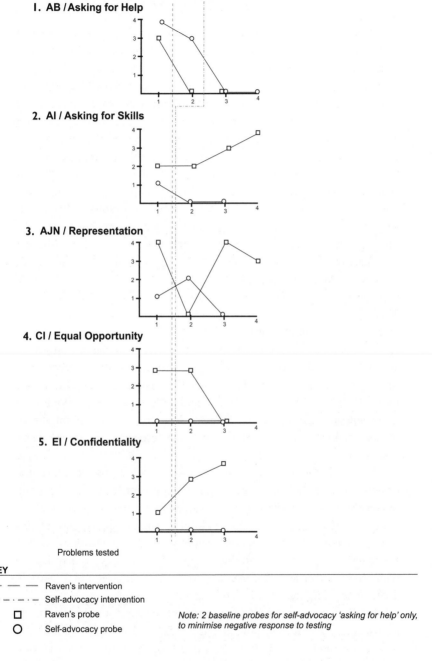

Figure 5.2 Case study responses to the scaffolding assessment procedure

is important to our consideration at Tier 2. These tools and ideas are summarised below.

A list of cognitive functions and dysfunctions in the mental phases of *input, elaboration* and *output* (see Chapter 4, and Howie 2003a, p.88) can be used by any teacher to explore the learning needs of a small group of learners, and then to develop an intervention approach which addresses those learning needs. A good example of this is provided by successful work with a tutorial group of Black South African students studying physics (Mehl 1991). Mehl gave each student a set of physics problem-solving tasks, questioning them about their problem-solving processes. He then used Feuerstein's listing of cognitive functions/dysfunctions to analyse the key difficulties displayed by the students (such as unplanned, impulsive and non-systematic exploration of the problem). Using this analysis, he provided the tutorial group with instruction which addressed the cognitive demands of the curriculum in ways that also addressed their particular learning difficulties. A similar approach was planned for work with Maori and Pacific Island students in their first year of financial accounting at the University of Auckland, as reported by Howie (2003a). This is an infused approach to the teaching of thinking, developed to meet shared exceptional learning needs.

The Learning Potential Assessment Device, a dynamic assessment approach, is widely used internationally with learners with exceptional needs (Feuerstein, Rand and Hoffman 1979; Feuerstein *et al.* 2002). This tool was developed when Feuerstein and colleagues were working with disadvantaged and culturally different learners, for whom traditional tests of cognitive ability were of little use, especially for determining intervention needs.

At this point it is of interest to us at Tier 2 that in the initial development of the tool there was a development for its use in group dynamic assessment, particularly for ascertaining the types of teaching assistance which would be most helpful to the group. The use of this tool for group assessment and intervention is detailed towards the end of Feuerstein's original book on the Learning Potential Assessment Device (Feuerstein, Rand and Hoffman 1979; see also Tzuriel and Feuerstein 1992 concerning dynamic group assessment).

In all of his work with this assessment device, Feuerstein is careful to discourage any idea of potential as a measurable and fixed entity, and indeed now prefers to call it the Learning Propensity Assessment Device. The aim is to understand what forms of assistance will best enable the learner to develop cognitively. A summary of the diverse groups and their exceptional needs for which assessment with the Learning Potential Assessment Device has been found to be helpful is given in Chapter 2 of Howie (2003a).

At Tier 2 level we should consider positively involving the parents of children in thinking enhancement programmes. A number of Feuerstein's colleagues have focused on ways of involving and training parents of learners with special needs. For example, one tool, the Mediational Intervention for Sensitising Caregivers (MISC), has been developed by Klein (2000). It is based on video observation of parental interaction with the young child, an analysis of the mediation criteria (using key mediated learning experience (MLE) criteria as outlined by Feuerstein, and further criteria relating to mediation of affect and developing empathy and the understanding of emotions), and workshops for parents to develop the criteria. It has been used in a variety of cultural contexts (e.g. Sri Lanka, Ethiopia, Israel, USA, Portugal), and with a variety of disadvantaged groups (including children with poor parent–child attachment, child maltreatment, etc.) It is important to enrich this tool with criteria valued by the culture involved. A full coverage of the work is provided by Coulter in the final chapter of *Changing Children's Minds* (Sharron and Coulter 1994). A paper on this work with MISC was presented by the present writer at a conference in Durham (Howie 2005).

We need to note the widespread use of Feuerstein's Instrumental Enrichment (FIE) programme for cognitive enhancement, with groups of learners with shared exceptional needs. This is one of the most common applications of this programme – not surprising, considering that it was developed to address the needs of severely disadvantaged learners, and also to support in a systematic way those mediation needs of the learners that were not adequately met in their past learning. Also, the aim of the programme is 'structural cognitive modifiability' which is unique to this programme and the reason why it is delivered intensively over two years.

The FIE programme is made up of a set of instruments, or tools, for teaching thinking strategies. The 14 instruments are:

1.   organisation of dots (teaching key metacognitive strategies)

2–4. orientation in space (three instruments, teaching the representation of space and person positions)

5–6. comparison and categorisation (two instruments, teaching verbal conceptual comparison skills)

7.   analytic perception (teaching description, categorisation, representation, and analysis)

8.   family relations (teaching relationships found in systems in everyday life)

9.   temporal relations (teaching relationships in time)

10. numerical progressions (teaching relationships in number)

11. instructions (teaching encoding and decoding processes)

12. illustrations (teaching application of problem-solving processes to real life)

13. representational stencil design (teaching complex representational thinking processes)

14. transitive relations and syllogisms (teaching formal reasoning including logico-verbal reasoning)

There are many reviews of the ways in which this programme (which addresses key metacognitive and cognitive processes, as well as motivational needs relating to these processes) has been used with groups of learners with exceptional needs. A number of these applications with a diverse range of learners with exceptional needs, including learners with disabilities and culturally different learners, are covered by Kozulin (2000).

A number of specific research studies which target groups with exceptional needs that the FIE programme has addressed, are covered by Feuerstein *et al.* (2006, p.430). These include learners who:

- have learning disabilities
- have specific reading difficulties
- are low-achieving
- are sensory-impaired
- are involved in rehabilitation programmes (e.g. learners who are neuropsychologically impaired, have psychiatric problems, and/ or are elderly)
- are gifted
- are in vocational training schemes
- are culturally different immigrants or from minority cultures.

A recent example of a long-term evaluation of Feuerstein's Instrumental Enrichment programme with 'learners who do not find learning easy' was carried out in Northern Ireland by Kate O'Hanlon (2011) as her doctoral research in the Psychology Department of Queen's University, Belfast. Five experimental schools throughout Northern Ireland were matched with five control schools. Three levels of Feuerstein's Instrumental Enrichment (the whole programme, for three years) were given to Key Stage 3 lower attaining pupils (aged 11–12 years) in the experimental schools. While the experimental pupils had two (40-minute) lessons in Instrumental Enrichment per week, the control pupils from similar classes in the control schools received an additional three to four (40-minute) lessons in extra English. In both cases, the pupils were withdrawn from lessons in Modern Languages for this enhancement work.

In spite of the curriculum advantage to the control pupils, there was a clear contrast between the achievements of the two groups, with 45 per cent of the Instrumental Enrichment pupils obtaining Grade A* to C in GCSE grades, while only 25 per cent of the control pupils did.

Twenty-four of the 87 Instrumental Enrichment pupils moved over their five years in their secondary school from their lowest attaining class to higher attaining groups, while in the control groups any pupils leaving only left the school or were expelled. According to Kate O'Hanlon's report: 'In one case, a boy from the Instrumental Enrichment group became Head Boy in his final year.'

Of particular interest to us is the increasing use of the FIE programme for learners who have social, emotional and behavioural needs. It should be noted that the original FIE programme addressed both cognitive and emotional needs, making it suitable for learners with such needs. Feuerstein comments 'The FIE framework of thinking and mediating does not divide the emotional from the cognitive' (Feuerstein *et al.* 2006, p.328).

The importance of motivational factors when enhancing the learning of people with significant underachieving in learning is recognised by Sternberg (1985) in discussing Feuerstein's inclusion of the motivational factors in the FIE programme.

One example of its use in the UK for learners with social, emotional and behavioural difficulties is provided by Head and O'Neill (1999). They chose to trial this programme with six learners experiencing these difficulties because of its insistence on a balance between the emotional and cognitive factors that determine behaviour. They state: 'The management team of the school decided to allocate four forty-minute periods a week for the teaching of IE to one group of pupils' (p.124) for twenty weeks – a considerable time commitment by the whole school, although clearly not the full two-year implementation advocated by Feuerstein. During this time they were only able to cover the first sections of the instruments 'organisation of dots' and 'orientation in space I'.

Evaluation was mainly through teacher observations, and the observers considered that the group which was taught IE had gained both academically and socially. They felt, in particular, that there was a decrease in impulsivity among the IE students. Teachers also responded to a questionnaire, which indicated that all except one of the six learners who completed the course showed an overall decrease in cognitive deficiency, which was accompanied by an overall decrease in inappropriate behaviour. The teachers drew attention to the importance of learners learning the processes of problem solving. Benefits to the individual learners, as case studies, are discussed. The writers conclude that a high level of commitment and input is required of the staff using such a programme. They state, 'The overall benefit of the IE programme can perhaps be summarised by saying that it lies in the realisation that the planning behaviour and self-regulation fostered by the programme lead to successful living' (Head and O'Neill 1999, p.128).

Both the Learning Potential Assessment Device and the FIE programme have been used successfully with gifted disadvantaged learners, for example by Kaniel in the Israeli context (Kaniel and Reichenberg 1993), and by Skuy *et al.* (1990) in South Africa.

Of particular interest is the way the work with gifted disadvantaged adolescents in Soweto combined FIE with a programme to develop creativity and socio-emotional development and academic enrichment. The overall intervention was carried out over two years, on Saturday mornings. Seven of the Instrumental Enrichment instruments were completed over this period, with work on the instruments interspersed with direct and explicit bridging to academic subjects and everyday life situations. For example, in teaching with the analytic perception instrument, a strategy called 'perspectivism' was used to mediate creativity, 'to promote self-awareness (e.g. in seeing the whole self in terms of the different "parts" others see in us), and develop a community and ecological consciousness' (Skuy *et al.* 1990, p.27). The particular programme to enhance creativity and socio-emotional development complemented and extended the Instrumental Enrichment programme, aimed at facilitating self-awareness, awareness of others and the environment, improved interpersonal communication, self-mastery, and a positive self-concept. The creativity aspect of the programme stimulated the assertion of individuality, enrichment of the imagination, and the expression of ideas through various modalities. (p.28)

The Instrumental Enrichment programme, enhanced in such a way, is particularly appropriate for learners whose cultural learning strengths include creativity.

New versions of the FIE programme have been developed for learners with shared exceptional needs, as described by Feuerstein *et al.* (2006) [revision of the book on Instrumental Enrichment]. For example, the 'Instrumental Enrichment-Basic' programme has been developed for younger children or older learners who have experienced significant cognitive developmental disabilities or delay. We should note that the four FIE-Basic instruments are 'directed towards helping the student learn about affective/emotional experiences with the help of the cognitive functions' (Feuerstein *et al.* 2006, p.328). These instruments are:

- 'identifying emotions'
- 'from empathy to action'
- 'compare and discover'
- 'thinking to learn to prevent violence'.

The instrument which focuses on the development of empathy is potentially of value not only to counteract bullying, but also for learners on the autistic spectrum who may have difficulty understanding the feelings of others. There is also a Braille version of the Instrumental Enrichment programme for learners with visual impairments.

Key studies carried out by Howie and colleagues in New Zealand using Instrumental Enrichment with a diverse range of learners included learners with mild learning disabilities in a special class; learners at the Kelston School for the Deaf; and Maori learners who were failing in the school system. It is of note that there were Maori and Pacific Island learners in the first two projects, and their very positive response to the FIE programme was one reason why it was subsequently offered to a South Auckland secondary school with a high percentage of Maori learners. (This is discussed in more detail at the end of this section, as the practical example of Tier 2 work with Feuerstein's approach.) All of these studies are summarised in Chapter 9 of Howie (2003a).

Aspects of the FIE programme were used by the present writer in a project on self-advocacy and real-life problem solving with young adults attending a sheltered workshop in Auckland (Howie 2003b). These young adults had a complex mix of learning difficulties and emotional difficulties. The results of the project suggest that enhancement of thinking skills is of value to older adolescents and young adults, who may well have experienced long-term failure in the school system, relating to a complex range of causes. The Instrumental Enrichment programme's attention to emotional and motivational factors, and systematic development of more positive thinking habits, make it appropriate for such learners.

With the increasing requirement in some countries for evidence that the teaching of thinking has a positive impact on academic achievement, especially in mathematics, there have been recent projects which use Feuerstein's approach very specifically to develop conceptual cognitive functions tools for the mathematics classroom. In their book *Rigorous Mathematical Thinking: Conceptual Formation in the Mathematics Classroom* Kinard and Kozulin (2008) outline how rigorous mathematical thinking can be fostered by developing the learner's cognitive tools and operations, using concepts from both Vygotsky and Feuerstein. There is evidence that this programme is particularly effective with learners who are educationally disadvantaged and culturally different.

We need to understand the distinction Feuerstein makes between *cultural disadvantage*, where the learner has not received sufficient mediation from his/her own culture, and *cultural difference*, where the learner has received this mediation, but where his/her culture is different to the prevailing one. (See Howie 2003a, Chapter 7 for a discussion of this distinction, and an application of it within the New Zealand context.) This distinction has implications for the mediational needs of these two groups of learners in the provision of more intensive teaching of thinking. In the case of cultural disadvantage, a very intensive systematic delivery of the Instrumental Enrichment programme will be required, with thorough use of MLE criteria. In the case of cultural difference, particular attention also needs to be given to mediation of the cognitive and curriculum demands of the learner's context.

A number of important studies using Instrumental Enrichment with learners from immigrant populations and minority cultural groups have been carried out by Professor Alex Kozulin, a Vygotskian expert and key researcher with Feuerstein's team in Israel. This is an exceptional shared need that is experienced worldwide. The studies are reported in Feuerstein *et al.*'s (2006) revision of the book on Instrumental Enrichment (pp.438–

442). As noted by the writers of this section, learners from immigrant and minority groups were the first recipients of the programme, which was developed for traumatised and disadvantaged learners coming to Israel.

The programme places emphasis on the general cognitive and learning strategies that are prerequisites for formal learning. It is also saturated with various graphic-symbolic devices, such as schemas, tables, graphs, plans and maps, which provide a basis for developing the psychological tools that are needed for formal learning (and which sometimes require mediation for learners from minority cultural groups).

Studies carried out by Kozulin and colleagues include:

- a study of intensive Instrumental Enrichment intervention as part of retraining for Ethiopian immigrant teachers

- a study of 15 adolescent girls receiving the programme three years after arriving in Israel, in a special 'immigrants' class. They had particular identified needs for understanding of superordinate concepts (such as 'size, form, origin, use, etc.), and were also poorly prepared for using contemporary learning materials which employ a range of graphic-symbolic devices (such as tables, graphs, etc.)

- a study with younger immigrant students using a relatively new form of FIE intervention for younger immigrant students called 'Concentrated Reinforcement Lessons (CoReL)'

- a study with young adults aged 18 to 26 whose pre-immigration schooling was insufficient for entry to more challenging pre-college programmes, but who were motivated toward college-level training and more challenging vocational training.

In all these studies, the goals of the Instrumental Enrichment training were met.

AN EXAMPLE FROM PRACTICE IN A SCHOOL SETTING

A detailed example carried out by the present writer examines the FIE programme in use for Maori learners within an Auckland (New Zealand) secondary school (Howie, Richards and Pirihi 1993). This application was previously discussed in the Tier 1 work (see Chapter 4, Section 2), with emphasis on the use of the three key mediation criteria. In this discussion of the same study (Howie, Richards and Pirihi 1993), attention will be focused on the overall use of the programme and its evaluation in culturally appropriate ways.

Feuerstein's Instrumental Enrichment (FIE) programme was chosen for the teaching of thinking to Maori adolescents in this largely Maori and Pacific Island South Auckland school because the programme had been developed within a multicultural context, its content was non-curriculum based, and so relatively adaptable to unique cultural values, and the teaching processes matched well those considered to belong to a traditional Maori way of teaching (Metge 1984).

The programme was taught by a team which included the writer and two Maori key classroom teachers for the Maori learners, so that ongoing aims, planning of the procedures, actual teaching, and ongoing evaluation of needs, could be collaborative (on a weekly basis). In any future application of the programme in such a cultural context, greater involvement of the wider cultural community would be sought to enhance the cultural collaboration with, and Maori ownership by, Maori elders and parents.

As examples in Chapter 4, Section 2 demonstrate, the Maori teachers mediated the teaching of the Instrumental Enrichment programme in culturally relevant ways. This involved not only use of the mediated learning criteria, embedded with Maori cultural meanings, but also enrichment of the content of the programme, including the bridging examples, with material and activities appropriate to their own Maori culture.

Chapter 9 of Howie (2003a) includes details on the results of the research project with Maori learners. There were particular issues of cultural appropriateness in the assessment which the researcher found a challenge, including cognitive assessment which did not rely on standardised data, use of an authentic achievement task (error correction – a process assessment – on a reading task, which linked to the self-monitoring work done in the programme), and use of a real-life problem-solving task.

The study used a group control design evaluation, which showed the greater shifts of learners receiving the Instrumental Enrichment programme as compared to learners who did not receive the programme, particularly on a verbal conceptual cognitive task ('Similarities' from the WISC-R measure) and on the reading error correction achievement measure.

The ways in which individual Maori learners were responding to the programme were also studied through single-subject design, which allowed the researcher to understand how individual learners were responding to each instrument as it was taught. There was strong evidence of successful teaching on the 'organisation of dots' instrument (a key instrument for teaching metacognitive skills), and learners appeared to be transferring this metacognitive learning to the real-life plan-of-search task.

Two of the learners had particular difficulty with the 'orientation in space I' instrument, and could be identified prior to the intervention as having orientation difficulties on the WISC-R Block Design test. Such learners appear to need more extensive training on this 'orientation in space' instrument. As noted above, the shifts on the 'comparisons' instrument were notable, and the learning from this appeared to generalise to the post-intervention 'Similarities' WISC-R measure.

Maori teachers commented on the considerable opportunities that the Instrumental Enrichment programme offered for gearing the teaching of it to Maori cultural needs, most often during the 'orientation in space I' instrument and the 'family relations' instrument. They also made considerable comments on their own professional development and increased feeling of confidence as they developed new skills in teaching the programme, and noted how they were generalising the teaching approaches used into their ordinary subject teaching with these learners. The teachers also made a number of statements relating to how the programme was addressing the learners' language needs, a typical comment being 'We have been generally giving them (the students) a low class of vocabulary and there is under-expectation. Children are retaining harder words' (Howie, Richards and Pirihi 1993, p.84). The teachers were also particularly impressed with motivational developments of the learners, such as increased perseverance on difficult tasks. The shift in teachers' attitudes to the learners appeared to be matched by a shift in learners' attitudes to their own abilities.

Approaches which include creative thinking

3. Howard Gardner's theory of Multiple Intelligences

This theory was discussed in detail in Tier 1, and is also discussed under this tier because it has a particularly inclusive approach that recognises the unique intellectual profile of all learners, and it suggests a number of group approaches to ensure that such unique and exceptional profiles of learning are recognised and their related learning needs met.

The concerns expressed in the 'issues' section, in relation to labelling and expectations, apply in particular to the use of this approach in attempts to meet shared and exceptional learning needs. There is increasing research literature on the successful use of Gardner's Multiple Intelligences when working with a wide range of learning needs. Points of note are the following:

1.   When grouping a class according to profile of intelligences, with work delivered in ways which suit these profiles, it is important to provide opportunities for learners to explore and strengthen their areas of weakness, as well as utilise their strengths. It is possible to modify and strengthen intelligences, according to Gardner, and he considers that 'the purpose of a school should be to develop intelligence' (Gardner 1993a, p.9). He also states that it is important for learners to observe competent peers or adults working with the different intelligences, so that they will 'readily come to appreciate the reasons for the materials as well as the nature of the skills that equip a master to interpret them in a meaningful way' (Gardner 1993b, p.206).

2.   Individuals have very unique combinations of the intelligences, so it is important to take these into account in determining what approaches may best suit and engage learners, including those usually regarded as less able. (One study with history learners used interviews to explore the learners' engagement in, and response to, various ways of utilising a Multiple Intelligences approach (Davies 2004). It is important to note that the students with initial lower history attainment showed a variety of unique Multiple Intelligences profiles, and they showed equal advantages to the students with initial higher history attainment for each of the Multiple Intelligences approaches used, which were: student choice of assessment approach from a variety of MI assessment approaches to match the intelligences, e.g. video assessment choice to match a strong visual-spatial intelligence; enrichment of whole-class teaching using Multiple Intelligences as 'entry points'; and small group work based on unique Multiple Intelligences profiles. Also, there were some surprises in what the learners enjoyed, with a much wider and more varied enjoyment of the different involvements with the Multiple Intelligences approaches than might have been expected.)

3.   Gardner makes a number of important points about assessment, which are relevant to work with learners who have exceptional

needs. He is critical of psychometric assessment of intelligence, and wants a more holistic approach. He states: 'we need to construct contextualised assessments which engage the distinct abilities of a number of intelligences' (Hatch and Gardner 2001, p.415). He even suggests that a school should have an 'assessment specialist' to provide a regular and updated view of individual learner profiles of intelligences (Gardner 1993a, p.72).

One approach to the assessment of the Multiple Intelligences, using the multiple and contextual approach advocated by Gardner, is that of Lazear (2004). He has developed the Multiple Intelligences Profile Indicator, where results from authentic real-life activities, such as a 'behaviour log', 'skills games', and 'inventing' are all entered on a circular pie chart, for each of the intelligences, allowing an overall view of the profile gained from multiple measures.

Another approach is offered by Shearer (2005), who devised the Multiple Intelligences Development Assessment Scales (MIDAS) to help create educational plans which maximise the learning, achievement, and personal development of those being assessed. This assessment tool is of particular interest to us at Tier 2 because the MIDAS scale was developed originally to assess the Multiple Intelligences of adolescents and adults undergoing cognitive rehabilitation for traumatic brain injury. It 'enquires about developed skill, levels of participation, and enthusiasm for a large variety of activities that are naturally encountered in daily life' (Shearer 2005, p.255). Gardner was involved in reviewing the large number of items to be field tested for the measure, and it has undergone tests for reliability and validity. There are now five versions of the MIDAS, for ages four through to adulthood. The ways in which this multiple-intelligences inspired assessment tool can be used are described by one teacher as follows:

> I think that Multiple Intelligences can really help to improve both the intrapersonal and interpersonal intelligences. The MIDAS can serve to make these more explicit aspects of the school curriculum. It can contribute to changing expectations and perceptions in positive ways. This is a very powerful instrument that can help teachers and students and parents. (Shearer 2005, pp.261–262)

4. The inclusion of the 'personal intelligences', that is, *intrapersonal intelligence* (the ability to have access to one's own feeling life) and *interpersonal intelligence* (the ability to understand the moods, temperaments, motivations and intentions of others), in the theory of Multiple Intelligences suggests that there may be a particular value in considering the use of this approach with groups of learners experiencing behavioural, social and emotional difficulties.

5. The meaningful use of the different intelligences in real-life settings, including in the wider school community, an approach which may be of particular value to learners with exceptional needs and from culturally different backgrounds, can be found in the following projects developed by Gardner and colleagues. For example, in the 'key school', as well as with outside specialists coming into the school, some learners are involved in projects at their community museum involving several months of 'apprenticeship' (Gardner 1993b, p.215). In the elementary McCleary School in Pittsburgh, Pennsylvania, as reported by Kornhaber, Fierros and Veenema (2004), an interdisciplinary curriculum has been developed which engages a variety of intelligences, and in covering a topic such as the water cycle, learners engage in field trips and group activities, such as drawing and constructing models of rivers, allowing for multiple entry points to learning. Another very common school practice called 'centres of work' ('learning' or 'activity' centres) within the school, as exampled in the eight learning centres within the Project Spectrum (Campbell, Campbell, and Dickinson 2004), including centres for arts, language, maths, mechanical movement, music, science, and social studies, allows for focus on particular intelligences in meaningful ways.

We need to remind ourselves that with any grouping involved with such an activity, it is important to ensure that all learners are encouraged to strengthen their weaker intelligences, and receive the opportunity to work with and observe peers functioning at a higher level.

The role of the intelligences within a cultural setting is of concern to Gardner, and he wants emphasis to be placed on those intelligences which are valued and important in a particular cultural context (Gardner 1983). He considers that intelligence should 'focus on those individual strengths that prove important within a cultural setting' (Chen and Gardner 2001, p.27). It is therefore important, when we are working with learners who are culturally different and disadvantaged, to understand the role of each of the intelligences in a particular cultural context, and ensure that any enhancement work is appropriate to related cultural meanings and values.

EXAMPLE FROM PRACTICE IN A SCHOOL SETTING

As an example of the use of Gardner's ideas on Multiple Intelligences for learners with shared exceptional needs, the work reported by Maura Sellars, of the University of Newcastle, UK (Sellars 2006) will be summarised. She identified a group of 27 learners considered to be low achievers in English. Their teachers were concerned not only at the literacy difficulties of these eight- and nine-year-olds, but also at their 'observable lack of motivation, task engagement, organisational skills, and self-efficacy' (p.3).

The intervention programme was developed to run for a ten-month period, integrated with the English activities. It was based on the results of individual Multiple Intelligences profiles assessments (McGrath and Noble 2003), and was designed so that learners had 'opportunities to use their relative strengths to help overcome their relative limitations in English' (Sellars 2006, p.4). The intervention programme of strategies was developed using the Bloom–Gardner planning matrix (McGrath and Noble 2005), which brings together Gardner's Multiple Intelligences and Bloom's well-known taxonomy of learning.

Let us look in a little depth at the Stage Two English Curriculum intervention which arose from this, utilising the Bloom–Gardner matrix for curriculum development to meet the learners' needs, both in literacy and emotion. Every Gardner intelligence was planned for, making provision for each of the Bloom skills of remembering, understanding, applying, analysing, evaluating and creating. For example, the intrapersonal intelligence area covered the following:

- *Remembering*: Recall favourite times at school, at home, with families, with friends, and alone. What skills and talents have you developed over the years? etc.

- *Understanding*: What were you doing during your favourite times? What were the others doing? Why was it a favourite time? Who helped you to develop these skills and talents? etc.

- *Applying*: Make a diary. Conduct a person search to find out who likes/dislikes the same things as you, etc.

- *Analysing*: Make lists of similarities and differences between yourself and one or two of your friends. Write several 'I can...' statements. Complete 'I learn best when...' etc.

- *Evaluating*: Evaluate your own habits, goals and strategies on several criteria, etc.

- *Creating*: Create a personal development chart. Create your own work schedule from weekly homework. Create personal learning goals and strategies, etc.

(Sellars 2006, p.14)

The programme was designed to offer 'task choices and differentiated strategies to suit each learner's individual strengths and weaknesses' (Sellars 2006, p.4), and self-choosing and self-management of goals were important features.

As a particular focus on intrapersonal intelligence in self-directed learning, the learners were encouraged to set individual learning goals in English, and to negotiate their learning environment to provide them with optimal support to meet those goals (such as timing of activities, types of activities of interest to them, social aspects of the group, etc.).

The learners' progress in their self-knowledge (i.e. intrapersonal intelligence, or metacognitive knowledge of self) was observed through a series of individual interviews, and details of learners' work habits were studied by means of teachers' observations and anecdotal records. Learners also kept journals to record their feelings and responses to the work being undertaken.

The learners had initial difficulty in setting learning goals. One group of eight students was unable to complete the SMART goal contract (independent student setting of a goal, and the strategies and resources needed to achieve it, as outlined above) (McGrath and Noble 2003), and had a modified process whereby they simply wrote a specific goal and discussed the remainder of the planning with an adult, who recorded their plans.

By the conclusion of the study, records showed that all learners had made progress and their work skills had improved. However, five of the learners still needed help, two in sustaining their on-task behaviours and organisational skills, and three in refocusing and reassurance.

The responses to the learner interviews indicated that the learners had 'developed a heightened awareness of the optimum learning conditions for each of them personally', and also indicated that the learners' 'use of strategies and thinking skills were both reflective and evaluative in nature' (Sellars 2006, p.6).

The Multiple Intelligences profiles (McGrath and Noble 2003) were re-administered at the end of the study, and indicated 'a considerable increase in the students' self-knowledge during this time' (Sellars 2006, p.7). From this measure there was statistical evidence to support teachers' observations of 'the increasing incidences of students initiating changes to the learning environment, approaching tasks intelligently, using a variety of strategies to solve difficulties and knowing when to access assistance' (Sellars 2006, p.7).

4. Edward de Bono's creative thinking skill methods

The programmes developed by de Bono are discussed at Tier 2 level because their easily appreciated value for the development of thinking, involving interesting, content-free material, suggests a range of values for learners with shared exceptional needs, and from different cultural contexts. They may have particular value in view of the following:

1. They are unique in their aim to develop creativity, and as such would be a natural choice for learners grouped for enhancement in relation to high ability. Indeed, Adey and Shayer (1994) suggest that the Cognitive Research Trust (CoRT) programme, with this aim, should be expected to show the greatest effect for above-average 14- and 15-year-olds. However, in one description of the programme de Bono (1991) asserts that

    > students' success in using the CoRT Program is not contingent upon their prior knowledge, ability to retain information, or reading or writing skills. In fact, by asking for a set of skills different from those traditionally measured by IQ instruments, CoRT may help teachers identify and cultivate talents that may not otherwise be evident. Therefore, students of varying ages and abilities benefit from CoRT thinking skills, including special-education students, gifted and talented students, at risk youth etc. (de Bono 1991, p.3)

2. The CoRT materials are designed to help learners develop alternative viewpoints, encouraging them to be much less egocentric, to think about other people's viewpoints, and to

develop lateral thinking about difficult everyday situations (as pointed out by McGregor (2007, p.157)) – so this approach may be particularly useful for groups of learners with behaviour, social and emotional difficulties.

The CoRT programme has been used in a variety of cultural contexts, including Singapore, Australia, Canada, Mexico and the USA (de Bono 2000, p.14), suggesting that the materials are accessible in a wide variety of contexts, for culturally different learners. Ritchie and Edwards (1994) report its use with Aboriginal children, and this example is described at the end of this section. This report reminds us that bridging or transfer of learning is very important for such learners. It is particularly important for culturally different learners that the bridging incorporates real-life problem-solving situations suggested by the learners themselves, which are therefore meaningful to them.

In the New Zealand use of the CoRT programme, known to the present author because of her involvement in the evaluation, as described in the previous chapter (Howie, Coombe and Lonergan 1998), interviews with a range of individuals receiving the programme did suggest that particular attention was needed to ensure that the material was made as meaningful as possible for culturally different learners, and that they needed to be encouraged to reflect on the application of the strategies within their own real-life problem-solving situations. For example, one learner of Chinese background, when asked about what she could do with the skills learnt, responded, 'I don't know how to use them.' However, later in the interview she did suggest, in relation to solving one real-life problem, that she could use 'minus and plusses' to address it. She did also mention that the teacher taking CoRT was 'making her think more about it. Not just sit there and listen to it' (an indication of reflective learning, important for learners from diverse cultural backgrounds). She also commented that she did enjoy the thinking skills programme.

Much use of CoRT has been with work-based learners. There is also an interesting use of CoRT in project-based technology instruction, reported by Barak and Doppelt (1999). This approach may be particularly suited to secondary-school pupils in danger of disengagement from the more formal school curriculum, and requiring sound preparation for problem solving in real-life work and social situations.

EXAMPLE FROM PRACTICE IN A SCHOOL SETTING

An example of use of the de Bono CoRT programme with a group of learners from a unique cultural background in Australia is now described. Professor John Edwards has been a leading researcher with de Bono's approaches, and this is a rigorous report of the use of de Bono's CoRT programme with learners from a cultural minority group who may have also experienced socio-economic disadvantage, in Australia. It also demonstrates well the matching of the thinking programme to the strengths and needs of a unique group of learners, and is in line with Vygotsky's concern to affirm the unique thinking skills of learners from a minority group (Ritchie and Edwards 1994).

Ritchie and Edwards note that 'Aboriginal children are one of the most disadvantaged minority groups in our school system' (Ritchie and Edwards 1994, p.242). However, divergent thinking had been found to be a relative strength of such groups, and the researchers sought to use a thinking programme which could build on this divergent or creative learning strength to enhance school success. They chose de Bono's CoRT thinking programme, which promotes divergent/creative thinking. They considered that applying this programme with this group of learners could be promising because it is free from academic content, and John Edwards had previously completed an Australian study of CoRT with learners in the mainstream, which showed that, after only about eight hours of instruction with CoRT, there were significant improvements, not only in originality and flexibility, but in scholastic ability and language achievement. The researchers felt that if this could be achieved with learners of Aboriginal cultural background, 'the habit of academic failure for many Aboriginal children might be broken' (Ritchie and Edwards 1994, p.244).

Six classes from four schools (schools which were classified as disadvantaged) with significant enrolments of learners of Aboriginal background were involved. Forty learners of Aboriginal background formed the study sample, 22 receiving the CoRT programme and 18 not (the control group). The groups had a mean age of 11 years 11 months and 11 years 10 months respectively. The CoRT lessons were taught once a week, following the regular implementation guidance, by classroom teachers.

Prior to the intervention no difference was found between learners from Aboriginal backgrounds and non-Aboriginal backgrounds in divergent learning, strengthening the assumption that underpinned the study.

There were statistically significant treatment group effects for the fluency, flexibility and originality constructs of the Torrance Tests of Creative Thinking (Torrance 1990), indicating the value of the programme for these learners of Aboriginal background, in terms of divergent and creative thinking.

The gains made in association with the CoRT programme on the Otis-Lennon School Ability Test (a measure of scholastic aptitude standardised for Australian children to take into account the ethnic composition of the population) were similar to those reported in John Edward's earlier (1988) study, but there was no statistically significant treatment effect. Also, school achievements for language, mathematics, social science and science, as rated by teachers, showed no significant treatment effects.

Steve Ritchie and John Edwards (1994) affirm in their discussion of these results that using the CoRT programme enhanced the creative production of the learners from Aboriginal backgrounds. They do note that there needs to be a shift from 'low' to 'high' road transfer (i.e. from a more automatic application to similar learning tasks, to more deliberate abstract application to a very different context or task) to enable these learners to generalise the learning from CoRT lessons to reading, writing and arithmetic, and state:

> For many disadvantaged students whose home experiences might be comparatively less similar to formal school learning contexts than mainstream students, incidental transfer may not occur – providing a barrier to future academic success… This means that teachers should purposely design discipline-related lessons which encourage the use of such skills. By setting up opportunities for students to apply general thinking skills to discipline-specific problems, teachers are more likely to provide essential scaffolding or bridging for transfer. (Ritchie and Edwards 1994, p.246)

They also make a plea to teachers to recognise and encourage the creativity of learners from Aboriginal backgrounds across subject disciplines, so that these learners experience success within the formal context of the school classroom.

Approaches which are more related to, or infused with, classroom learning

5. The Lipman 'Philosophy for Children' programme

As noted in Tier 1 coverage, the Philosophy for Children approach has been used for a variety of learners from differing socio-economic backgrounds and differing cultural backgrounds. We need to consider the following points in relation to its use for learners with shared exceptional learning needs at Tier 2:

1. Its progressive complexity, its focus on aspects such as rationality, ethics, science reasoning etc., and its delivery around reading material, may mean that it is a good choice for learners of high ability.

2. It presents problems and dilemmas which are set in the context of the learners' lives, and which can be engaged in as a community of enquiry (Adey and Shayer 1994), so it may be very useful for learners who have experienced behavioural, emotional and/or social difficulties, or who are preparing for real-life problem-solving in the work situation.

    •   There is a particular focus on how to develop not only critical and creative thinking, but also caring thinking while using the philosophical tasks. Lipmanz suggests that social good may arise from the approach, including a reduction of violence in society (Lipman 2003; McGregor 2007). A review of research studies on this programme found among the positive outcomes improvements in listening and talking skills, confidence levels, appreciation of another's viewpoint, and reduction in angry behaviour, all of particular relevance to this shared needs focus (Trickey and Topping 2004).

    •   Another review of research with this programme noted that it did appear to be motivating, and to lead to widespread gains in verbal tests of critical thinking, but the reviewers also mention the importance of the role of the trained teacher in delivering this programme, and this would apply particularly when delivering it to learners in danger of disengagement from the formal school curriculum (Sternberg and Bhana 1996).

- Gains on critical thinking and inference for a small group of learners with learning difficulties and emotional difficulties were found in an early study by Simon (1979).

Several early studies with learners of mixed ethnic background gave evidence of gains, the first two in reasoning, and the last in reading comprehension, after only short periods with the programme, as follows: Lipman's (1970) US study with white and black learners; Shipman's (1978) study with public-school learners of mixed ethnic and socio-economic backgrounds; and Haas' (1975) US study with white, black and Hispanic learners from low socio-economic areas (see also Howie 2003, p.150). Lipman reported in a published interview (Fisher 2004) that new materials for the Philosophy for Children approach have been developed in countries as culturally diverse as Taiwan, Korea, Ukraine and Iceland. There is a summary of recent research in the UK, Hawaii, and Iceland contexts by Lipman (2002). A detailed description of the use of Philosophy for Children in South Africa is presented by Green (2008). She notes that the programme is attractive because it can incorporate aspects of moral and citizenship education, as well as mediating thinking. Stories have been developed which are meaningful for that context, and for the National Curriculum Statement. (Further details of this work in South Africa are given below, as an example of using the programme with learners from culturally unique shared backgrounds.)

It is essential when using Philosophy for Children with learners from differing cultural backgrounds to work with material that is meaningful and valued by them.

In New Zealand, this programme has been applied with a wide range of learners, in terms of age and socio-economic background, as reported by Howie (2003). Dr Kovack, a leader in the use of Philosophy for Children in New Zealand, reported that experimental use of this programme with young adults who had intellectual disabilities had proved to be a real challenge. The work in New Zealand is supported by strong training opportunities through the New Zealand Philosophy for Children Association, and a volume of philosophical support material to go with stories from the *School Journal* has been published (Olley 2000).

EXAMPLE FROM PRACTICE IN A SCHOOL SETTING

We have a valuable description of the use of Philosophy for Children in South Africa, and particularly with teachers and children from the

'Colored' community, by Lena Green (2008), Professor of Educational Psychology at the University of the Western Cape, South Africa.

She introduces the report with a careful discussion of the classroom community of enquiry, stating that 'A community of enquiry is characterised by respect for persons, for truth, and for the procedures of enquiry' (Green 2008, p.140). She also notes that Lipman, like Vygotsky, emphasises in Philosophy for Children the developmental importance of a shared social context and the centrality of language. Green considers that the program is valuable because

> it combines the development of concepts (thus being able to incorporate aspects of moral or citizenship education) with the mediation of desirable thinking practices. It recognises the social nature of knowledge construction and acknowledges the creativity of both children and teachers. (Green 2008, p.147)

After an initial 'Stories for Thinking' project funded by the Western Cape Province in 1999 (Green, Faragher, and Faasen 2000), which was a relatively short intervention, a project was developed with all teachers in one primary school for a more in-depth development of the Philosophy for Children approach. Teachers worked together as a community of enquiry to produce stories and manuals for the programme which reflected the conditions in local schools and were designed to take account of the National Curriculum Statement. The stories, therefore, had local and cultural relevance, and the teachers also felt a sense of ownership of them, and motivation to use them.

The teachers were free to choose when and how to introduce the new ideas involved in the programme. Green reports:

> according to the teachers...the children do acquire some of the characteristics valued in a community of enquiry. They become more respectful of each other and appreciate the structure provided by negotiated ground rules. They become more reflective. Their responses are more thoughtful and less impulsive. They begin to develop sensitivity towards areas of agreement and disagreement and to appreciate the need to offer and examine reasons. (Green 2008, p.149)

Perhaps the most important outcome noted by the teachers in this example is the way it encouraged learners to have a voice. Green notes:

> by far the most frequent and significant change noted by teachers was in the children's willingness to own and express opinions. This necessary

precondition for thinking and learning cannot be taken for granted in South African classrooms. The country's history of oppression and authoritarian educational practices has had a pervasive effect on the self-concept of individuals and of entire communities, something that still shows itself in certain social norms. Adult teachers who themselves were deprived of the right to speak are still discovering how to make this possible for the children in their care. As one teacher said '[this is] a challenge to our community to express themselves. This is the hardest thing that the so-called "Colored" community is faced with – not speaking up…living under the former repressive regime gave impetus.' (Green 2008, p.149)

Green sees the programme as a non-threatening way of mediating the teaching of thinking to teachers so that they begin to see themselves as thinkers and connect this understanding to their professional roles as mediators of thinking.

6. Swartz and Parks: an infused approach

Chapter 4, Section 11 covered this approach at Tier 1 in detail, including both the initial approach, as developed by Swartz and Parks, and the Activating Children's Thinking (ACTS) approach by McGuinness, which was modelled on that. It is now discussed at Tier 2, as it has a number of features that make it relevant to work with smaller groups of learners with exceptional shared needs.

1.   Metacognitive self-regulation is important for such learners, especially those experiencing social, emotional and behavioural difficulties. Two key strands in metacognition, knowledge about thinking and self-regulation were identified by Professor Carol McGuinness in her presentation at the Harrogate International Conference on Thinking (McGuinness 2002). She asserted that there was research backing for the belief that improvements in metacognition can compensate for 'low aptitude' and act as a lever for cognitive development. Some of the ingredients of her ACTS programme would appear to be particularly suited to learners with 'low aptitude' – for example, developing vocabulary for talking about thinking, using thinking diagrams, and making links and connections (transfer). As an example of self-regulation in classroom dialogue, McGuinness presented a transcript of a video in which learners were discussing decision

making, critiquing their own thinking method, and discussing the degree of prompting and scaffolding they needed. However, as noted in the report on the evaluation of Activating Children's Thinking (ACTS) at Tier 1 in Northern Ireland (see Chapter 4, Section 11), such work with learners of lower ability requires careful support, and learners of lower ability in the study did not achieve the same positive outcomes as the learners of higher ability (McGuinness *et al.* 2005). McGuinness (2006) notes that 'particular attention should be paid to children with poorer cognitive and social resources' (p.1).

2. In line with our concern to link the teaching of thinking to high-quality subject teaching, McGregor (2007) states, in discussing the approach developed by Swartz and Parks (1994), 'the aim of infusion in the critical and creative thinking approach is to improve student thinking *and* [italics hers] enhance content learning' (p.128). This may be a strength for some groups of learners who require both the development of metacognitive skills and enrichment of the curriculum, with transfer of the thinking skills being taught to meaningful curriculum content. Both the vertical (throughout years) and horizontal (throughout subject areas) integration of the approach can be developed, and this should contribute to lasting curriculum reform, as argued by Swartz, Fischer and Parks (1998).

Of particular interest is the wide range of graphic organisers (called thinking diagrams by McGuinness) which have been developed by Swartz and Parks (1994) to support each of the thinking skills. These are seen as focusing on and clarifying the thinking steps to reach a solution. (They are described well in McGregor (2007)). One would expect such visual support to be of particular interest and value to learners with strength in visual intelligence (according to Gardner), and/or with a learning style which prefers learning through this modality.

Teachers' beliefs and professional development appear to be important components in successful use of this approach, including for learners with lower ability. Professional development is included as a very important feature of the ACTS programme. We can see the importance of professional development for influencing teacher beliefs and attitudes in relation to an intervention in a UK study involving an infusion of critical thinking approach, discussed by Baumfield, Hall and Wall (2008). Details of the approach are not given, but two Year 6 classes were involved, the teacher in one using the infusion programme, and the teacher in the other (i.e. the control class) not. Although the writers use this example to caution care in interpreting the compared outcomes, they do point out that the infusion programme raised the scores of all the learners involved (presumably standardised achievement scores) 'although the range suggests that the effect is variable and some children get more out of it than others' (p.106). However, this class was already scoring higher than the control class on the outcome measure prior to intervention, suggesting that the teacher had been using critical thinking skills in her teaching already, and that there may well have been a cumulative effect in the gains made by this class, leading to the later significant advantage to the 'infusion of critical thinking' group. The very brief report raises the importance of teachers' beliefs and attitudes in the choice of this intervention: 'it suits her beliefs and the way she likes to work with children' (p.106).

The infusion approach by Swartz and Parks is widely used internationally. Also, there is increasing international use of McGuinness' ACTS programme. It is used in Wales, with teachers trained bilingually in its use, and in Thailand (McGuinness 2008). In Thailand, schools like the Prathomsuksa Thammasat School (see www.pts.ac.th/thinking. html) have involved all of their teachers in a training seminar 'Activating Children's Thinking Skills'.

One aspect that needs thinking about is how well tools such as graphic organisers (thinking diagrams) reflect the unique thinking strengths and values of each cultural group involved. The present writer found it difficult to locate a study using either the approach of Swartz and Parks, or that of McGuinness, that reflected in depth on how to match the approach to the unique cultural needs of the population. Carol McGuinness, who developed ACTS within Northern Ireland, with its great creative poetry tradition, commented in her presentation to the Harrogate International Conference on Thinking (McGuinness 2002), on her use of the thinking diagrams, noting the particular value of the 'brainstorming' diagram, which allowed for creative combining of ideas. This tool may be of particular value for learners from cultural groups who have this ability as a strength.

EXAMPLE

Swartz has discussed how to cater for the needs of learners who have particular difficulties within an inclusive classroom, when using this approach (Swartz, Kiser and Reagan 1999), and an account of this has been given by Martin (2001) as follows:

> Swartz and Reagan underscore the usefulness of 'streamlining' in which a teacher diagnoses the degree of complexity and abstraction that special students can be expected to achieve and simplifies the thinking tasks as needed, while still involving all students in the tasks. Here the teacher develops a repertoire of techniques for each thinking task in a lesson and includes a range of tasks of varying difficulties, tailored to the individual student in ways that complement each other while demanding quality thinking on the part of each student participating. (p.214)

We could consider this to be use of a 'differentiation of tasks' approach within an ordinary classroom, to meet the shared exceptional needs of learners (a practice already common internationally).

We need to remember that in applying differentiation it is important to move each learner to the highest level of abstraction possible, without under-expectation.

Approaches with a strong emotional or motivational focus

7. Goleman's Emotional Intelligence

Chapter 4 covered this approach with reference to Tier 1. At Tier 2 as well, it has clear whole-school applications for all learners, and is also an approach which is applicable to groups of learners with shared exceptional needs, as discussed in the following:

1. Learners with behavioural, emotional and social difficulties would clearly benefit from intensive work on some of the skills involved in such programmes for developing emotional intelligence, such as the W.T. Grant Consortium Programme (Goleman 1995/6), addressing self-talk (to cope with challenging behaviours), and using steps for problem solving, decision making (including controlling impulses, setting goals, and anticipating consequences), understanding the perspectives of others, and developing a positive attitude to life.

2.   The material developed in the UK for addressing the social and emotional aspects of learning (SEAL) (DfES 2005), as discussed with reference to Tier 1, is clearly suitable not only for whole-school approaches, but also for particular groups of learners, such as those in a separate unit or other provision for learners with behavioural, emotional and social difficulties. The material presents a number of ways of addressing each of the key aspects of emotional intelligence (i.e. perceiving and identifying emotions, assimilating emotions, understanding emotions, and managing emotions) in an infused way – that is, through the whole of the school curriculum and procedures.

Goleman has developed his own programme for use in the work situation. It involves identifying emotional issues in the workplace, deciding to bring about change, and group work with feedback to bring about change. This 'Mastering Emotional Intelligence Programme' (reviewed by Stys and Brown (2004) would clearly be applicable for work with older learners in work placement situations.

In writing about emotional competence, which he defines as 'a learned capability based on emotional intelligence that results in outstanding performance at work' (1998, p.24) Goleman assures the reader that we each have a unique emotional competence profile with its individual pattern of strengths and limits, and that it is possible to achieve outstanding performance with strengths in only some of these competency areas. (Groups of competencies match the emotional intelligences, as he outlines them.) This indicates that focusing on the strengths of all learners, including those with special educational needs, can be a very inclusive approach. For groups of learners who share a learning need in the area of social competence (such as those diagnosed as on the Autistic Spectrum, who may, for example, have difficulty in empathising with others) we need to consider the pattern of each individual's unique profile, affirming and utilising the strengths, while building up areas of weakness.

AN EXAMPLE FROM PRACTICE IN A SCHOOL SETTING

As an example of using Goleman's ideas with learners with shared exceptional learning needs, a study with older adolescents and young adults with learning and emotional difficulties in an Auckland sheltered workshop setting was carried out by the present writer (Howie 2003a,

2003b). This work, which focused on the assessment and teaching of real-life problem-solving behaviours, and in particular, self-advocacy skills, could be considered to be in line with Goleman's approach to enhancement of emotional intelligence. It focused particularly on perceiving emotions, and assimilating and understanding emotions, in its work on information gathering in problem solving; and on managing emotions in its work on developing strategies for problem solving and self-advocacy.

In particular, work in the assessment part of the project focused on the understanding of self as a learner, along with the emotions involved. Learners were shown both open-ended question forms and cartoon forms of each self-advocacy dilemma, and among the questions asked in relation to each situation were the following:

- 'What should your attitude towards yourself be?' (tapping into metacognitive emotional/affective aspects and attribution aspects). The cartoon cards depicted possible choices on the dimensions of effort attribution, strategy attribution and internal or external attribution.

- 'What sort of feelings is it best to have?'

In the full intervention training, the work on perceiving, assimilating and understanding emotions was carried out with each example discussed (including real-life problem solving and self-advocacy examples brought by the young people themselves, from their own experience). Each example was described and discussed with the help of a standard form that covered the key aspects involved (including the emotive/affective aspects), using the following questions:

- 'What did you feel when that happened?'
- 'What did you say to yourself when that happened?'(tapping into private speech, as advocated in one of the programmes cited by Goleman).

Some of the learners had difficulty in identifying and describing their feelings precisely, using broad terms such as 'good feelings' and 'positive feelings' in response to the assessment question 'What sort of feelings is it best to have?' This appeared to limit their ability to discriminate and judge feelings that would be appropriate in solution planning.

The researcher used as an extra resource the 'Illustrations' instrument from Feuerstein's Instrumental Enrichment programme, which is a set of cartoons depicting novel real-life problem-solving situations. Learners were encouraged to add 'speech thoughts' as 'speech bubbles' concerning what the key players in the illustration were saying to themselves about feelings. This helped in both discrimination and labelling of feelings, and in identification of helpful and unhelpful feelings.

Managing emotions was dealt with as part of the actual real-life problem solving. Even learners who had mastered earlier work on identifying and labelling helpful feelings found it difficult to apply this learning to new real-life examples of problem solving and decision making, even when they brought the example from their own experience. Through modelling and role play, the learners were taught and encouraged to express their own feelings positively in giving reasons for a self-advocacy request. If this failed, they were taught to talk about the rights involved (which had formed part of the content of the training).

Even some of the learners who were more able in self-advocacy found it difficult to respond positively and effectively if the person they were addressing gave a negative response. The young people were supported in exploring and working on their feelings in such a situation. However, more time and considerable practice in working on self-monitoring and self-reinforcement would have been useful to encourage them to produce helpful rather than unhelpful thoughts about themselves, particularly when they encountered initial failure in the self-advocacy process. These young people often demonstrated long-term and habitual negative self-statements which were readily replayed in new and possibly unexpected challenges, or when self-advocacy was not initially successful.

In confirmation of Goleman's claims concerning the importance of emotional intelligence, it can be said that for these young people it was the motivational and emotional aspects of real-life problem solving and self-advocacy that were more difficult to shift, and which required more attention, than the more cognitive aspects.

8. Meichenbaum's cognitive-behavioural approach to the teaching of thinking

This approach is covered only at Tier 2 because it is best suited to small group or individual work, and the research on it has tended to be conducted in such contexts.

It is also covered in this section because an underlying principle of the approach is that learners' expectations and appraisals as to what will happen in a problem situation are important cognitive factors in how they behave in addressing or solving the problem. Work is done to alter self-talk with:

- positive appraisals (perceiving the situation in a positive way)
- ongoing self-talk to manage a pre-prepared set of steps to solve a problem or manage a behaviour
- positive post-event attributions (attributing success or failure to causes in a positive way).

It is included in this section on approaches with a strong emotional or motivational focus because its main use has been with learners with difficulties in managing their own emotions and behaviours.

The approach combines a talk-aloud self-instruction process which utilises a problem-solving set of steps much like that outlined in Sternberg's problem-solving cycle at Tier 1 (see Chapter 4, Section 3). For example, a set of self-instructions to self-regulate on task behaviours could be as follows:

1. 'Let's see, what am I supposed to do?' (problem definition)

2. 'I have to look at all the possibilities.' (problem approach and plan)

3. 'I'd better concentrate and focus in, and think only of what I'm doing right now.' (focusing of attention)

4. 'I am meant to be choosing only one.' (self-guiding while performing the task)

5. 'Great! I did a really good job.' (self-evaluation and self-reinforcement) or 'Oh, I made a mistake. Don't worry. Next time I'll try to go slower and concentrate more and maybe I'll get the right answer.' (coping statement)

(adapted from Kendall and Braswell 1993, p.124)

These steps are developed and taught to learners by modelling a regulative speech process, which uses the same three processes as Vygotsky's social, egocentric and private speech. First, the procedures for self-instruction, once agreed with the learners, are modelled aloud by the teacher while the teacher is solving the problem; then whispered; and finally just demonstrated, with the self-instruction as covert (spoken to self, as inner speech or thought). Learners are then asked to copy the modelling of each of the three speech procedures while solving the problem. This allows for internalisation of the regulative process. This approach has been demonstrated as particularly valuable for the following groups of learners sharing exceptional needs:

1. Learners with Attention Deficit Hyperactivity Disorder (ADHD). Considerable work with individuals with these difficulties is reported by Meichenbaum and his research associates (Meichenbaum 1985). Programmes for learners grouped for such needs have incorporated the teaching of talk-aloud strategies for managing emotions and behaviours on a group basis. It becomes like a group plan for managing classroom behaviour. There can be reframing of self-talk with individual members of the class modelling appropriate self-guiding statements to manage a behaviour, which is reinforced when back in the classroom – as suggested by Rogers (1994).

2. Pupils with behavioural, social and emotional difficulties. This approach is widely used in anger management, as outlined by Novaco (1979). An example of the kind of self-instructions used by a learner to manage their behaviour would be as follows:

    a. 'This could be a rough situation, but I know how to deal with it.' (preparing for provocation)

    b. 'There's no point in getting mad. Think of what you have to do.' (impact and confrontation)

    c. 'My muscles are getting tight. Relax and slow things down.' (coping with arousal)

    d. 'Don't take it personally. It's probably not so serious.' (conflict unresolved)

    e. 'I handled that one pretty well. That's doing a good job.' (conflict resolved).

3. Learners with shared difficulties in the processes involved in reading, writing and mathematics. The approach could be developed on a group basis. Research in New Zealand has shown the value of such an approach in reading and mathematics for learners (Cameron and Robinson 1980, and James 1980). Howie supervised a dissertation in Hull on the enhancement of control of writing processes using Meichenbaum's procedures, which was very successful (involving a whole classroom intervention)

(Thompson 2003). (See the Tier 1 example for Vygotsky in Chapter 4, Section 1 for a coverage of this work.)

4. A programme has been provided aimed at metacognitive self-regulation for learners with language difficulties who require visual support, by Camp and Bash (1985). Cards depicting a bear using a series of problem-solving self-instructions, with the private speech in 'speech bubbles', are provided.

A whole chapter on cognitive-based approaches which include self-instruction training particularly for learners who are aggressive, and for increasing the self-management of learners who have more severe disabilities, so that they can become more self-reliant, is presented by Shapiro and Cole (1994).

A think-aloud technique to address assessment, intervention and consultation needs has been used by Ward and Traweek (1993).

It is important that the mediator of this approach works in partnership with the learners to develop self-instruction statements and processes that are appropriate to the learners' own language use and cultural values (Kendall and Braswell 1993). This is particularly the case when working with learners from different cultural backgrounds.

EXAMPLE FROM PRACTICE IN A SCHOOL SETTING

This self-instruction approach was used by John Thickpenny with two groups of high-achieving and able learners in an Auckland learning enrichment study, as part of the real-life problem-solving processes being taught. (See Howie 2003 for details of this project.) The aim was to help the learners gain greater control over their thinking, and an example of the procedures from the tape used is given in Howie (2003). Part of this example is reproduced below, as the self-regulative statements are modelled to the learners by John Thickpenny:

'I am going to think aloud while following the steps for problem solution which I have given you.

The first step I must take is to examine all of the information to get some idea of what the problem is all about...[demonstrates]. I've tried to stop guessing what it is about but have looked at all of the information carefully.

Now I need to look at all of this information again and consider if it is relevant...[demonstrates].

The next step is to see if there is any missing information. I look over all of the information and see if there is anything that is missed out. Are there any sets of information that I still need to know?

...Finally, I make a clear statement on what I have to do, including all of the relevant information.' (Howie 2003, p.113)

(This work focused on the information-gathering part of the project.)

The learners were taught about overt and covert self-instruction, and asked to work through problems given to them, when they were at home, first talking aloud overtly with a tape recorder, friends or a family member, then covertly, to themselves, following guidelines given.

The tasks for which the groups involved in these procedures showed clear gains included 'Picture interpretation', where the pictures depicted problems – which suggests that the enrichment programme was indeed increasing creativity in real-life problem-solving skills.

The learners were interviewed at the end of the enrichment programme, and in the report on these interviews it is noted that

> [students] found it enjoyable, interesting and useful. Many commented that they used the problem-solving techniques in real-life situations (e.g. at home, with personal relationships, with thinking about their future plans, with school work). Several commented that they felt they were better organised, or doing better at school, enjoying school work more. (Howie 2003, p.117)

Self-reflective questions

☐ Within your own school community, what are the key issues for the teaching of thinking at Tier 2?

☐ Which of the approaches covered at Tier 2 might best meet the exceptional and shared learning needs of small groups of learners in your school community, and why?

☐ How would these approaches need to be implemented and evaluated to meet the specific exceptional and shared needs identified in these groups of learners?

References
Introduction

Feuerstein, R., Rand, Y. and Hoffman, M.B. (1979) *The Dynamic Assessment of Retarded Performers: The Learning Potential Assessment Device: Theory, Instruments and Techniques.* Baltimore, MD: University Park Press.

Feuerstein, R., Feuerstein, Ra.S., Falik, L.H. and Rand, Y. (2002) *The Dynamic Assessment of Cognitive Modifiability: The Learning Propensity Assessment Device–Theory, Instruments and Techniques.* Jerusalem: International Centre for the Enhancement of Learning Potential.

Gipps, C. (2005) *A Framework for Educational Assessment.* London: Falmer.

Hatch, T. and Gardner, H. (2001) 'If Binet Had Looked Beyond the Classroom: The Assessment of Multiple Intelligences.' In B. Torff (ed.) *Multiple Intelligences and Assessment.* Palatine, IL: Skylight.

Howie, D. (2003) *Thinking about the Teaching of Thinking.* Wellington: New Zealand Council for Educational Research.

Howie, D.R., Thickpenny, J.P., Leaf, C.A. and Absolum, M.A. (1985) 'The piloting of 'Instrumental Enrichment' in New Zealand with eight mildly retarded children.' *Australia and New Zealand Journal of Developmental Disabilities 11*, 1, 3–16.

Lidz, C.S. and Macrine, S.L. (2001) 'An alternative approach to the identification of culturally and linguistically diverse learners: The contribution of dynamic assessment.' *School Psychology International 22*, 1, 74–96.

Sternberg, R.J. (1985) *Beyond I.Q.: A Triarchic Theory of Human Intelligence.* New York: Cambridge University Press.

Vygotsky, L.S. (1978) *Mind in Society: The Development of Higher Psychological Processes.* Cambridge, MA: Harvard University Press.

Vygotsky, L. (1986) *Thought and Language* (revised by Kozulin). Cambridge, MA: Harvard University Press.

Vygotsky

Das, J.P. and Kendrick, M. (1997) 'PASS Reading Enhancement Program: A short manual for teachers.' *Journal of Cognitive Education 5*, 3, 193–208.

Gupta, R.M. and Coxhead, P. (eds) (1988) *Cultural Diversity and Learning Efficiency.* London: Macmillan Press.

Haywood, H.C., Brooks, P.H. and Burns, S. (1992) *Bright Start: Cognitive Curriculum for Young Children.* Watertown, MA: Charlesbridge Publishers.

Haywood, H.C. and Lidz, C.S. (2007) *Dynamic Assessment in Practice: Clinical and Educational Applications.* New York: Cambridge University Press.

Howie, D.R. (2003a) *Thinking about the Teaching of Thinking.* Wellington: New Zealand Council for Educational Research.

Howie, D.R. (2003b) 'The assessment and training of decision-making and self-advocacy skills.' *Journal of Cognitive Education and Psychology 3*, 1, 1–26.

Kozulin, A. (1998) *Psychological Tools: A Socio-cultural Approach to Education.* Cambridge, MA: Harvard University Press.

Kozulin, A. and Gindis, B. (2007) 'Sociocultural Theory and Education of Children with Special Needs.' In H. Daniels, J. Wertsch and M. Cole (eds) *The Cambridge Companion to Vygotsky.* New York: Cambridge University Press.

Lidz, C.S. (2000) 'The Application of Cognitive Functions Scale (ACFS): An Example of Curriculum-based Dynamic Assessment.' In C.S. Lidz and J.G. Elliott (eds) *Dynamic Assessment: Prevailing Models and Applications.* Amsterdam: Elsevier Science.

Robson, S. and Lin, M. (2002) 'Thinking skills interventions and young people with disabilities in China.' *International Journal of Learning 9*, 1, 447–459.

Rogoff, B. (1990) *Apprenticeship in Thinking: Cognitive Development in Social Context.* Oxford: Oxford University Press.

Rogoff, B. (2003) *The Cultural Nature of Human Development.* Oxford: Oxford University Press.

Sutton, A. (1988) 'L.S. Vygotskii: The Cultural-Historical Theory, National Minorities and the Zone of Next Development.' In R.M. Gupta and P. Coxhead (eds) *Cultural Diversity and Learning Efficiency.* London: Macmillan.

Vygotsky, L.S. (1978) *Mind in Society: The Development of Higher Psychological Processes.* Cambridge, MA: Harvard University Press.

Vygotsky, L. (1986) *Thought and Language* (revised by Kozulin). Cambridge, MA: Harvard University Press.

Wood, D., Bruner, J.S. and Ross, G. (1976) 'The role of tutoring in problem solving.' *Journal of Child Psychology and Psychiatry 17*, 2, 89–100.

Wood, D. and Wood, H. (1996) 'Vygotsky, tutoring and learning.' *Oxford Review of Education 22*, 1, 5–16.

Feuerstein

Feuerstein, R., Rand, Y. and Hoffman, M.B. (1979) *The Dynamic Assessment of Retarded Performers: The Learning Potential Assessment Device: Theory, Instruments and Techniques.* Baltimore, MD: University Park Press.

Feuerstein, R., Feuerstein, Ra.S., Falik, L.H. and Rand, Y. (2002) *The Dynamic Assessment of Cognitive Functions: The Learning Propensity Assessment Device, Theory, Instruments, Techniques.* Jerusalem: International Centre for the Enhancement of Learning Potential.

Feuerstein, R., Feuerstein, Ra.S., Falik, L.H. and Rand, Y. (2006) *Creating and Enhancing Cognitive Modifiability: The Feuerstein Instrumental Enrichment Program.* Jerusalem: International Centre for the Enhancement of Learning Potential.

Head, G. and O'Neill, W. (1999) 'Introducing Feuerstein's Instrumental Enrichment in a school for children with social, emotional and behavioural difficulties.' *Support for Learning 14*, 3, 122–128.

Howie, D.R. (2003a) *Thinking about the Teaching of Thinking.* Wellington: New Zealand Council for Educational Research.

Howie, D.R. (2003b) 'The assessment and training of decision-making and self-advocacy skills.' *Journal of Cognitive Education and Psychology 3*, 1, 1–26.

Howie, D.R. (2005) 'Early learning and mediation.' Paper presented to the 10th International Conference of the Association for Cognitive Education and Psychology, Durham, July 2005.

Howie, D., Richards, R. and Pirihi, H. (1993) 'Teaching thinking skills to Maori adolescents.' *International Journal of Cognitive Education and Mediated Learning 3*, 2, 70–91.

Howie, D.R., Thickpenny, J.P., Leaf, C.A. and Absolum, M.A. (1985) 'The piloting of 'Instrumental Enrichment' in New Zealand with eight mildly retarded children.' *Australia and New Zealand Journal of Developmental Disabilities 11*, 1, 3–16.

Kaniel, S. and Feuerstein, R. (1989) 'Special needs of children with learning difficulties.' *Oxford Review of Education 15*, 2, 165–179.

Kaniel, S. and Reichenberg, R. (1993) 'Dynamic Assessment and Cognitive Programs for Disadvantaged Gifted Children.' In B. Wallace and H. Adams (eds) *Worldwide Perspectives on the Gifted Disadvantaged.* London: Academic Press.

Kinard, J.T. and Kozulin, A. (2008) *Rigorous Mathematical Thinking: Conceptual Formation in the Mathematics Classroom.* Cambridge, MA: Cambridge University Press.

Klein, P.S. (2000) 'A developmental mediation approach to early intervention: Mediational Intervention for Sensitising Caregivers (MISC).' *Educational and Child Psychology 17,* 3, 19–31.

Kozulin, A. (2000) 'The Diversity of Instrumental Enrichment Applications.' In A. Kozulin and Y. Rand (eds) *Experience of Mediated Learning: An Impact of Feuerstein's Theory in Education and Psychology.* London: Pergamon.

Mehl, M.C. (1991) 'Mediated Learning Experience at University Level: A Case Study.' In R. Feuerstein, P.S. Klein and A.J. Tannenbaum (eds) *Mediated Learning Experience (MLE): Theoretical, Psychological and Learning Implications.* London: Freund.

Metge, J. (1984) 'Culture and Learning: Education for a Multi-cultural Society.' In J. Metge (ed.) *Learning and Teaching: He Tikana Maori.* Wellington: Department of Education (based on Metge, J. (1983) *Learning and Teaching. He Tikinga Maori Report on Research carried out as Captain James Cook Fellow 1981–83.*Wellington: Maori and Islands Division, The Royal Society of New Zealand).

O'Hanlon, K. (2011) Personal communication. 'Changing children's minds: Instrumental Enrichment.' A thinking skills programme research report, 2004–2009.

Sharron, H. and Coulter, M. (1994) *Changing Children's Minds: Feuerstein's Revolution in the Teaching of Intelligence.* Birmingham: Sharron Publishing Company.

Skuy, M., Mentis, M., Nkwe, I., Arnott, A. and Hickson, J. (1990) 'Combining Instrumental Enrichment and creativity/socioemotional development for disadvantaged gifted adolescents in Soweto.' *International Journal of Cognitive Education and Mediated Learning 1,* 2, 25–31 (Part 1) and 93–102 (Part 2).

Sternberg, R.J. (1985) 'Instrumental and Componential Approaches to the Nature and Training of Intelligence.' In S.F. Chipman, J.W. Segal and R. Glaser (eds) *Thinking and Learning Skills Vol. 2: Research and Open Questions.* Hillsdale, NJ: Erlbaum.

Tzuriel, D. and Feuerstein, R. (1992) 'Dynamic Group Assessment for Prescriptive Teaching: Differential Aspects of Treatments.' In H.C. Haywood and D. Tzuriel (eds) *Interactive Assessment.* New York: Springer-Verlag.

Gardner's Multiple Intelligences

Campbell, L., Campbell, B. and Dickinson, D. (2004) *Teaching and Learning through Multiple Intelligences* (3rd edition). Boston, MA: Allyn and Bacon, Inc.

Chen, J. and Gardner, H. (2001) 'Alternative Assessment from a Multiple Intelligences Perspective.' In B. Torff (ed.) *Multiple Intelligences and Assessment.* Palatine, IL: Skylight.

Davies, R. (2004) 'What are the effects of using MI theory on the teaching and learning of history in an English secondary school?' Unpublished MA thesis, University of Hull, UK.

Gardner, H. (1983) *Frames of Mind: The Theory of Multiple Intelligences.* New York: Basic Books.

Gardner, H. (1993a) *Multiple Intelligences: The Theory in Practice.* New York: Basic Books.

Gardner, H. (1993b) *The Unschooled Mind: How Children Think and How Schools Should Teach.* London: Fontana Press.

Hatch, T. and Gardner, H. (2001) 'If Binet Had Looked Beyond the Classroom: The Assessment of Multiple Intelligences.' In B. Torff (ed.) *Multiple Intelligences and Assessment.* Palatine, IL: Skylight.

Kornhaber, M., Fierros, E. and Veenema, S. (2004) *Multiple Intelligences: Best Ideas from Research and Practice.* USA, NJ: Pearson Education Inc.

Lazear, D. (2004) *Multiple Intelligences: Approaches to Assessment.* Carmarthen: Crown House Publishing.

McGrath, H. and Noble, T. (2003) *Bounce Back! Classroom Resiliency Program.* Sydney: Pearson Education.

McGrath, H. and Noble, T. (2005) *Seven Ways at Once: Classroom Strategies based on the Seven Intelligences – Book 1.* Melbourne: Longman Australia.

Sellars, M. (2006) 'The role of intrapersonal intelligence in self-directed learning.' *Issues in Educational Research 16,* 95–115. Available at www.iier.org.au/iier16/sellars.html, accessed on 23 April 2007.

Shearer, C.B. (2005) 'Enhancing Cognitive Functions via a Multiple Intelligences Assessment.' In O. Tan and A. Seng (eds) *Enhancing Cognitive Functions: Applications Across Contexts.* Singapore: McGraw Hill.

de Bono

Adey, P. and Shayer, M. (1994) *Really Raising Standards: Cognitive Intervention and Academic Achievement.* London: Routledge.

Barak, M. and Doppelt, Y. (1999) 'Integrating the Cognitive Research Trust (CoRT) Programme for creative thinking into a project-based technology curriculum.' *Research in Science and Technology Education 17,* 2, 139–151.

de Bono, E. (1991) *The CoRT Thinking Programme.* Columbus, OH: SRA Macmillan/McGraw Hill.

de Bono, E. (2000) *De Bono's Thinking Course* (revised). London: BBC Worldwide Publishing.

Edwards, J. (1998) 'The direct teaching of thinking skills: CoRT-1, an evaluative case study.' Unpublished PhD thesis, James Cook University, Queensland, Australia.

Howie, D.R., Coombe, P. and Lonergan, J. (1998) 'Using single subject research design in an Auckland study of the CoRT thinking skill programme.' Paper presented to Conference on Teaching for Successful Intelligence, Auckland.

McGregor, D. (2007) *Developing Thinking, Developing Learning: A Guide to Thinking Skills in Education.* Maidenhead: McGraw Hill/Open University Press.

Ritchie, S.M. and Edwards, J. (1994) 'Creative thinking instruction for Aboriginal children.' *Learning and Instruction 6,* 1, 59–75.

Torrance, E.P. (1990) *Manual for Scoring and Interpreting Results. Torrance Tests of Creative Thinking. Verbal, Forms A and B.* Bensenville, IL: Scholastic testing Service.

Lipman's Philosophy for Children.

Adey, P. and Shayer, M. (1994) *Cognitive Intervention and Academic Achievement.* London: Routledge.

Fisher, R. (2004) 'Philosophy for Children: Simple gifts.' (Interview with Lipman) *Teaching Thinking and Creativity,* Winter 2004, 42–47.

Green, L. (2008) 'Cognitive Modifiability in South African Classrooms: The Stories for Thinking Project.' In O. Tan and A. Seng (eds) *Cognitive Modifiability in Learning and Assessment: International Perspectives.* Singapore: Cengage Learning.

Green, L., Faragher, L. and Faasen, N. (2000) *Cognition in Curriculum 2005 Project Report.* Cape Town: Western Cape Education Department.

Haas, H.J. (1975) *Philosophical Thinking in the Elementary Schools: An Evaluation of the Educational Program, Philosophy for Children.* Report prepared for the National Endowment for the Humanities, Rutgers University, Institute for Cognitive Studies, New Jersey.

Howie, D.R. (2003) *Thinking about the Teaching of Thinking.* Wellington: New Zealand Council for Educational Research.

Lipman, M. (1970) *Philosophy for Children.* Montclair, NJ: Institute for Advancement of Philosophy for Children.

Lipman, M. (2002) *Philosophy for Children: A Systematic Review.* Research Papers. Available at www. montclair.edu/pages/iapc/experimentalinfo.html, accessed on 16 May 2011.

Lipman, M. (2003) *Thinking in Education* (2nd edition). Cambridge: Cambridge University Press.

McGregor, D. (2007) *Developing Thinking Developing Learning: A Guide to Thinking Skills in Education.* London: Open University Press/McGraw Hill.

Olley, A. (2000) *Thinking About… A Guide to Thoughtful Discussion.* Invercargill: Essential Resources.

Shipman, V.C. (1978) 'Evaluation replication of the Philosophy for Children program: Final Report.' *Thinking: The Journal of Philosophy for Children 5*, 2, 28–35.

Simon, C. (1979) 'Philosophy for students with learning disabilities.' *Thinking: The Journal of Philosophy for Children 1*, 1, 21–34.

Sternberg, R. and Bhana, K. (1996) 'Synthesis of research on the effectiveness of intellectual skills programs: Snake oil remedies or miracle cures?' *Educational Leadership 44*, 2, 60–67.

Trickey, S. and Topping, K.J. (2004) 'Philosophy for Children: A systematic review.' *Research Papers in Education 19*, 3, 363–378.

Swartz and Parks' infused approach

Baumfield, V., Hall, E. and Wall, K. (2008) *Action Research in the Classroom.* London: Sage.

Martin, D.S. (2001a) 'Thinking and the Special-Needs Learner.' In A.L. Costa (ed.) *Developing Minds: A Resource Book for Teaching Thinking* (3rd edition). Melbourne: Hawker Brownlow.

Martin, D.S. (2001b) 'Thinking and the Special-Needs Learner'. In A.L. Costa (ed.) *Developing Minds: A Resource Book for Teaching Thinking.* Pacific Grove, CA: Critical Thinking Press and Software.

McGregor, D. (2007) *Developing Thinking Developing Learning: A Guide to Thinking Skills in Education.* Maidenhead: Open University Press/ McGraw Hill.

McGuinness, C. (2002) 'Metacognition in classrooms.' Paper presented to the International Conference on Thinking, Harrogate.

McGuinness, C. (2006) 'Building thinking skills in thinking classrooms: ACTS (Activating Children's Thinking Skills) in Northern Ireland.' *Teaching and Learning Research Programme 18*, September 2006, 1–4. Available at www.tlrp.org/pub/documents/McGuinness_RB_18.pdf, accessed on 25 March 2011.

McGuinness, C. (2008) 'A metacognitively-rich pedagogy in primary classrooms. What is it?' Paper presented to the National Pedagogy Conference, Cardiff, Wales.

McGuinness, C., Curry, C., Eakin, A. and Sheehy, N. (2005) 'Metacognition in primary classrooms: A pre-ACTive learning effect for children.' Paper to TLRP Annual Conference, Warwick.

Swartz, R.J., Fischer, S. and Parks, S. (1998) *Infusing the Teaching of Critical and Creative Thinking into Science.* Pacific Grove, CA: Critical Thinking Books and Software.

Swartz, R.J. and Parks, S. (1994) *Infusing the Teaching of Critical and Creative Thinking into Content Instruction.* Pacific Grove, CA: Critical Thinking Books and Software.

Swartz, R., Kiser, M.A. and Reagan, R. (1999) *Teaching Critical and Creative Thinking in Language Arts: A Lesson Book Grades 5 and 6.* Pacific Grove, CA: Critical Thinking Books and Software.

Goleman's emotional intelligence

Department for Education and Skills (DfES) (2005) *Excellence and Enjoyment: Social and Emotional Aspects of Learning (SEAL).* Nottingham: DfES.

Goleman, D. (1995/6) *Emotional Intelligence: Why it Matters More than IQ.* London: Bloomsbury.

Goleman, D. (1998) *Working with Emotional Intelligence.* London: Bloomsbury.

Howie, D.R. (2003a) *Thinking about the Teaching of Thinking.* Wellington: New Zealand Council for Educational Research.

Howie, D.R. (2003b) 'The assessment and training of decision-making and self-advocacy skills.' *Journal of Cognitive Education and Psychology 3*, 1, 1–26.

Stys, Y. and Brown, S.L. (2004) 'A review of the emotional intelligence literature and implications for corrections.' Available at www.csc-scc.gc.ca/text/rsrch/reports/r150/r150_e.pdf, accessed on 25 March 2011.

Meichenbaum

Cameron, M.I. and Robinson, V.M.J. (1980) 'Effects of cognitive training on academic and on-task behaviour of hyperactive children.' *Journal of Abnormal Child Psychology 8*, 3, 405–419.

Camp, B. and Bash, M. (1985) *Thinking Aloud: Increasing Social and Cognitive Skills-Applying a Self-regulating Private Model to Classroom Settings.* Ardmore, PA: Workbook Publishing.

Howie, D.R. (2003) *Thinking about the Teaching of Thinking.* Wellington: New Zealand Council for Educational Research.

James, M.E. (1980) 'Cognitive training: A component analysis.' Unpublished MA thesis, University of Auckland.

Kendall, P.C. and Braswell, L. (1993) *Cognitive-Behavioural Therapy for Impulsive Children.* New York: The Guilford Press.

Novaco, R.W. (1979) 'The Cognitive Regulation of Anger and Stress.' In P.C. Kendal and S.D. Hollon (eds) *Cognitive-Behavioural Interventions: Theory, Research and Procedures.* London: Academic Press.

Meichenbaum, D. (1985) 'Teaching Thinking: A Cognitive Behavioural Perspective.' In S.F. Chipman, J.W. Segal and R. Glaser (eds) *Thinking and Learning Skills, Vol. 2: Research and Open Questions.* Hillsdale, NJ: Lawrence Erlbaum.

Rogers, B. (1994) *Behaviour Recovery: A Programme for Mainstream Schools.* Harlow: Longman.

Shapiro, E.S. and Cole, C.L. (1994) *Behaviour Change in the Classroom.* New York: The Guilford Press.

Thompson, J.E.M. (2003) 'Children's self-talk and writing: How can self-instruction be used to raise attainment in writing in Key Stage Two pupils?' Unpublished MEd dissertation, University of Hull.

Ward, L. and Traweek, D. (1993) 'Application of a metacognitive strategy to assessment, intervention and consultation: A think-aloud technique.' *Journal of School Psychology 31*, 4, 469–485.

CHAPTER 6

Tier 3 – Working with Individuals who Need Further Attention, Beyond Tier 2

Introduction

Tier 3 level aims to address approaches that can be used to meet unique individual needs arising from characteristics of the learner which are so considerable and unique to the person concerned that they require individual intervention in the teaching of thinking further to that provided at Tier 2 level. For example, this could apply to individuals who experience a major barrier to learning through disability, which has not been fully overcome through Tier 2 work, and to individuals with complex learning needs, such as a learning disability and a unique emotional need. Figure 6.1 represents Tier 3.

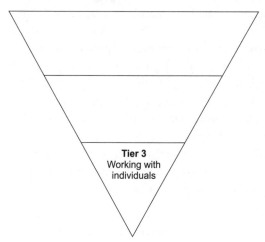

Figure 6.1 Teaching thinking in Tier 3 – individual work

It is important to provide such individualised, one-to-one instruction in thinking in order to ensure 'personalised learning', a policy focus in the UK and emerging in the concerns expressed in, for example, New Zealand for meeting the needs of all learners. It involves understanding the learning progress being made by the individual, in terms of past progress and future learning needs, addressing individual learning needs in a holistic way, and maximising partnership and choice in the learning process.

Some of the issues that require our particular attention at Tier 3 level are the following:

1. Individuals with these unique needs must first be identified by carrying out an individual assessment of needs which will allow that individual's unique profile of strengths and needs to be understood in a holistic way, and appropriate strategies to be chosen to enhance thinking by that individual. A dynamic assessment approach is considered the most useful for this task. The latest comprehensive coverage of dynamic assessment approaches for clinical and education work, by Haywood and Lidz (2007), is recommended as a resource. Educational psychologists internationally are increasingly adopting such dynamic assessment processes as the Feuerstein Learning Potential Assessment Device (Feuerstein *et al.* 2002) for this purpose. This assessment tool includes as one of its measures adaptations of Raven's Progressive Matrices. This Raven's measure may be particularly applicable for use in culturally diverse countries because of its culture-reduced nature (i.e. it incorporates less culturally specific content than traditional tests of intelligence). In some countries the testing component used before and after the teaching component could use the Raven standardisation for that population, as is done in New Zealand for its culturally diverse population (Raven 1985). (i.e. the population on which it is standardised is a representative New Zealand population including representation from its different cultural groups.) Further suitable dynamic assessment approaches are covered later in this section.

2. The assessment approach and individualised intervention used need to be holistic, paying particular attention to motivational and emotional needs, as well as cognitive enhancement needs. It is probable that learners requiring further support at Tier 3 level will have experienced some failure in the school system,

so that original disabilities and difficulties will have become more complex with the addition of unique motivational and emotional needs. It is particularly important, before any unique intervention, to assess these needs both within the dynamic assessment approach and with reference to any other additional measures used (such as those developed for the aspects of self-concept and attribution). There needs to be an individual interview to discuss these issues, and careful ongoing observation in relation to them throughout the intervention. A metacognitive individual interview approach would look at:

- individuals' perceptions of their learning strengths and needs (metacognitive knowledge of the self)

- perception of the thinking requirements of the task (metacognitive knowledge of the task)

- thinking strategies which would be useful in carrying out that task (metacognitive knowledge of strategies).

(See Butler and Meichenbaum 1981; Meichenbaum *et al.* 1985.)

3. For learners at Tier 3, it is particularly important that we focus on the learning process itself, and not just on the outcome/output of the learning. This is so that the mediator/teacher can perceive where in the problem-solving process the learner is experiencing difficulty and requires assistance. In all of the approaches covered in this chapter attention to the learning process is seen as significant and detailed examples are chosen to illustrate this.

4. Process evaluation of the enhancement is needed, to inform users of how well each component is meeting the learners' unique learning needs, and to inform ongoing intervention. This is a very formative approach to assessment. Even when work is being undertaken within a group, a single-subject research approach can be used for evaluation, with the learner acting as their own control. In a formal single-subject evaluation approach, we would obtain a baseline on the cognitive skills being taught *prior* to the intervention, *throughout* the intervention, and in follow-up *after* the intervention. (Examples of a single-subject evaluation approach in use, along with a group control design are reported in Chapter 9 of Howie (2003).)

5.   It is important that we carry out assessment and intervention in a partnership approach. Not only is this important as part of the personalisation of learning, it is essential to ensure engagement of the learner and internalisation by the learner of the aims and goals of the enhancement and the strategies taught, to support the learner in becoming an independent and lifelong learner.

6.   Finally, it is important to plan opportunities for the individual learner to engage with other learners in both a group situation and a full classroom situation, to ensure the fullest possible benefits from positive peer learning interaction. Planning to link the individual assessment and thinking enhancement approach into the small-group and whole-class context also requires careful thought in order to achieve as much consistency as possible between all delivery settings, and make it possible for the strategies and habits of thinking covered in one setting to be generalised to, and rewarded in, the other settings.

Approaches of varying types

1. Vygotsky's socio-cultural approach

This approach is fundamental to thinking enhancement at every tier level. Some of its particular contributions that we have not yet considered at depth are important at Tier 3 level, as discussed below.

The importance of understanding individual uniqueness and difference, including the unique cultural factors which impact on such difference, is stressed by Vygotsky. He believed that 'a functional learning system of one child may not be identical to that of another, although there may be similarities at certain stages of development' (Vygotsky 1978, p.125). His own experiences led to this emphasis on unique learning difference. Vygotsky took a particular interest in the rehabilitation of children with disabilities, becoming the Scientific Director of the Institute of Defectology in Moscow. He also took a major interest in the learning of children from national minority groups in Russia, coming himself from the Jewish minority population. His experiences led him to construct a very positive view of the role of culture in an individual's learning, with, according to Sutton (1988), a wish to understand the unique characteristics of the culture which impact on a child's learning development. Vygotsky states:

The child grows and develops in an extremely individual cultural-social environment which reflects the complex path of the historical development of the given people and the complex system of economic and cultural conditions of its present-day existence. Hence: the primary task for paedology is the study of children of national minorities not in an isolated fashion, not cut off from their specific cultural-social forms, but above all against the background of these peculiarities, in connection with them, in vital interaction with them. (Vygotsky 1929, cited in Sutton 1988, pp.96–97)

This is in full accord with the UK personalised learning policy (see p.40 for more details), and with a Tier 3 individualised approach. An example of such positive understanding is given by Vygotsky himself in describing a bilingual Tatar girl (from a nation within the then Russian Federation) who was diagnosed as having 'mental retardation'. In fact, her poor performance on standardised tests was due to social and cultural deprivation and related to her limited mastery of both Russian and her native language. Gindis, reporting this example, notes:

The most appropriate evaluation tool in this case would have been an assessment that, as Vygotsky pointed out, would concentrate on mental processing and certain qualitative metacognitive indicators. Examples are the cognitive strategies employed by the child, the type and character of the mistakes, the ability to benefit from help provided by the examiner, and emotional reactions to success and failure...' (Gindis 2003, pp.207–208)

As can be seen in this example, the importance of studying the learning process and how it comes about was also stressed by Vygotsky. He stated: 'we need to concentrate not on the *product* of development but on the very *process* by which higher forms are established' (Vygotsky 1978, p.64; italics his). This notion underpins the work on dynamic assessment of cognitive functioning with a 'test, teach and retest' format which allows for exploration of the learning process within the zone of proximal development (Haywood and Lidz 2007; Lidz 1987; Lidz and Elliott 2000).

It also underpins the attention to the process, and not just the output, of education in basic skills (reading and arithmetic), and the teaching of them in process ways such as those used within the UK literacy and numeracy programmes, both for quality teaching for all at Tier 1 level, and in individualised work at Tier 3. Tools such as the 'number line' (a technique used in UK to visually and verbally map the mathematical process) and a shared language for talking about process are encouraged in the UK literacy and numeracy programmes.

Basically, using Vygotsky's idea of the zone of proximal development, and scaffolding through systematic individualised mediation within that zone, many of the approaches outlined in Tier 1 could be intensified at Tier 3 to suit the unique needs of individual learners. 'Scaffolding' involves a teaching/mediation process that enables a learner to solve a problem or carry out a task which would be beyond his/her normal unassisted efforts (Wood, Bruner and Ross 1976). The teacher/mediator provides the assistance needed for success with the task, and as the learner becomes more competent, the assistance is gradually faded. It is important to provide only the minimal help required for success, the overall goal being for control of learning to be passed to the learner.

There is also a particular programme called 'Bright Start' (Haywood, Brooks and Burns 1992) which, although normally delivered to small groups of young learners who have pervasive developmental disorders or who are at risk of failure, is discussed here because of its strong application of Vygotskian theory, and particularly because of the way it seeks to remediate by means of attention to the cognitive processes. It includes a mediational teaching style which 'consists of methods of mediating the children's basic thinking skills, generalising meanings of the children's own experiences, and managing their metacognitive processes'. It uses process-oriented questioning such as 'Why do you think it is better to count this way?' Gindis, describing the programme, concludes: 'As one can see, the type of questions asked in process-oriented lessons differs from the type of questions asked in content-oriented lessons' (Gindis 2003, p.215).

In individualised work with a child with special educational needs, Vygotsky's ideas on how private speech or talk is used by the learner to manage their own thinking could be an important tool. Some extensive exploration of the private talk of learners, by Nuthall in his fascinating book *The Hidden Lives of Learners* (2007), shows us how each learner lives in their own personal and social world within the classroom. (Microphones were attached to selected children, and interviews used to explore their memories of their learning through a unit of work.) The way we internalise our thinking about what we have experienced in our social worlds, a Vygotskian idea, is explained by Nuthall, who says:

> Working with our mental model of the social and physical worlds in our minds is what we call thinking. Much of this 'working with

our mental model' occurs through language, an internal version of language, or talking to oneself. (p.74)

He gives wonderful examples from this exploration of how learners make sense of their learning experience, and 'construct' their own unique meanings. Of particular interest to us at Tier 3 is that he found that 'what students learn during a unit is largely unique' (p.100), that 'there are considerable differences in how individual students make use of available resources and create their own learning activities', relating particularly to their own background knowledge and level of interest (p.101) and (in relation to the children of differing abilities in the classroom) that 'all the students learned when they had sufficient relevant experiences, and did not learn when they did not have those experiences' (p.97).

This all indicates the importance of understanding the reality of each learner's unique learning experiences and processes as they develop new knowledge and skills – a truly personalised approach.

An example of the possible value of internalised 'private speech' in a unique cultural setting, was covered in a seminar paper given by one of the writer's masters students at the University of the South Pacific. Mere Vadei, an ethnic Fijian who was a teacher trainer, emphasised in her seminar the role of private speech in self-guiding the functions of the child. She drew attention to research which showed that learners with learning disabilities showed the same pattern of private speech development as other children without disabilities (Berk and Landau 1993). She felt that teachers of such children in Fijian classrooms should be encouraged to make more use of private speech, for example, with special study corners in the classroom to allow for these learners to use audible self-regulatory speech without disturbing their peers, in contrast to the 'absolute quiet classroom' so common in Fiji. She also noted the strong role that older sisters played in the care of their younger siblings, and the use of private speech by these children to help themselves in that care, in this cultural context. She considered that private speech could be utilised as a strength.

EXAMPLE

The Reading Recovery programme developed by the late Dame Marie Clay is an example of a Vygotskian approach to enhancement, as affirmed by Clay in her article 'A Vygotskian Interpretation of Reading Recovery' (Clay and Cazden 1990). (The writer is also very familiar with the programme, as Marie Clay supervised the writer's own PhD and they were colleagues in the same Department of Education at the University of Auckland.)

This programme is used for individual intervention when the learner is falling behind in reading after one year at school, no matter what the cause, and is widely used internationally, including in the UK, as a Tier 3 reading intervention. It is reported to have large positive effect sizes, not only for decoding and oral reading, but also for reading comprehension (Hattie 2009).

Reading Recovery uses a process diagnostic approach to identify the unique reading characteristics of the individual learner, as outlined in Clay (2005). It uses a Vygotskian understanding of the process itself, not just of the final outcome (such as a word recognition or comprehension score). Marie Clay's 'running records', taken while the learner is reading aloud, allow the mediator to understand the learner's unique knowledge and use of reading strategies and how best to enhance them. (The writer found this assessment approach to be very useful with Maori adolescents, to explore to what extent learners are able to transfer the error correction strategies taught in Feuerstein's 'organisation of dots' Instrumental Enrichment instrument, to error correction in reading. See Howie, Richards and Pirihi (1993).)

Reading Recovery also uses the Vygotskian idea of scaffolding to help the individual learner to construct a self-improving system of knowledge and strategies by 'creating a lesson format, a scaffold, within which [the teacher] promotes emerging skill' and 'passes more and more control to the child and pushes the child, gently but consistently, into independent, constructive activity' (Clay and Cazden 1990, p.212). The child is carefully introduced to a new text in a way which highlights potentially difficult syntax, unusual vocabulary, or a less predictable story line. The teacher emphasises strategies which are undertaken as part of the 'covert' internal processes, and the child is encouraged to internalise these strategies as a 'voice in the head' so as to self-instruct when coming to a new word.

These, then, are a number of ways in which the Reading Recovery programme infuses a Vygotskian approach in a number of its assessment and teaching aspects. Teachers trained in Clay's Reading Recovery programme would have an excellent theoretical and experiential base for applying a programme for the teaching of thinking in such an individualised way.

2. Feuerstein's theory of mediated learning experience

This approach is useful to us at all tier levels. There are a number of assessment and intervention tools designed by Feuerstein and his team specifically to address cognitive needs of learners with a variety of learning difficulties, and which are appropriate for the individual teaching of thinking. They address both individual cognitive needs and motivational/emotional needs. Increasingly, as all learners are included in the ordinary classroom, professionals responsible for supporting them in their learning in that context are equipping themselves with these tools, including educational psychologists, occupational therapists, and counsellors (Kozulin 2008b). One of the members of Feuerstein's team, Professor Louis Falik, has been involved in a number of publications pertinent to individual therapists.

Outlined below are some examples of the ways in which available tools are being used for both assessment and intervention, to give an idea of the wide range of possibilities for work on an individual basis. All of the tools require a very interactive approach to the process of learning involved, and use careful questioning as a form of mediation. In discussing this, the 'modes of questioning in the learning process' are drawn to attention by Shmuel Feuerstein (2000). He states: 'the way a question is formulated…is of critical importance to the successful outcome of learning… Teachers need to have question strategies that are clear and adapted to their students' (pp.136–137). 'Learning to ask questions and to answer them satisfactorily enters into what are termed higher order skills, which include critical thinking, logical reasoning, metacognitive and cognitive strategies' (p.137). Such successful communication he sees as being coordinated and structured by the parameters of mediated learning experience (MLE) (Feuerstein and Feuerstein 1991), which were discussed in the Tier 1 coverage of this approach in Chapter 4, Section 2.

An important aspect when we are working with individual needs at this tier level is to take a holistic approach, so that motivational and emotional needs are addressed, in a way which is integral to the intervention. One of the key goals of Feuerstein's Instrumental Enrichment (FIE) programme is the development of intrinsic motivation. Using Instrumental Enrichment in Belgium with learners with learning disabilities and behaviour problems in special schools, both the mediating attitude of teachers, as well as their approach in a holistic way, were important for learner change (Schnitzer, Andries and Lebeer 2007).

Feuerstein gives a list of cognitive functions/dysfunctions, based on the learning process involving *input*, *elaboration* and *output* of information processing (what he calls the three phases of the mental act). (See Chapter 4 and Howie 2003, p.88). It is useful to analyse individual learners' learning needs and progress while undergoing the FIE programme. We could review learning with the learner, through individual interview, using this list of cognitive dysfunctions in order to jointly identify, in partnership, the unique profile of learning strengths and needs – as suggested by Falik and Feuerstein (1990). It may also be possible to carry out this exercise again, after a period of individual intervention to address the difficulties. Even where needs are more strongly emotional, it has been suggested that links between cognitive functions/dysfunctions and Beck's idea of cognitive distortions (1976) can be used in addressing the cognitive dysfunctions of individuals in a counselling session for emotional disorders such as depression (Wong 2008).

We are particularly interested in individual self-reflection on, and self-management of, learning. A set of procedures which the learner can use to describe the changes in themselves in response to Instrumental Enrichment intervention has been outlined by Falik and Feuerstein (1993). They call this 'internalised mediation'. It involves using regularly through the intervention a form of metacognitive interview looking at:

- task knowledge (such as knowledge of the name of the instrument, its components, and the requirements of the task)

- the 'mental activities which the learner employs' (i.e. the strategies)

- the learner's own perceived difficulties with the task.

These three levels equate to the three key metacognitive knowledge aspects (knowledge of self, task and strategies, as described in the introduction to this chapter). The questions which could be asked in such an 'internalised mediation' process are detailed by Falik and Feuerstein (1993).

The Learning Potential Assessment Device (now called the Learning Propensity Assessment Device (LPAD)) developed by Feuerstein and his team (Feuerstein et al. 2002) is now probably the most widely used dynamic assessment tool with learners who have considerable and complex learning needs. As a dynamic assessment approach, it looks at the learning process in an interactive way. It is normally used on an individual basis, with the choice of testing measures (from within a wide range of possibilities) determined by hypotheses concerning the unique learning needs. The teaching phase uses adaptations of those measures for training on the strategies involved. It can be used to inform intensive individual intervention – but approaches developed by Feuerstein for intervention do not depend on this demanding assessment approach. (It is also important to note that this assessment tool is not used either to predict the future functioning of the learner, or to compare the learner's learning potential with that of other learners. The learner is their own point of reference.) In discussing this focus upon the learner, Kozulin notes that this dynamic assessment process is more like art than science. As an art 'the emergence of cognitive functions revealed during the LPAD procedure is a unique event engendered by the interaction between the mediator and the child' (Kozulin 2008a, p.27).

An example of the way in which the LPAD and Instrumental Enrichment can be used to address unique individual learning needs is given to us in a case study by Cohen, Williams and Keane (1993) called 'Mediating a single student: A case study'. After it was realised that 'Ron' would have difficulty accessing the Instrumental Enrichment programme being used in the classroom, an initial evaluation with the LPAD was carried out. It found that 'Ron' had multiple cognitive deficiencies, so an individualised programme was designed for him which incorporated a strong focus on the mediation of meaning, using an extra early instrument involving colouring to develop rapport, careful building up of mastery on the instruments, and later introduction of a reading programme. Subsequent assessment showed significant improvements for 'Ron'.

The Cognitive Abilities Profile (CAP) was developed to overcome some of the challenges of time, training, and application to classroom curriculum and teaching needs in using dynamic assessment, by Ruth Deutsch (a leading UK trainer in dynamic assessment and a colleague of Feuerstein) and Michelle Mohammed (2008). It includes observing the learner within their own typical learning context, consultations with all key mediators for the learner, bringing the dynamic assessment methodology into formative assessment within ordinary classrooms, and addressing the three key elements of *the task, the learner* and *the mediator* in the assessment process. In relation to these three key aspects (identified by Feuerstein):

- Section A of the CAP addresses the cognitive abilities of the learner, adapted from Feuerstein's Deficient Cognitive Functions

- Section B addresses responses to teaching and mediation, based on the Mediated Learning Rating Scales of Lidz

- Section C addresses analysis of the task, based on Feuerstein's Cognitive Map.

An increasing number of studies use Feuerstein's MLE criteria in an intensive and individualised way to provide an intervention to meet the complex and unique learning needs of a learner. For example, Sharma (2002) used a unique process of mediation over a considerable time-frame to meet the unique learning needs of a boy who had undergone a left hemispherectomy.

The FIE programme has always been used with individuals with severe learning disabilities, on an individual basis. The ways in which young adults with severe learning difficulties taught Instrumental Enrichment to each other were explored in a unique study by Kaufman (2001). It shows that individualised intervention with the FIE programme can be successfully used with learners with severe learning difficulties, mediated by their peers with similar learning difficulties under the direction of a skilled mediator. Another exemplary aspect of the study was the evaluation of the mediation processes taking place between the individuals, using a microanalysis of videotaped observations to analyse the mediation processes, based on Feuerstein's criteria.

Particular individual therapeutic applications of Feuerstein's approach were discussed by Professor Lois Falik (2008), a member of Feuerstein's team and a specialist in counselling, at the 2008 Feuerstein International Workshop in Jesolo (Italy). He saw the 'therapeutic application' as involving two different perspectives. First, he outlined the perspective of educational and cognitive teaching and learning, where increasingly the FIE programme is being used as a powerful intervention for small groups and therapeutic one-to-one work. The power in the tools and the mediation given can be enhanced through exploration of the individual's cognitive functions/dysfunctions, and the application of the FIE programme can be focused more specifically on the needs of the learner. One can also bridge very directly to the individual learner's experience, such as aspects of the curriculum that they are struggling with. Second, Falik addressed the perspective of the range of problems identified in social and emotional development. The mediator needs to observe closely while working with Instrumental Enrichment, to see where there are links between cognitive skills and social/emotional skills (including conditions like anxiety, depression, social confusion etc.), and to develop alternative ways of responding through appropriate cognitive strategies.

There has always been a very inclusive approach towards sharing the tools available with all learners, and with key persons in their lives (such as parents), on the part of Feuerstein and his team. Parents attend

Instrumental Enrichment training workshops, and the most advanced 'training for trainers' workshop that the writer has attended included a parent who had a child with severe learning difficulties. Some of the unique opportunities of home-based mediated learning interaction, including a closer, more informal and more permanent relationship, as well as the opportunity to work with a wider range of stimuli relating to the learner's immediate needs, have been identified by Moshe Egozi (1986), a former key training member of Feuerstein's team.

EXAMPLE

An example of individual use of the FIE programme is some work done by the writer in partnership with a parent. The Instrumental Enrichment mediation was carried out by the parent, whose child was of above average ability but experiencing specific learning difficulties in reading and written expression. (A full report of this work can be found in Howie 2003, Chapter 5.) This parent, who was a science teacher, had read of success using the FIE programme for learners with such difficulties (e.g. Messerer, Hunt, Meyers and Lerner 1984).

A minimal intervention was carefully planned, to be carried out by the parent under the writer's guidance to target her son's learning needs and strengths, as identified by the mother and by the writer's very specific assessment using task examples from several instruments of the programme. Sessions were taped so that they could be reviewed by the writer, and feedback given to the mother on her mediation processes.

The mother showed a very interactive type of questioning and discussion about the problem-solving process, and the son showed strengths in reciprocating and appeared to feel free to correct his mother's approach as they worked at task requirements together. There was therefore considerable joint mediation of intentionality and reciprocity in the learning process. For example, the mother successfully encouraged this partnership and reciprocity by saying to her son, 'Suggest a strategy for me to use.' By the time the mother had reached the 'organisation of dots page 11', she was showing considerable skills in direct and precise questioning aimed at increasing her son's reflection on his thinking process.

She also showed considerable understanding of the learning requests that might arouse anxiety in her son, and real skill in devising novel, game-like activities in order to overcome it. For example, in emphasising strategic and metacognitive behaviours, and to encourage reflection, the mother shared with her son the development of a model of how a bomb disposal expert might work. This idea was introduced in an 'organisation of dots' lesson in which strategy was discussed in some depth. In this game her son 'pretended to be a strategy expert and fed her strategy advice, speaking to her through a tube and referring to a checklist of cues that had been jointly drawn up' (Howie 2003, p.45).

In order to address some of the specific learning needs identified, in many of the 'organisation of dots' exercises the mother chose to incorporate recall tasks and the teaching of strategic memory skills.

She was also able to question for detailed generalisation. For example, in careful summary at the end of one of the 'organisation of dots' lessons, the following dialogue occurred:

> *Mother:* Would you say in this exercise that you had to think of more than one thing at a time, rather than eliminate one thing at a time?
>
> *Son:* Yes.
>
> *Mother:* Can you give me an example in real life – for example, in driving, where you have to think of about steering, road conditions, etc.?
>
> *Son:* Diving.
>
> *Mother:* What things do you have to think of?
>
> *Son:* Be careful not to pull on the air monitor, speed of coming up, mouthpiece in mouth, look out for sharks.
>
> *Mother:* A good example.

(Howie 2003, p.45)

The mother showed the same ability to draw out systematic organisation and recall of attributes in work within the comparisons and categorisations instruments.

In reflecting on her own learning from this shared experience of Instrumental Enrichment, the mother included the following in her comments:

I learnt the following:

- The use of praise, as a means of showing that something specific had been noticed and appreciated, is a powerful tool.

- An awareness of the metacognitive aspects of learning opens the doors to learning at a more deep-seated level.

- The skill of directing learning can be imparted to parents so that learning in a one-to-one situation is enhanced.

- This skill, once acquired in a specific setting, is transferable to other settings.

(Howie 2003, pp.48–49)

3. Robert Sternberg's problem-solving cycle and metacomponents

We covered this approach in detail at Tier 1 in Chapter 4, Section 3. As noted in that coverage, it arises from the use of an information-processing theoretical framework, and looks at the cognitive components and metcomponents used in the problem-solving process (Sternberg 1979). It is therefore a key approach through which we can look at how an individual addresses the learning process, what difficulties they have in the cognitive components of the process, and what metacognitive strategies they require to regulate their thinking processes. It is an approach which lends itself to work with individuals with unique and complex difficulties, in the following ways and examples.

We could use the metacomponents identified by Sternberg and outlined in his problem-solving cycle in cognitive self-instructions for learners requiring greater regulation of their thinking process. For example, we could use these problem-solving procedures in talk-aloud protocols (see Meichenbaum, Tier 2, p.182). Such cognitive self-instruction is used with a variety of learners with exceptional learning needs. The procedures are very frequently taught on a one-to-one basis.

In the intervention we can draw on findings from a detailed individualised metacomponential interview already developed to address the key metacomponents which Sternberg has identified as important, including: defining the nature of the problem, problem representation, strategy planning, and monitoring. The metacomponential measure initially designed by Clements and Nastasi (1990) uses a dynamic assessment approach, so is in line with the Vygotskian concepts of the zone of proximal development and guided assistance within that zone, and focuses on the learning process. Some work with this assessment tool, both with classroom learners in Ireland, some of whom had disadvantaged backgrounds (Barry-Joyce 2001; Barry-Joyce and Howie 1998) and with adults with brain damage in Hong Kong (Fong 2004; Fong and Howie 2007; Fong and Howie 2009) has shown that it is able to identify individual differences in use of these metacomponents, and changes in use of these metacomponents in response to a cognitive enhancement intervention aimed at developing these metacomponential problem-solving behaviours.

A thinking strategy intervention based on Sternberg's meta-componential theory and problem-solving approach can address both more academic related tasks or problems (as in the case of Barry-Joyce's work, which focused on mathematical problems) and real-life problem solving (as in the case of Fong's work). It requires a careful analysis of the component processes involved in the tasks/problems being addressed, so that 1) any metacomponential interview approach used is adapted to these tasks, and 2) the intervention itself addresses the task needs as well as the learner and strategy intervention needs.

The published research to date on the use of this metacomponential thinking strategy approach does indicate its value with a range of learning needs and within a range of cultural contexts, but it would be useful to see more evaluation and published research to support this.

EXAMPLE

A more detailed example of the use of an explicit problem-solving approach, which taught Sternberg's metacomponential strategies, as compared to a conventional cognitive training approach, was carried out with outpatients with brain injury in Hong Kong by Fong (2004), supervised by the writer. It is included here because Fong carried out this metacomponential training with learners with very considerable learning needs, especially in real-life problem-solving processing, and the training was given either in small groups of four to five participants, or individually, if the participants could not work in such a small group.

Twenty-two sessions of training were given, two sessions per week, each with a 45-minute educational session covering the metacomponential facet being addressed, followed by a 30-minute computer-based cognitive training session for the participant to make use of the metacomponential strategies just taught. These strategies were as follows:

- Defining the problem: verbalising and thinking-aloud activities were used for this facet.

- Planning: brainstorming and means–end analysis were taught as part of this strategy.

- Problem representation: forward and backward chaining were used, in both cases with visual representation.

- Self-monitoring: self-awareness was particularly targeted as it has been found to be a common need with patients with brain injury. Participants were taught to monitor feedback so that they could review and reflect on their own performance.

(Fong and Howie 2009, p.529)

The participants who received this metacomponential training showed a statistically significant advantage over participants receiving conventional cognitive training, on the representation correctness score and the total correctness score of the metacomponential interview measure. There were also advantages to these participants receiving metacomponential training on a social problem-solving video measure, a means–end problem-solving measure, and the 'six elements' test, all focusing on real-life problem-solving skills, but the small numbers involved, as well as the limited length of the training programme, may have contributed to the advantages not being statistically significant.

A study of some of the individual participants in depth, to look at their response to each training facet, was carried out through single-subject trend analysis. This suggested that for some participants not only the full length of the intervention but also the follow-up time was required to consolidate the use of the metacognitive strategies (Fong and Howie 2007). For example, one of the four participants selected for more detailed single-subject analysis not only made gains, as did the other experimental participants undergoing single-subject analysis, in association with training on the 'nature of the problem' component, but made marked gains on this component through the follow-up phase.

For the planning metacomponent, all of the single-subject participants in the metacomponential training showed remarkable reduction of planning errors when this planning facet of the programme was introduced, and in the follow-up measure maintained their low level of errors.

For the 'representation' metacomponent, the individual responses to teaching of this metacomponent were more variable, and there was an indication that two of the participants had benefited on this metacomponent subtest prior to the specific training phase for it, meaning from the overall intervention already covered. Two of the participants who were trained in this metacomponent made important gains over the follow-up period.

The self-monitoring metacomponent was not able to be measured in this single-subject trend analysis.

It was suggested in the reports of this research project that further work on application of the learning of these metacomponents to real-life problem-solving situations which the participants were engaged in, and more detailed interviewing of the participants about their perceptions of the programme, would have been of value.

4. Jensen's MindLadder model

The MindLadder learning model includes dynamic assessment with a wide range of tasks and modalities to explore and enhance the development of the learner's knowledge construction processes, as well as classroom learning and parent-education components. This model is unique in that it brings together three key theoretical developments, the first two of which we are already familiar with from coverage in this book: Vygotskian constructivism (active learner involvement with the process of meaning-making), Feuerstein's cognitive functions and mediated learning experiences, and problem-based learning and novice-to-expert transitions (the 'steps' of the 'mind's ladder'). (Jensen 2000, 2003). It is also a process model of assessment and intervention which is well suited to work with individuals with unique and complex learning difficulties, for the following reasons:

1. We can consider it to be in line with this Tier 3 because Jensen sees it as a 'reach-to-teach' model, with high expectations for all learners. In his 2007 article on how it can be used for meeting the needs of learners with academic difficulties and learning disabilities, within the ordinary classroom, details are described of how it addresses the individual needs of the learner, noting the importance of careful attention not only to cognitive processes, but also to subject area content, motivation, affect, behavioural skills, self-perception and attitudes, all within a developmental context (Jensen 2007).

2. It is also of interest that Jensen links this individual approach as useful within the Response to Intervention (RTI) American requirement, since the delivery is based on the learner's response to intervention, as assessed by a dynamic and interactive assessment approach.

3. It uses a process model of dynamic assessment and learning in its MindLadder dynamic assessments, which gives the assessor freedom and opportunity to explore the development of any area of the learner's functioning which can help in understanding how to provide the best intervention for knowledge construction. A particular value to us is the way it can be used to look at change over time, because the assessment includes data covering baseline skills, acquiring of further skills, retaining of the newly learnt skills, and the way they can be used flexibly, transformed and generalised.

The programme for classroom learning based on the MindLadder Classroom Learning Model has been developed to give the classroom teacher the freedom and opportunity to be a mediator in the development of the learner's knowledge construction functions (the cognitive processes underpinning the construction of knowledge and skills). These are the 'brain tools' in the programme. The programme integrates these functions with curriculum objectives and academic standards. For example, the knowledge construction function or 'brain tool' called 'traces, signs and symbols' helps the learner to infer something from a thing that points to it. The 'traces, symbols and signs' are three types of information that point to something else. Ability to develop this knowledge construction function is important not only for the decoding of information (drawing out of information) in order to develop images and ideas in the mind, but important also for encoding (expressing information) and communicating thoughts and feelings. An example of teacher–student dialogue in mediating this knowledge construction is given by Jensen in an Appendix to his 2003 paper as follows:

> *Teacher*: When you walk in the sand or snow what do you leave behind? What have you noticed? [Teacher waits for students to reply.]
>
> *Students*: You leave footprints.
>
> *Teacher*: Yes. If we walk in the sand or the snow, we leave behind our footprints. Now, if you were walking in the snow and you saw some footprints along the way, what would you know?
>
> *Student*: That someone else was there.
>
> *Student*: Or, depending on the print you saw, it could be an animal.

Teacher. Yes, good. You could see different kinds of prints in the snow. The footprints are clues or signs that something or someone was there. We often call this kind of clue a trace. A trace is a mark left by a person, animal, thing or event... Traces point to something else. That is, a sound, smell, taste, feel or mark of an object can stand for the object when it is not wholly present or visible. Like the footprint stands for the person. The trace enables you to think about something else that it is pointing to. The trace enables us to infer something. When we infer we use one piece of information to reach another. For example, when we see smoke we infer that something is burning.

(Jensen 2003, pp.137–139)

The MindLadder Classroom Learning Model encourages high expectations of learners. Jensen states that, 'The overall goal is to enable students to achieve high academic standards while learning how to assemble and use knowledge' (Jensen 2003, p.121). Teachers are given a MindLadder Learning Guide to help them in implementing the classroom learning model, and in using a variety of outcome measures such as standardised achievement tests, portfolios tied to reflective self-evaluation, and other authentic real-life assessments.

Another unique aspect of this model is that it includes a MindLadder Parent-as-Mediator Programme. This can stand alone or be used with the school-based programme (Jensen and Jensen 1996), and provides a wide range of practical approaches that parents can use to foster their children's emotional, social, language, and cognitive development. There is emphasis on parents using their own unique and cultural heritage as well as daily life events to foster their children's knowledge construction skills. It helps parents to contribute meaningfully to their children's learning objectives, as full partners.

AN EXAMPLE FROM PRACTICE IN A SCHOOL SETTING

An example of use of this approach, is a carefully constructed study carried out by Mogens Jensen to test the ability of the MindLadder Classroom Learning Model to improve students' learning and achievement in the upper elementary grades in a school district north of Atlanta, Georgia (Jensen 2003). The learners were in ordinary classrooms, but these classrooms included some learners who had learning disabilities and remedial reading or maths needs.

The teachers involved in the study carried out the MindLadder Classroom Learning Model while also studying and implementing the MindLadder Parent-as-Mediator Programme. They also used the MindLadder Learning Guide as they chose, and they learnt from dynamic assessments of a small number of learners in their classrooms.

The teachers themselves, following initial training for the project, carried out a needs assessment of their own needs and wishes for assistance, coaching and support for themselves, as they carried out the new teaching approach, and 'planning for mediated instruction' and 'organising and managing the classroom for active learning' were the top needs identified. They were given help with their identified needs by coaches who spent time in their classrooms regularly. Teachers were supported in teaching the knowledge construction functions ('brain tools'), in how to model the use of a function, and how to provide students with opportunities to use the function and talk about its meaning.

> Teachers learned to connect the function to other situations, places and subjects by providing illustrations, by eliciting examples from students and by discussing the significance of its application... Teachers were taught how to start and use portfolios where students could keep a record of their emerging understanding of their knowledge construction functions ('brain tools'). (Jensen 2003, p.127)

The results of the study showed that the MindLadder learners outperformed the control learners in achievements (reading, language, maths, social studies sources, and the composite score on the ITBS, an academic measure) and in verbal reasoning and non-verbal reasoning ability (CogAT, a cognitive ability measure).

In line with our interest in the wider learning environment, Mogens Jensen also used the Classroom Learning Environment Scale in his evaluation, which was specifically designed to measure qualities in the learning environment that are targeted by the MindLadder programme (including 'a supportive learning environment where one can talk about ideas, learn how to think, feel safe while taking risks and receive help and encouragement as needed' (Jensen 2003, p.131). It was rated by learners themselves. It was able to measure in the classroom three different factors, two of which are central to the theories underpinning the programme – that is, the 'teacher mediation' factor, and the 'facilitation of participation' factor. The third factor was called the 'school experience' factor. The 'facilitation of participation' factor appeared to be the most important in relation to the higher scores of the learners in the experimental group.

Discussing the link between learner ratings of their classrooms using this Classroom Learning Environment Scale, and their achievements, Mogens Jensen states:

> The experimental programme appears, in a sense, to have 'rubbed off' on students that ordinarily might be somewhat harder to reach... Perhaps this was most clearly suggested by the finding that experimental students that self-reported below median levels of overall school experience nonetheless scored significantly higher on the ITBS [academic measure] than control students who reported above median levels of school achievement. (Jensen 2003, p.13)

This suggests that the programme could be valuable for learners who are at risk of school disengagement.

Although this study did not make specific attempts to assess and follow learners with particular needs in the classroom, a later analysis carried out by Jensen and reported in his 2007 paper on using MindLadder to meet the needs of learners with learning disabilities, yields some positive results for the use of the intervention with such learners. When he compared the children who were eligible for participation in special programmes for those with learning disabilities, remedial reading or maths, children from poor families more than two years behind in achievement, and children with emotional and behavioural difficulties (EBD) in both the experimental and control classes, there was a significant positive effect for academic achievement on the ITBS (an academic measure), for these children undergoing the MindLadder intervention. In fact, these students exposed to the MindLadder programme showed a similar level of achievement to children in the control group who did not qualify for such special provision – a wonderful 'bridging of the gap'.

Another unique aspect of this model, important at Tier 3 level, is that it brings together the enhancing of cognitive processes with curriculum learning. In his discussion of the study, Mogens Jensen notes that one of the strengths of the MindLadder model is that it develops the cognitive functions 'within a rich and meaningful curriculum' and 'enhances the role of the teacher by stressing the need to mediate the development of the students' cognitive and knowledge construction functions and to do so in combination with instruction and real learning events' (Jensen 2003, p.134). He also notes as another strength its aim to enable all who contribute to a learner's educational outcomes – teachers, students, parents, psychologists, speech therapists, etc. – to share a common language and series of applied programmes which support each other, within a shared approach to meet a learner's educational need.

Self-reflective questions

☐ Within your own school community, what are the key issues for the teaching of thinking at Tier 3 level?

☐ Which of the approaches covered at Tier 3 might best meet the exceptional learning needs of individual learners in your school community who need further individual intervention?

☐ How would any chosen approach need to be implemented and evaluated in order to meet the unique learning needs of the individual it was chosen for?

References

Introduction

Butler, L. and Meichenbaum, D. (1981) 'The Assessment of Interpersonal Problem-Solving Skills.' In P.C. Kendall and S.D. Hollon (eds) *Assessment Strategies for Cognitive Behaviour Intervention.* New York: Academic Press.

Feuerstein, R., Feuerstein, Ra.S., Falik, L.H. and Rand, Y. (2002) *The Dynamic Assessment of Cognitive Functions: The Learning Propensity Assessment Device, Theory, Instruments, Techniques.* Jerusalem: International Centre for the Enhancement of Learning Potential.

Haywood, H.C. and Lidz, C.S. (2007) *Dynamic Assessment in Practice: Clinical and Educational Applications.* Cambridge: Cambridge University Press.

Howie, D.R. (2003) *Thinking about the Teaching of Thinking.* Wellington: New Zealand Council for Educational Research.

Meichenbaum, D., Burland, S., Gruson, L. and Cameron, R. (1985) 'Metacognitive Assessment.' In S.R. Yussen (ed.) *The Growth of Reflection in Children.* London: Academic Press.

Raven, J.C. (1985) *Standard Progressive Matrices: Sets A, B, C, D, and E.* Wellington: New Zealand Council for Educational Research.

Vygotsky

Clay, M.M. (2005) *The Early Detection of Reading Difficulties.* Auckland: Heinemann.

Berk, L.E. and Landau, S. (1993) 'Private speech of learning-disabled and normally achieving children in classroom academic and laboratory contexts.' *Child Development 64,* 2, 556–571.

Clay, M.M. and Cazden, C.B. (1990) 'A Vygotskian Interpretation of Reading Recovery.' In L. Moll (ed.) *Vygotsky and Education.* Cambridge: Cambridge University Press.

Gindis, B. (2003) 'Remediation through Education.' In A. Kozulin, B. Gindis, V. Ageyev and S. Miller (eds) *Vygotsky's Educational Theory in Cultural Context.* New York: Cambridge University Press.

Hattie, J. (2009) *Visible Learning: A Synthesis of over 800 Meta-Analyses Relating to Achievement.* London: Routledge.

Haywood, H.C., Brooks, P.H. and Burns, S. (1992) *Bright Start: Cognitive Curriculum for Young Children.* Watertown, MA: Charles Bridge.

Haywood, H.C. and Lidz, C.S. (2007) *Dynamic Assessment in Practice: Clinical and Educational Applications.* New York: Cambridge University Press.

Howie, D.R., Richards, R. and Pirihi, H. (1993) 'Teaching thinking skills to Maori adolescents.' *International Journal of Cognitive Education and Mediated Learning 3*, 2, 70–91.

Lidz, C.S. (ed.) (1987) *Dynamic Assessment: An Interactional Approach to Evaluating Learning Potential.* New York: Guiford Press.

Lidz, C. and Elliott, J. (eds) (2000) *Dynamic Assessment: Prevailing Models and Applications.* Oxford: Elsevier Press.

Nuthall, G. (2007) *The Hidden Lives of Learners.* Wellington: New Zealand Council for Educational Research.

Sutton, A. (1988) 'L.S.Vygotskii: The Cultural-Historical Theory, National Minorities and the Zone of Next Development.' In R.M. Gupta and P. Coxhead (eds) *Cultural Diversity and Learning Efficiency.* London: Macmillan.

Vygotsky, L S. (1978) *Mind in Society.* Cambridge, MA: Harvard University Press.

Wood, D.J., Bruner, J.S. and Ross, G. (1976) 'The role of tutoring in problem solving.' *Journal of Child Psychology and Psychiatry 17*, 2, 89–100.

Feuerstein

Beck, A.T. (1976) *Cognitive Therapy of the Emotional Disorders.* New York: Penguin Books.

Cohen, L., Williams, S. and Keane, K.J. (1993) 'Mediating a single student: A case study.' *International Journal of Cognitive Education and Mediated Learning 3*, 1, 39–46.

Deutsch, R.M. and Mohammed, M. (2008) 'The Cognitive Abilities Profile.' In O. Tan and A. Seng (eds) *Cognitive Modifiability in Learning and Assessment: International Perspectives.* Singapore: Cengage Learning.

Egozi, M. (1986) Personal communication. 'Instrumental Enrichment (FIE) and mediation.' Paper presented at the MLE Conference.

Falik, L.H. (2008) 'Therapeutic applications.' Paper presented to the Feuerstein International Workshop, Jesolo, Italy; author's notes.

Falik, L.H. and Feuerstein, R. (1990) 'Structural cognitive modifiability: A new cognitive perspective for counselling and psychotherapy.' *International Journal of Cognitive Intervention and Mediated Learning 1*, 2, 143–150.

Falik, L.H. and Feuerstein, R. (1993) 'Assessing internalised mediation in cognitive learning.' *International Journal of Cognitive Education and Mediated Learning 3*, 1, 47–59.

Feuerstein, S. (2000) 'Questioning as a Form of Mediation.' In A. Kozulin and Y. Rand (eds) *Experience of Mediated Learning: An Impact of Feuerstein's Theory in Education and Psychology.* London: Pergamon.

Feuerstein, R. and Feuerstein, S. (1991) 'Mediated Learning Experience: A Theoretical Review.' In R. Feuerstein, P.S. Klein and A.J. Tannenbaum (eds) *Mediated Learning Experience (MLE): Theoretical, Psychosocial and Learning Implications.* London: Freund.

Feuerstein, R., Feuerstein, Ra.S., Falik, L.H. and Rand, Y. (2002) *The Dynamic Assessment of Cognitive Functions: The Learning Propensity Assessment Device, Theory, Instrumental Techniques.* Jerusalem: International Centre for the Enhancement of Learning Potential.

Howie, D.R. (2003) *Thinking about the Teaching of Thinking.* Wellington: New Zealand Council for Educational Research.

Kaufman, R. (2001) 'The process of experiencing mediated learning as a result of peer collaboration between adults with severe learning difficulties.' Unpublished PhD thesis, University of Exeter.

Kozulin, A. (2008a) 'Sociocultural Paradigm.' In J. Clegg (ed.) *The Observation of Human Systems: Lessons from the History of Auto-Reductionist Empirical Psychology.* London: Transaction Publishers.

Kozulin, A. (2008b) Personal communication.

Messerer, J., Hunt, E., Meyers, G. and Lerner, J. (1984) 'Feuerstein's Instrumental Enrichment: A new approach for activating intellectual potential for learning disabled youth. *Journal of Learning Disabilities 17*, 6, 322–325.

Schnitzer, G., Andries, C. and Lebeer, J. (2007) Usefulness of cognitive intervention programs for socio-emotional and behavioural difficulties.' *Journal of Research in Special Educational Needs 7*, 3, 161–171.

Sharma, R. (2002) 'My two years in the life of Alex: Mediated learning experience with a boy who had undergone a left hemispherectomy.' Doctoral dissertation, University of Exeter.

Wong, S. (2008) 'Cognitive Modification of Cognitive Dysfunctions and Distortions in a Learner.' In O. Tan and A. Seng (eds) *Cognitive Modifiability in Learning and Assessment: International Perspectives.* Singapore: Cengage Learning.

Robert Sternberg's metacomponents

Barry-Joyce, M. (2001) 'The effects of a logo environment on the metacognitive functioning of Irish students.' Unpublished PhD thesis, University of Hull.

Barry-Joyce, M. and Howie, D. (1998) 'Using single subject design to investigate the development of metacognition (Sternberg's metacomponents) in a computer based thinking skills program.' Paper presented to the teaching for Successful Intelligence Conference, July, Auckland, New Zealand.

Clements, D.H. and Nastasi, B.K. (1990) 'Dynamic approach to measurement of children's metacomponential functioning.' *Intelligence 14*, 1, 109–125.

Fong, K.N. (2004) 'Training of metacomponential functioning in problem-solving performance for patients with brain injury in Hong Kong.' Unpublished PhD thesis, University of Hull.

Fong, K.N. and Howie, D. (2007) 'Metacomponential assessment and training in real-life problem solving.' *Journal of Cognitive Education and Psychology 6*, 2, 165–184.

Fong, K.N. and Howie, D.R. (2009) 'Effects of an explicit problem-solving skills training program using a metacomponential approach for outpatients with Acquired Brain Injury.' *The American Journal of Occupational Therapy 63*, 5, 525–534.

Sternberg, R.J. (1979) 'The nature of mental abilities.' *American Psychologist 34*, 3, 214–230.

Jensen's MindLadder model

Jensen, M.R. (2000) 'The MindLadder Model: Using Dynamic Assessment to Help Students Learn to Assemble and Use Knowledge.' In C.S. Lidz and J.G. Elliott (eds) *Dynamic Assessment: Prevailing Models and Applications.* Amsterdam: JAI/Elsevier Science.

Jensen, M.R. (2003) 'Mediating knowledge construction: Towards a dynamic model of assessment and learning. Part II: Applied programmes and research.' *Educational and Child Psychology 20*, 2, 118–142.

Jensen, M.R. (2007) *Students Moving up the Mind's Ladder: Meeting the Needs of Students with Academic Difficulties and Learning Disabilities.* Roswell, GA: Center for Mediated Learning. Available at www.mindladder.com/mindladder%20article%202006.pdf, accessed on 8 March 2011.

Jensen, M.L. and Jensen, M.R. (1996) *The Parent as Mediator Parent Education Program.* Atlanta, GA: Cognitive Education Systems.

Jensen, M.R. (for direct contact in obtaining programme) e-mail: mj@mindladder.com, website: www.mindladder.org

CHAPTER 7

Decision Making for a Whole-school Approach to Teaching Thinking for All

Introduction

There are many decisions that a school community must make in adopting, implementing and evaluating the teaching of thinking for all. The importance and complexity of the thinking required in making such decisions have been drawn to our attention by a number of writers. For example, in discussing one of the complex decisions concerning what approach to adopt for the teaching of thinking, Haywood (2004) writes: 'There are currently more than 200 programs that are commercially available, all of which are called in some way "cognitive" by the authors or publishers. One needs to exercise great care in choosing among them' (p.250). Another writer draws our attention to the care needed in making such complex decisions, stating: 'Hence, no matter what program is used, careful selection should be made, taking into consideration the needs of the school district and the children' (Sternberg 1987, p.256).

There are extensive coverages already available concerning the kinds of questions which need to be asked by a school community when implementing a chosen programme. For example, the final chapter in the book *Developing Thinking; Developing Learning* by McGregor (2007) is called 'School Development to Support Thinking Communities'. In her section on clarifying the issues, problems or challenges, she states: 'Managers, decision makers and participants of learning within a school need to clarify what should be done' (McGregor 2007, p.299). A very inclusive stance is taken in this chapter, reminding us that all participants in the development of a thinking school community need to grow in their thinking about thinking. McGregor states:

Just as schools are places of growth for children, they should also be places of growth for teachers and administrators, where the pursuit of intellectual activity and professional collaboration are supported and encouraged. A successful learning organisation should enable all members of the school community to collaborate in the processes of goal setting, monitoring and evaluation, creating a dynamic system that changes as the needs and the vision of the community changes. (p.303)

She also presents a chapter on professional development that can support teachers in this growth, based largely on her own innovative work with professional development activities that can foster growth in the teaching of thinking.

The present writer has decided to focus, in this final chapter, on an inclusive metaphor for the decision-making process which may be useful in addressing the many decision-making issues raised in relation to each tier of the three-tier model. She was fortunate to be present when Professor David Perkins gave a paper entitled 'King Arthur and the Round Table' at the International Conference on Thinking in Harrogate, UK, in 2002. She was impressed by the way in which he used this metaphor, a culturally meaningful one in the the UK, to address the potential for an inclusive approach to decision making. Perkins has subsequently, in 2003, published a book titled *King Arthur's Round Table*, which is a more extensive coverage of this metaphor.

In this chapter the writer will first comment on some of the key characteristics of the metaphor of King Arthur's Round Table, drawn largely from what Perkins has stated in his paper and written in his book, but with some small additional content from the writer's own knowledge.

She will then take each of the key dimensions which need to be addressed in the teaching of thinking, as outlined in Chapter 2 (i.e. a belief system; the embracing learning environment; the task; the mediator; and the learners); and for each dimension discuss how the King Arthur's Round Table metaphor can guide the decision making involved in that dimension.

The metaphor: King Arthur's Round Table

First, Perkins (2003) uses this metaphor to address decision making, which is based on collaborative conversation, within any organisation. A round table is seen as a 'smarter' table, in which people can 'put their heads together'. At the Round Table of the mythical King Arthur, the knights sat around a large marble table, with their backs against the wall, to discuss and decide key matters for political ordering. The roundness of the table meant that every person could be heard by all when they spoke. The importance of equal voice and regard available with the round table arrangement is pointed out by Perkins. In contrast, with a long table, positions such as closeness to the King, the source of the power, become important – as does the possibility of not being heard by the King. Regrettably, Perkins notes, today these aspects of position and closeness to the source of power continue to be important to each person's decision-making power.

Perkins then discusses the importance of the collaborative conversations which are possible around such a Round Table. We know from our coverage of Vygotsky earlier in this book how central interactive conversation is for high-quality thinking. Such successful Round Table conversation and decision making involves knowledge processing by all, attention to the evidence, clear discussion, with appropriate questions of clarification, and exploratory and imaginative consideration of solutions, according to Perkins.

Aims and beliefs

Having a shared vision, aims and beliefs, is central to a Round Table approach to decision making concerning the teaching of thinking within a whole-school community. In discussing King Arthur's Round Table Perkins notes: 'Central to the legendary Arthur's agenda of unifying England and fostering peace and prosperity were the knights of the Round Table... He wanted a *smart* Camelot, a collective enterprise that functioned intelligently' (Perkins 2003, p.1). He notes: 'His knights would converse as equals – proposing, challenging, debating, reaching accords, and solving the problems of the kingdom' (p.2).

There appears to be a consensus in the literature on the teaching of thinking that an overriding aim is the growth in every individual's thinking capacities, an inclusive notion. For example, McGregor, a key writer on the teaching of thinking, states:

> All teachers need to be cognizant of, and actively support, the ultimate aim, which is to enable pupils to *develop* a wide variety of cognitive skills; *apply* and *transfer* their thinking capacities usefully, from an academic setting to everyday life; and to *enhance* and *extend* their problem solving abilities, for the future. (McGregor 2007, p.312; her italics)

This is endorsed by a further statement: 'Thinking programmes should scaffold for successive cognitive experiences that become more complex so that the students grow in their capacities' (McGregor 2007, p.307).

However, there can be barriers in the organisation to sharing of the ultimate aim, as noted by Perkins. For example, he states:

> often, a person's current frame of reference – established beliefs and attitudes – generates resistance to an innovation (i.e. it won't work, it won't work here, or I already do that, or it's a fad, or it's a good thing in principle but won't take hold, or it's a threat to how I've set things up, or I'm tired of all these initiatives that never really accomplish anything). (Perkins 2003, p.226)

Perkins tells us that one of the simplest strategies for challenging such frames of reference is to give really good reasons to try. Chapter 1 of this book provides a number of rationales or reasons for the shared ultimate aim of enhancing the cognitive potential of all learners.

There are, regrettably, barriers not only in terms of individual persons' resistance to innovation, as described by Perkins above, but also individual agendas which can form barriers to joint aims and beliefs. For example, regressive patterns in the Round Table conversations and decision making can occur, according to Perkins, when there are 'people bent on attaining, maintaining and taking advantage of power positions, even though they serve the general interests of the group less well' (Perkins 2003, p.84). We need to put aside individual aims for power, status and territory need, for the Round Table beliefs.

Also regrettably, there may be confusion or tension between aims, even where dictated by government and wider policy. For example, there is in the UK a clear government aim for individual, inclusive enhancement of potential (for example in 'personalised learning'; see p.40). However, the way in which the status of schools is determined by standardised attainment testing and the publication of school league tables appears to foster practices that raise such measured attainment to the status of a main aim. In the writer's view, aiming to enhance cognitive and metacognitive skills, which underpin all learning, should impact positively on school subject attainment, where there is the expected teaching for transfer of these skills, and high-quality subject teaching for all.

If there are unclear or conflicting aims, it may help to reflect on a guiding principle which is stated within 'supreme law', that is, the rights and best interests of each child, as espoused in the United Nations Convention on the Rights of the Child (1989). This is increasingly becoming a guiding principle in the education legislation of countries who are strongly affirming an inclusive approach to school development (Howie 2010).

Further, there may be subsidiary aims for the teaching of thinking which often relate to the unique needs and situation of the whole-school community, as pointed out by McGregor. She states: 'if school aims are to focus on the process of professional development and/or higher pupil performance and/or redesign for the curriculum, different approaches or programmes provide different opportunities related to thinking skills' (McGregor 2007, p.307).

The wider organisation and the learning environment

In discussing the wider organisation involved in Round Table decision making, Perkins notes the importance of the culture of the wider group, saying that the culture of the organisation is 'a matter of the tacit belief systems that people hold and that underlie their behaviour...they resurface in the way people say things and the way they behave' (Perkins 2003, p.28). According to him it is largely through this symbolic conduct that the culture of the group is expressed and reinforced. He is careful to point out that organisations have their own distinctive and unique cultures, and states: 'in asking about the relevance of the Round Table model across cultures, we should bear in mind not just national and ethnic but organisational cultures' (Perkins 2003, p.141). He considers that his general model of the Round Table conversational processes and interactions could apply in any organisational cultural context, but that 'the symbolic significance of different styles of interaction certainly varies across community, organisational, ethnic and national cultures' (Perkins 2003, p.142).

This reminds us of the importance of understanding the complex values and needs of the wider school learning community as a culturally unique organisation, in decision making concerning the teaching of thinking.

In the international literature on the teaching of thinking, attention is drawn to the wider school community values that should be encouraged in the teaching of thinking, because they endorse an ethos of thinking. For example, Robson and Moseley (2005) state that a school-wide environment should value such characteristics as open-mindedness, objective thinking, impartiality, intellectual integrity and independent judgement. They also consider that it should be a supportive environment which encourages autonomy, choice and self-reflection.

This is in line with some of the writing specifically about schools as communities of enquiry. In building such communities of enquiry, discussion about the teaching of thinking can be broad enough to take into account wider school and community issues such as target setting and formative assessment, as noted by Baumfield (2000), a leading researcher on the teaching of thinking and building a community of enquiry.

A particularly inclusive approach towards building communities of practice in schools (a concept which overlaps with communities of enquiry) has been put forward by Wearmouth, Berryman and Glynn (2009). It includes compelling examples of culturally relevant ways of building such communities of practice.

Another leading international researcher on the teaching of thinking, McGuinness (2005), notes: 'Several writers have gone beyond skills and dispositions to focus on developing communities of learners that have norms and practices for sustaining high-quality learning and self-regulation' (p.119). She draws attention to the work of Brown and Campione (1994) on 'learning communities' and points out the key role of ideas about metacognition and self-regulation in such communities. As McGuinness notes, this work is built on considerable early research by Brown and Campione on metacognition, self-regulated and strategic learning.

This focus on members of a learning community all taking responsibility for thinking about their thinking, being self-regulated and strategic, fits well with the writing on the Round Table by Perkins (2003) in relation to the symbolic conduct which is expected from Round Table discussion, not only from a facilitative leader but from all participants. He notes that 'collaboration benefits from responsible citizenship, with its high commitment to the common enterprise and high process awareness' (p.168) and the importance of people acting as 'good citizens' prepared to 'monitor and guide their behaviour in ways that advance the collective effort. Being a good citizen of collaboration involves spirit and commitment at least as much as technique' (p.167). Further, 'authentic participation in a collaboration means not only taking the mission, goals and progress for granted but participation in the construction, reconstruction and monitoring of them' (p.170).

In developing a whole-school community that is working towards decision making in the teaching of thinking, we should include all key players in the community in that decision making, including administrators, teachers, parents, and learners themselves. In this way the decision making is a proper partnership process.

Perkins has written an earlier book called *Smart Schools: Better Learning and Thinking for Every Child* (1991). He outlines as one principle of 'Smart Schools' as learning organisations, that they are places of growth for all. The successful learning organisation puts in place structures that enable all members of the school community, as noted above, to collaborate in the processes of decision making and self-monitoring, which creates a dynamic system able to change as the needs and vision of the whole-school community change. Perkins (1991) notes that Smart Schools 'revitalise everyone's interest by asking them all to be thoughtful and responsible, not just for the school in general, but for each individual child' (p.171).

Further, Baumfield draws attention to the wider role of the school community and its links to other agencies in supporting thinking developments, which could include decision making regarding the teaching for thinking. She notes: 'impact within the schools is evident in the emphasis on building capacity for long-term development, through action research focused on issues arising from the teachers' own practice and linked to school priorities' (Baumfield 2000, p.77). Support for this, in her view, includes support through links with tutors at university, local education authority advisors, and partnerships with other schools.

Finally, we should ensure that the Round Table model of decision making operates across all dimensions of the whole-school community, and informs all of them, for inclusion. These include the culture, policies and practices of the whole-school community, according to the *Index of Inclusion* (Booth and Ainscow 2002), as discussed in Chapter 2.

The task and decision making

The decision making carried out by the Round Table conversation is aimed at choice making and problem solving in relation to the teaching of thinking for the whole-school community. McGregor (2007) suggests that problem-solving steps could be applied to 'guide schools when considering the steps they might take to improve the thoughtful learning within their institutions' (p.298). These steps are identified as:

- clarifying the issues, problems or challenges

- considering how to address the issues and challenges, including considering all of the possible ways that each issue or problem could be approached

- deciding on which method would be best and why

- putting all that is needed in place
- evaluating how well the solution is working.

This problem-solving approach is very similar to that discussed in Chapter 4, Section 3 on Sternberg's problem-solving cycle (1995). It covers the following steps.

1. *Recognising the existence of a problem.* In this case, it is our general need to form a consensus and plan concerning how best to meet the needs for the teaching of thinking within a school community.

2. *Defining the nature of the problem.* In this stage, we will require information gathering to understand what the overall aims and subsidiary aims of the development will be. It will involve us in accessing information on national and local requirements for the teaching of thinking, accessing assessment information, and even doing further assessment to determine the needs for cognitive enhancement for all learners in the school community, as well as accessing information about the approaches to the teaching of thinking which might meet those needs. As part of this process, we could represent the complex factors involved during discussion – for example, on a whiteboard and in shared minutes – to help the decision-making process to move forward with all involved recognising the complex factors.

3. *Formulating a problem-solving strategy or set of strategies – an action plan.* It is particularly important that we make this a collaborative, Round Table process. Perkins (2003) discusses the stakeholders talking together in this part of the decision-making process. He states: 'The feeling of common decision and common cause may be much more core to future success than the efficiency of the deliberation' (p.155). We will need, in this strategy or action planning, to include planning to ensure that the resources required to implement the decisions effectively, are available. The literature on the teaching of thinking, as well as the writer's experience, suggest that resources will be needed for professional development of all concerned; organising for ongoing support in the innovations; adequate physical resources in terms of materials, etc; and adequate time resources to allow for any separate teaching of thinking classes, and for team work

and sharing concerning the development and teaching of the programme/s.

4. *Implementing the action plan.* Collective and collaborative implementation of the action is important to maximise support for those carrying out the actions. Reflective thinking in collaborative ways about the actions would enhance growth in thinking for all involved. McGregor's (2007) final chapter on school development to support thinking communities has much useful information for this implementation stage.

5. *Monitoring and evaluating the problem solving.* Robson and Moseley (2005) highlight the importance of this monitoring and evaluation stage. Further, we also need to carry out this stage collaboratively, with all stakeholders, including the learners themselves, consulted for their opinions.

Perkins (2003) notes that perhaps the best way for a group to move from an idea to an action is to embrace the spirit of action research. Action research models generally follow a cyclical pattern similar to Sternberg's problem-solving cycle, with evaluation of the needs for action and evaluation of the action itself being strong aspects of the research method. For example, Baumfield, Hall and Wall (2008) in their book on *Action Research in the Classroom* (which draws on considerable action research with projects concerning the teaching of thinking), present action research cycles adapted from Kemmis and McTaggart (1988). The initial cycle involves:

- definition of the problem
- needs assessment
- developmental action plan
- implementation of plan
- evaluation of action
- and then reflection and review of the first cycle of action research, leading to decision making for the second cycle of action research (which follows the same stages as the first cycle, starting with redefinition of the problem).

The mediator/facilitator/leader

The facilitation required for enhancing the Round Table conversations, in terms of communicative feedback by all, and especially by the facilitator or leader, is discussed by Perkins (2003). This communicative feedback clarifies the ideas 'on the table', and examines them specifically in terms of what the participants like about an idea, what might be the problems with it, and how these problems can be solved. He states that the leader 'who guides concrete and reflective discussion, allowing for divergent points of view, can foster insight and practical action by pooling the thoughts and perspectives of the participants' (Perkins 2003, p.9).

He sees such a leader as engaging in the following communicative activities:

> sending positive messages about the ability, knowledge and judgement of others beside the leader...declaring trust in the others to act in the collective interests...respecting the multiple enriching perspectives of the others...acknowledges the legitimate individual interests of others...views positively the strength of the collective effort, and the potential to work together effectively. (Perkins 2003, p.32)

Several particular characteristics of leaders come in for some extensive discussion by Perkins. One relates to how the leader views policies or rules in relation to decision making and problem solving. The facilitator of the Round Table conversation signals not that 'you are here for the organisation' (an inhibitor), but 'the organisation is here for you' (a facilitator). In the case of the 'inhibitor', the message given by the leader is that the Round Table can't carry out a particular suggestion, because of policy so-and-so. In contrast, the 'facilitator' gives the message that an action may be difficult to carry out because of policy so-and-so, but the challenge is to find a way to do it. In communicating this more positive message the facilitator engages in 'a genuine intellectual partnership with the participants' (Perkins 2003, p.95).

Another aspect of leadership discussed by Perkins (2003) focuses on what he terms an 'enquiry-centred leadership'. He states:

> An enquiry-centred leader would also encourage others' questions, facilitate conversation, initiate investigations, welcome multiple viewpoints and the like. Enquiry-centred leaders let others do a lot of the thinking and let them take credit for it. Beyond direct personal contact, an enquiry-centred leader fosters organisational structures that support enquiry, for instance small teams composed of diverse

expertise, matrix structures that promote organisational crosstalk, or support for small-scale testing of risky innovations with high potential. (Perkins 2003, p.99)

In the present writer's view, such 'enquiry-centred leadership' would be particularly useful to adopt when we engage in development of whole-school policies which incorporate the teaching of thinking and address the needs of the whole school. McGregor (2007) suggests that 'Teaching and learning policies for school development plans can highlight and emphasise the thinking that pupils should engage in' (p.304).

Further, curriculum reform and development in relation to the teaching of thinking is another area of whole-school development which would benefit from such 'enquiry-centred leadership'. For example, McGuinness (2005) notes 'the challenges that would face a scaled-up thinking curriculum' (p.123). She sees such challenges to include:

- developing a path within a curriculum area for growth and progression

- dealing with existing national curriculum expectations and assessment requirements that are not aimed at evaluating higher order thinking

- overcoming systemic barriers within the school itself, such as differing classroom cultures.

Reflection on how characteristics of 'enquiry-centred leadership' would help to address such challenges would be helpful.

Finally, Perkins does not see such leadership and facilitation as provided always by a single leader, or by the obvious 'boss'. It could be provided by people who can introduce progressive styles of interaction, who can seed the organisation in more progressive patterns, lead towards collective intelligence, and cultivate other developmental leaders. Such 'developmental leaders' can 'function as exemplars, facilitators, and mentors within the group, helping it to move towards a progressive culture' (Perkins 2003, p.219). He discusses how those individuals can learn, through commitment and habit, to take the lead in progressive interaction, so that eventually there is the mixing of such people across the groups in an organisation, and the carrying of such progressive styles of conversation to other groups in which they participate.

Soon a community will emerge with mostly round tables, a community in which most interactions have a progressive character most of the time, a community that, because of superior knowledge processing and symbolic conduct at all levels, is more intelligent. (Perkins 2003, p.224)

So, for transformation of an organisation, we need not only vision and leadership from the top, but active developmental leaders throughout the organisation.

It is of interest that the UK guidance which has been provided for school leaders, and is aimed at supporting the development of thinking skills in Years 7, 8 and 9, within the school environment (DfES 2005), follows this pattern to some extent. In its four-phased development of focusing, developing, establishing and enhancing thinking skills at Key Stage 3, a trio of teachers is suggested as the lead thinkers. This trio could work across curriculum departments, or within them. Eventually, it is hoped that new lead thinkers will develop through whole-school years and over the three school years, through coaching and collaboration, to build a portfolio of good practice groups.

Learners/members of the Round Table

A key feature of Round Table decision making is commitment to equal regard and voice. The Round Table allowed everyone to be heard, so building a sense of belonging and commitment. Perkins believes that in Round Table decision making there can be the building of collaborative understanding and support. In order to achieve this in the original Round Table counsel, 'chivalry' was involved, with principles such as members speaking one at a time.

There are similar expectations in group sharing practices used widely in the UK, such as 'circle time' and restorative practice, which we use to build shared problem solving in the school community. Such procedures can be used by groups of staff members for their own decision making, as well as by pupils.

A number of the approaches to the teaching of thinking covered in this book, such as the development of a community of enquiry in Lipman's Philosophy for Children, and the infusion approaches of Swartz and Parks, and McGuinness, require and foster good practices for group sharing of ideas.

As noted earlier in this chapter, participants in Round Table decision making should be representative of all of the key stakeholders in the whole-school community. It is particularly important that those sectors of the school community that we may find to be generally least heard or most vulnerable should be represented, so that the decision making regarding the teaching of thinking can be truly inclusive, and meet the needs of all. We need to ensure the proper involvement of representatives of individuals with disabilities, and members of different cultural groups. In their discussion of an integrated framework for the teaching of thinking Robson and Moseley (2005) have drawn attention to the under-representation of members of minority groups in enhancement programmes for learners who are gifted. They call for greater recognition of the needs of learners of low socio-economic status and learners with disabilities.

McGregor (2007) draws attention to the unique social and cultural influences which each participant brings to group resolution, in her own professional development activities for the teaching of thinking. She advocates a societal mix of co-learners for cognitive development, and enhancing understanding of how social and cultural experiences can influence 'perceptions, interpretations and understandings' (p.289). We can apply these concerns to Round Table members' development within progressive Round Table decision making concerning the teaching of thinking.

Perkins (2003) suggests the importance of such Round Table discussion and communicative feedback focusing on 'ideas, products or behaviours, not core character or abilities' (p.43). This means that we consider all ideas fairly and objectively. It also requires us to avoid what Perkins calls 'emotional oversimplification'. To counter this, he emphasises the importance of not being egocentric in discussion, but being able and willing to take the other's viewpoint and perspective, 'putting yourself in the other's shoes'. He draws attention to Goleman's writing on emotional intelligence (1998) where

> Goleman makes empathy a key dimension of emotional competence, including such features as awareness of others' feelings and perspectives, perceptiveness about developmental needs, alertness to political relationships, and the adoption of a service orientation. Clearly these traits have a progressive character. (Perkins 2003, p.80)

Emotional intelligence is a fundamental requirement in Round Table decision making. This book, as well as covering Goleman's approach to the enhancement of emotional intelligence, covers approaches to the teaching of thinking, such as those of Feuerstein and de Bono, which have components specifically designed to address empathy and perspective taking.

Perkins gives considerable attention to the role of collaborative conversations in which *everyone* engages in Round Table decision making, regardless of role, status or position. Perkins writes:

> King Arthur's dream had people coming together to coordinate their thoughts and efforts smoothly, effectively, intelligently. But, when such collectives work, what wires them together? As neurones connect one part of the brain to another, conversations connect the different parts of communities and organisations. Conversations are the virtual neurones of a collective mind. (Perkins 2003, p.18)

Just as neural action is important in meaning-making, so, in decision making about the teaching of thinking, the development of shared language and a shared understanding of each person's unique contribution (McGregor 2007) will help in the development of shared meanings, leading to shared decisions.

Not only shared meanings, but the opportunity to share what really interests us, is important. Perkins wants negotiations within the Round Table context to take place from a frank statement of positions of interests, rather than 'non-negotiable demands' and 'compromise', with a search for mutually beneficial solutions.

Perkins (2003) hopes that collaborative conversation will lead to more being done, sooner, of greater quality ('taking advantage of diversity for creativity and greater critical perspective'), as a 'committed, unified group (as in stakeholders collectively talking through a decision)' (p.155). Finally, it will lead to more in terms of learning more, 'generating considerable individual and collective learning that becomes a resource for the further endeavour of the community and the organisation' (p.156).

Such development by us of learning and thinking for the whole-school community is the aim of this chapter and this whole book.

Self-reflective questions

☐ How 'Round Table' is the decision making concerning the teaching of thinking in your school community?

☐ How well are you carrying out a facilitative role in developing progressive conversations in such decision making?

References

Baumfield, V.M. (2000) 'Inquiry made public: Thinking skills and professional development.' *Education Review 14*, 1, 76–79.

Baumfield, V.M, Hall, E. and Wall, K. (2008) *Action Research in the Classroom.* London: Sage.

Booth, T. and Ainscow, M. (2002) *The Index for Inclusion.* Bristol: CSIE.

Brown, A.L. and Campione, J.C. (1994) 'Guided Discovery in a Community of Learners.' In K. McGilly (ed.) *Classroom Lessons: Integrating Cognitive Theory and Classroom Practice.* Cambridge, MA: MIT Press.

Department for Education and Skills (DfES) (2005) *Leading in Learning: Developing Thinking Skills at Key Stage 3. School Training Manual.* London: DfES.

Goleman, D. (1998) *Working with Emotional Intelligence.* New York: Bantam Books.

Haywood, H.C. (2004) 'Thinking in, around, and about the curriculum: The role of cognitive education.' *International Journal of Disability, Development and Education 51*, 3, 231–252.

Howie, D.R. (2010) 'A comparative study of the positioning of children with special educational needs in the legislation of Britain, New Zealand and the Republic of Ireland.' *International Journal of Inclusive Education 14*, 8, 755–776.

Kemmis, S. and McTaggart, R. (1988) *The Action Research Planner.* Geelong: Deakin University.

McGregor, D. (2007) *Developing Thinking; Developing Learning. A Guide to Thinking Skills in Education.* Maidenhead: Open University Press/McGraw Hill.

McGuinness, C. (2005) 'Teaching thinking: Theory and practice.' *Pedagogy-Learning for Teaching,* BJEP Monograph Series II, 3, 107–126.

Perkins, D. (1991) *Smart Schools: Better Learning and Thinking for Every Child.* New York: Free Press.

Perkins, D.N. (2002) 'King Arthur and the Round Table.' Paper presented to the International Conference on Thinking, Harrogate, 2002.

Perkins, D. (2003) *King Arthur's Round Table: How Collaborative Conversations Create Smart Organisations.* Hoboken, NJ: John Wiley and Sons.

Robson, S. and Moseley, D. (2005) 'An integrated framework for thinking about learning.' *Gifted Education International 20*, 1, 36–50.

Sternberg, R.J. (1987) 'Questions and Answers about the Nature and Teaching of Thinking Skills.' In J.B. Baron and R.J. Sternberg (eds) *Teaching Thinking Skills: Theory and Practice.* New York: Freeman and Company.

Sternberg, R.J. (1995) *In Search of the Human Mind.* Orlando, FL: Harcourt Brace. (The problem-solving model is on p.13.)

United Nations (1989) *United Nations Convention on the Rights of the Child.* Geneva: United Nations.

Wearmouth, J., Berryman, M. and Glynn, T. (2009) *Inclusion through Participation in Communities of Practice in Schools.* Wellington: Dunmore Publishing.

Subject Index

Author Index

Sternberg, R.J. 11, 16, 17, 21,
  28, 39, 42, 58, 59, 71, 72,
  73, 74, 79, 80, 81, 82, 83,
  84, 86, 94, 97, 113, 117,
  118, 120, 122, 142, 143,
  157, 173, 207, 218, 225
Stys, Y. 180
Sutcliffe, R. 98
Sutton, A. 150, 196, 197
Swartz, R.J. 39, 105, 106, 177,
  178, 179

Tam, S.K.T. 130–1
Tebar Belmonte, L. 20
Thompson, J.E.M. 64, 185
Thomson, C. 76
Todd, E. 32
Toft, P. 116
Topping, K.J. 97, 173
Torrance, E.P. 90, 172
Traweek, D. 185
Trickey, S. 97, 173
Tunstall, P. 128–9
Turnure, J. 78
Twist, J. 101
Tzuriel, D. 43, 154

United Nations 12, 12–13,
  22, 221

Veenema, S. 166
Vygotsky, L.S. 19, 20, 21, 60,
  61, 62, 63, 143, 145,
  146, 147, 148, 196, 197

Wake, E. 84
Wall, K. 74, 95, 97, 177, 226
Wallace, B. 77
Walters, R.H. 76, 77, 79
Walters, S. 90
Ward, L. 185
Watts, B. 94
Wearmouth, J. 223
Weiner, B. 127
Wellborn, J.G. 129
Wertsch, J.V. 60
Williams, S. 98, 203
Williams, W.M. 81
Winyard, J. 97, 98
Wong, S. 202
Wood, D. 147, 198
Wood, H. 147

Yeung, A.S. 104

Zigler, E. 78